M000237940

The Unstoppable Jesus Christ:
How Your Faith Can Triumph in a World Gone Mad

The Unstoppable Jesus Christ:
How Your Faith Can Triumph in a World Gone Mad

Jerry Newcombe, D.Min.

Creators Publishing
Hermosa Beach, CA

The Unstoppable Jesus Christ:
How Your Faith Can Triumph in a World Gone Mad
Copyright © 2016 Jerry Newcombe, D.Min.

All rights reserved. No part of this book may be reproduced or transmitted in any form or by any means, electronic or mechanical, including photocopying, recording or by any information storage and retrieval system, without permission in writing from the author.

Cover Image: Jesus Christ Pantocrator-ancient mosaic from Hagia Sophia. Photo by Edal Anton Lefterov

Cover art by Peter Kaminski

FIRST EDITION
Creators Publishing
Hermosa Beach, California 90254
310-337-7003

ISBN 978-1-945630-39-2
CREATORS PUBLISHING

* * *

Dedication to my grandchildren,
Elizabeth and Isaac,
who bring a great deal of joy into my life

* * *

Contents

Foreword by William J. Federer   1
Additional Endorsements   4
Author's Introduction   7

Part 1. Jesus Christ   8
The Unstompable Jesus Christ   9
The Historical Jesus   11
Passover and Good Friday   12
Easter Hope---Based on Facts of History   14
On the Resurrection---Just the Facts, Ma'am   16
The Alleged "Lost Tomb of Jesus"   19
Global Warming or Crucifixion Day?   21
Jesus Is Coming back---But Not as Saturday Night Live   23
Depicted
Judgment Day on May 21? Let's Talk It Over---on May 22   26
A Challenge to Skeptics: An Easter Message   28
New Theory Tries to Debunk the Original Easter   30
The Non-Jesus Religion   33
The Answer to Muslim Violence: Jesus   35

Part 2. Hollywood and the Media   38
Is Hollywood Poised to Slander George Washington?   39
Moviegoers Tend Not To Relish Their Values Being   41
Assaulted
On the Lighter Side   43
Robo-Christ?   45
Hollywood and the Siren Song of Socialism   47
Is Scripture-Quoting a Sign that You're Nuts?   50
Great New Movie---"God's Not Dead"   52
So, Roseanne, You Want to Go Back to the French   54
Revolution?
Oh the Profanity   57
Shocked No More?   59
Fighting Media Bias---and Winning   61
Is Religion Box Office Poison?   63
The Alternative Media---A Lifeline of Freedom   66

Part 3. The Bible   70
Are Adam and Eve Just an Allegory?   71
The Gods of Egypt   72
A Great Injustice to the New Testament   74
Rebuttal to *Newsweek*'s Cover Story on "The Myths of Jesus"   79
Is the New Testament Forged?   81
Time to Give the Gnostics a Rest   83
Prescription for a Truly Happy New Year   86
The Price Paid to Get the Bible into English   88
The Lost Art of Bible-Meditation   90

Part 4. The Church   93
Would Jesus Side with the Wall Street Protesters?   94
Church for Atheists   96
Where Have All the Bold Pastors Gone?   98
"Go to Church, Live Longer"   100
Martyrdom Comes to America?   103
Church---Antidote to Loneliness?   104
More Jesus, Less Crime   106
How Christianity Benefits Even "Angry Humanists"   109
Four Myths about Church to Avoid, Lest They Become Self-   111
Fulfilling Prophecies
Is the Atheist Population Skyrocketing?   113
Will NYC Implement the ABC Principle---Anything But   116
Christ?

Part 5. Christian-bashing   119
Can Your Pro-Life Bumper Stocker Actually Get You in   120
Trouble?
Do Christians Want "Jews to Die" to Hasten the Second   122
Coming?
Shooting at FRC: Overcoming Hate with Love   124
A New Low in the War on Christmas   126
"The Advent of Controversy"   129
Is Christianity Really to Blame for Much of What is Wrong in   131
our World?
The Blessings of "Christian Hegemony"   133
The War on the Cross   136

Part 6. Christmas   139
This Christmas, Defy the Atheists---Worship the Truth   140
Prophecies Jesus Fulfilled in His First Coming   142
'Tis the Season to Attack the Gospels?   147
It's Time to Call is "Black-eye Friday"   150
Away With the Manger?   152
'Tis the Season to Jettison Reason?   154
The Birth of a Classic: Handel's Messiah   156
Are We Winning or Losing?   159
Disputing the Pagan Roots of Christmas   161
Which Side of History Are You On?   163

Part 7. Christian History   166
Love, Commitment, and Valentine's Day   167
In Remembrance of a True Hero of the Faith---St. Patrick   169
What Changed the Vikings?   171
A Significant Milestone: The King James Bible at 400   173
In the Arena   174
On the 100th Anniversary of the *Titanic*   177
The Christian and Civil Disobedience   179
Maria Von Trapp, RIP   181

Part 8. Science   184
Does Science Disprove God?   185
Is Evolution Just a Shell Game?   187
God and Science---A Comment on the "Hands of God" in   189
Space
"Darwin's Doubt"   191
On Religion and Climate Change   193
A Baby Reflects the Glory of the Creator   196

Part 9. Islam   199
A Warning to the West   200
Please, Don't Burn the Qur'an   202
What Part of "Death to America!" Don't We Understand?   204
"Enough, Enough, Enough"   206
Faithful, Even Unto Death   209
The Hundredth Anniversary of a Tragedy---Eerily Familiar   210

Political Correctness on Islam Can Lead to More Killings 213
What Was Left Out of the 9/11 Memorials? 215
Vengeance is *Ours*, Says the Islamist 217
Praising Allah at the National Cathedral 219
Shariah Law—Incompatible with Basic Rights 221
Plans to Take Over the World---Temporarily Put on Hold 223
Why Did The Marathon Bombers Do It? 225
The Scapegoating of the Christians in Egypt 228
Forgotten Heroes of 9/11 230
Killing Christians With Impunity? 232
Celebrating Christmas Can Be Dangerous---in Egypt 235
Multiculturalism Is Disproven by Europe's Immigration Crisis 237
Europe's Only Hope is Christian Revival 239
Who Are the Real Terrorists? 241
What Good Is the Right of Free Speech If You Can't Exercise It? 243

Part 10. Miscellaneous Musings 246
"Truth" in a Post-Christian West 247
On Avoiding Scandalous Sin 248
A Hymn for Our Time 250
"The Music of the World" 252
A Pope Named Francis? Well, it's About Time 255
The End of the World? Been There. Done That. 257
Ten Trends to Watch in 2012 259
Has the Milk of Human Kindness Curdled? 261

Part 11. The Seven Deadly Sins 265
Pride—the Sin Behind Many Headlines 266
Greed---The Bible Proven Right Yet Again 268
Envy, the Green Monster 270
The Antidote to our Culture's Sexual Anarchy 272
A Sad State of Affairs 275
The Deadly Sin of Anger on the Rise 277
If My Body is the Temple of the Holy Spirit, Then Why Do I Look Like the Buddha? 280
Food for Thought on America's Obesity Problem 282
Overcoming the Sun of Sloth 284

Part 12. Apologetics, the Defense of the Faith   287
Is Heaven Just a "False Hope"?   288
Why Does God Allow Hurricanes?   290
God Is Not a "Psychotic Mass Murderer"   292
Whatever Happened to Hell?   295
A Dark Night Indeed: Trying to Make Sense Out of Another   297
Senseless Act of Violence in Modern America
Does Believing in Hell Make One "Evil"?   299

Part 13. Death   303
Entrepreneur Wants to Find "Cure" for Death   304
Reflections on Death with the Passing on my Mother   306
Chuck Colson, Trophy of God's Grace   308
Shakespeare and "Death with Dignity"   310
Omnipresent: Video Cameras---And the Lord   312
Breaking News From AD 33   314
Are Your Ready for the Test?   317

Epilogue: "The Stone That Become a Mountain"   320
Acknowledgments   325
About the Author   326
Index   327

Foreword

It has been said, "The past is prologue." History is important. But what many people don't realize are the incredible lessons from history, especially when it comes to the ultimate worldwide prevailing of the Christian faith, not through force but persuasion.

Pulitzer Prize-winning historian Arthur Schlesinger, who was on President John F. Kennedy's staff, wrote in an op-ed titled "Folly's Antidote" (the *New York Times*, January 1, 2007), wherein he said, "History is to the nation as memory is to the individual."

So if you can imagine an individual who's lost his memory, maybe he has Alzheimer's. He does not know who he is. He doesn't know who you are, and you can take advantage of him.

In America, we have national Alzheimer's. Here we are in America, and we have been the freest most prosperous country that planet earth has ever seen, but recently we've lost our memory. We don't know who we are; we don't know all the sacrifices and all the faith and courage that were necessary for us to have the freedom of deciding who are you going to marry, where are you going to live and work, and go to church if so inclined, and so on.

If we don't understand the things that made America and the West in general great, particularly the Judeo-Christian tradition, the freedoms we have enjoyed---that grow out of that tradition--- will slip through out fingers like sand. In world history, the most common form of government is a king, though called by different names, such as chairman, chieftain, czar, monarch, prime minister, sultan or communist totalitarian dictator. But our founders gave us this country where we get to decide our fate.

Ronald Reagan stated in 1961: "In this country of ours took place the greatest revolution that has ever taken place in the world's history ... Every other revolution simply exchanged one set of rulers for another ... Here for the first time in all the thousands of years of man's relation to man ... The founding fathers established the idea that you and I had within ourselves the God-given right and ability to determine our own destiny."

But there are always tendencies for the powerful to assume power and to take away our freedoms. Freedom is at risk, and each generation has to do its part to preserve it.

In all my studies of the past, there are two threads that I trace throughout history: greed and the Gospel. You always find people motivated by greed. And you always have some people motivated by the Gospel. You have the ones digging wells in poor countries, and starting orphanages and hospitals. But you also have those that sell people into slavery, that take land from the Indians, or those, in a less egregious example, that vote for candidates that they think will help their pocketbook, but they don't care about the moral implications of voting for that candidate. So you have these two: greed and the Gospel. As you examine your own life, are you helping to promote greed in this world or the Gospel?

In our cultural context today, we see that lies are silencing Christians, and it's primarily because we have not educated ourselves in history. There is a Communist tactic called deconstruction, where you specifically have to unhook the train car from one engine before you can hook it to another. You have to separate a culture from its past before you can make it a Communist. Karl Marx put it this way, "The first battlefield is the rewriting of history."

Europe went from a Judeo-Christian past, being Catholic and Protestant with Jewish neighborhoods, then with the French Revolution and with mostly German higher criticism that undermined faith in the Bible, Europe transitioned into a secular free sex neutral. Today Europe seems poised to be entering into an Islamic future.

Karl Marx put it this way, "Take away the heritage of a people and they are easily destroyed."

Poet Carl Sandburg wrote: "When a nation goes down, or a society perishes, one condition may always be found; they forgot where they came from. They lost sight of what had brought them along."

George Orwell wrote in *Nineteen Eighty-Four*: "'Who controls the past,' ran the Party slogan, 'controls the future: who controls the present controls the past.'"

George Orwell added: "The Party could thrust its hand into the past and say of this or that event, it never happened ... Past events, it is argued, have no objective existence, but survive only in written records and in human memories. The past is whatever the records and the memories agree upon. And since the Party is in full control

2

of all records, and in equally full control of the minds of its members, it follows that the past is whatever the Party chooses to make it ... The past, he reflected, had not merely been altered, it had been actually destroyed ... Everything faded into mist. The past was erased, the erasure was forgotten, the lie became truth."

That's what China did when they got rid of 5,000 years of their culture before they could become the People's Republic of China. Well, in America, there's been an effort from the early 1900s on to deride and ridicule and separate us from our Judeo-Christian past, so that we become secular before we become completely godless. We have seen Europe engaged in this anti-Christian crusade ahead of us by a couple of centuries. And the results have been devastating. Such as two world wars and the Holocaust.

History matters. And understanding history and current events from a Christian perspective is critical. That's why I'm very pleased with this new book.

Dr. Jerry Newcombe has hit another home run! His book, *The Unstoppable Jesus Christ: How Your Faith Can Triumph in a World Gone Mad* is absolutely brilliant. Jerry's in-depth decades of historical research and interviews with national and global leaders has given him a unique and fascinating perspective into what the problems are facing Western Civilization, and what the answer is.

With chapter topics ranging from Hollywood to Socialism to refuting myths about Jesus, Dr. Newcombe brings apologetic excellence together with a keen, entertaining wit. It is a masterpiece that every America must read. I highly endorse Dr. Jerry Newcombe's soon-to-be-classic book, *The Unstoppable Jesus Christ: How Your Faith Can Triumph in a World Gone Mad.*

--*William J. Federer*,
Best-selling Author & Nationally Known Speaker

Additional Endorsements

When you witness the anti-Christian bias in our modern culture, it is almost hard to believe this nation was founded on religious liberty. In his important new book, *The Unstoppable Jesus Christ*, Dr. Jerry Newcombe urges us to re-embrace our Christian values and fight back against forces seeking to repress our Christian liberties, which are increasingly in jeopardy. Whether we rise to that challenge, or continue to descend into complacency and cowardice could determine the future of this great nation.

--David Limbaugh
NY Times bestselling author, syndicated columnist

* * *

The title of the book says it all – Jesus Christ is Lord of All, the Kings of Kings, the Redeemer and transformer of chaos into order and darkness into light. In short, Jesus is unstoppable. He takes broken history and reorders it. When those who call on the name of Jesus follow Him and apply his radical teachings, history is changed and lives are enriched for good. The incarnation of God into His own human creation shook the universe and transformed the culture. Dr. Jerry Newcombe captures the incredible transformative power of Jesus in this must read book.

--Mathew D. Staver
Founder and Chairman, Liberty Counsel

* * *

As social scientists argue over the very definitions of "Culture," and as some theologians try to make sense of the Christian's responsibility within the culture, the rest of us just know: "something has changed: drastically." Indeed, the West has undeniably passed into a Post Christian, Secular age that is marked by an increasing hostility to the Biblical truths that make up the very foundation stones of Western civilization and Western democracies. Some believe, and I am one, that the current Secular age is unsustainable, that a new Post-Secular age will certainly follow the present difficult period of history. Yet, that doesn't promise anything better, necessarily. Through it all, though, we know that Jesus Christ shines as a beacon of transformative hope to human beings caught in the oppressive cycle of sin and the sinful culture that their hearts produce. Mercifully, the Lord raises up prophetic and scholarly

4

voices to help us who sojourn through such times. My long-time friend and colleague, Dr. Jerry Newcombe, is one of those voices. His best-selling books and his on-air personality have guided many through the labyrinth of postmodernity's inconsistencies and cultural traps to find peace with God. His latest book, *The Unstoppable Jesus Christ: How Your Faith Can Triumph in a World Gone Mad*, demonstrates that he is not only a faithful minister of the Gospel, but also a wise observer of the conservative movement in America, and one of its better scholars. Those who are engaged in the day-to-day skirmishes with destructive ideas will benefit from this book. Certainly, all of us who care about the Christian voice in the "naked public square" will want to get this book, read it, and keep it handy for reference in the on-going struggles. I commend the book and pray the lessons in it will be applied with prayerful determination and humility.

--Michael A. Milton, Ph.D.
President, Faith for Living, Inc., Ragsdale Chair of Missions and Evangelism, Erskine Theological Seminary; President, D. James Kennedy Institute

* * *

Much of today's Christianity has regrettably become a watered-down, truthless, hyper-grace-filled counterfeit. We have forgotten that God's Law was given to shine a bright light on the reality of our need for salvation, because we are hopelessly lost in our sin, which leads to death, without it. In his new book *The Unstoppable Jesus Christ*, my friend Dr. Jerry Newcombe gives a comprehensive look at the full counsel of scripture in the context of our modern times. He displays in his salient way how Christ, though full of grace, also represents the only way, truth and life.

--Matt Barber
Associate Dean, Liberty University School of law and founder of BarbWire.com

* * *

In the 21st Century age of ignorance, *The Unstoppable Jesus Christ: How Your Faith Can Triumph in a World Gone Mad* by Jerry Newcombe, D.Min is a beacon of wit and wisdom to encourage those who have faith and help others to understand the power of Grace. It is must reading. Since it is comprised of short vignettes, it is a book to be enjoyed as bedside reading or in timely

moments. I highly recommend *The Unstoppable Jesus Christ: How Your Faith Can Triumph in a World Gone Mad* by Jerry Newcombe, D.Min and urge everyone everywhere to read it.
--*Dr. Ted Baehr*
Publisher, "Movieguide"® and author of *The Culture-Wise Family*

* * *

Did you ever wish you had one book that you could go to for a quick reference on various topics? Here it is---a wonderfully, unexpected book. An essential volume for living in today's world. A great book written with authority and insight.
--*Jennifer Kennedy Cassidy*
Co-host, *Truths that Transform*, and daughter of Dr. D. James Kennedy

* * *

Jerry Newcombe understands faith and freedom and warns about the threats that are attacking both. His keen observations highlight what we must understand in our nation and what is happening around the world. This book is an important must-read! Our nation needs this book now more than ever.
--*Attorney David Gibbs III*
Founder/director of the National Center for Life and Liberty (NCLL)

* * *

Author's Introduction

Jesus is the most important person who ever lived. He has been the inspiration for more positive changes the world has ever seen than anyone else by far.

On balance, historic Christianity has greatly benefitted humanity. About a hundred years ago, James Russell Lowell, who wrote the hymn "Once to every man and nation" (which Dr. Martin Luther King, Jr. quoted when he made it to Selma) once said this: "I challenge any skeptic to find a ten square mile spot on this planet where they can live their lives in peace and safety and decency, where womanhood is honored, where infancy and old age are revered, where they can educate their children, where the Gospel of Jesus Christ has not gone first to prepare the way. If they find such a place, then I would encourage them to emigrate thither and there proclaim their unbelief."

But in our day the skeptics seem to be in full force. *The Unstoppable Jesus Christ* aims to show who the real Jesus is; why His mission will not fail; why we can trust His Word, the Bible; why the Hollywood left and the Christian-bashers are on the wrong side of history; and that science and the arts are tools of His creation.

Jesus said the day would come when men will kill you and think that in so doing they are worshiping God. And so the book deals with the very real threat of radical Islam and even the threat of death itself. Jesus is unstoppable, and His movement is unstoppable. And everyone, regardless of past actions and socio-economic background and religious upbringing, is welcome to join His Kingdom, on His terms.

Napoleon was well acquainted with political power, and he once observed, "I search in vain in history to find the similar to Jesus Christ, or anything which can approach the gospel. . . . Nations pass away, thrones crumble, but the Church remains." There is no one with the authority of Jesus.

Jerry Newcombe, D.Min.
Ft. Lauderdale, FL
June 2016

Part 1.

Jesus Christ

The Unstompable Jesus Christ

3/27/13

By now, it seems most everyone has heard about an inane assignment that boggles the mind. Earlier this month a professor at FAU, Florida Atlantic University (the Davie campus, near Ft. Lauderdale), had his students participate in a bizarre exercise.

He told his students to take out a sheet of paper and write on that paper in large letters, the name "Jesus." Then he said to take the paper, put it on the floor, stand up, and then stomp on the paper.

I'm not exactly sure what the point of the assignment was---other than to prove how absurd some modern higher academia has become. What if it had said "Mohammed"?

One student, a Mormon, picked up his "Jesus" paper, put it back on his desk, and respectfully told the professor he could not participate. That student was suspended from the class. Initially, the school stood by the teacher. But now they've apologized and said that that exercise will not be repeated. The student has been reinstated in the class, thanks to the help of the Texas-based Liberty Institute.

"What's wrong with those people?" asks my son-in-law, who has a BA from FAU." They truly are cowards. They hide behind their diplomas and degree. You can't spew that kind of hate without repercussions---except on the college campuses, I guess."

My son-in-law met my daughter there when she was earning her BA there. I've had a positive view of the school, but this incident was quite troublesome.

There's an incredible irony of this professor's actions. Just as there is irony in all the Christian bashing we seem to find in this culture. Like Jamie Foxx thanking his "Lord and Savior"---Barack Obama, on a television appearance a few months back.

Here's the irony: every beat of the heart is by the grace of Jesus Christ. When He says, "Enough," life is over. And to Him we must all give an account. Contrary to all the St. Peter at the Pearly Gates jokes, Jesus is the one to whom we must answer for our lives.

How can I say that? Because of the original Easter. Two thousand years ago Jesus walked out of His tomb in Jerusalem. This is a fact of history that changed all of history.

The change of the disciples' hearts and minds after His resurrection was such that they were convinced He was risen.

Because of His death for sinners and His resurrection, they were transformed, from men who hid behind locked doors to fearless missionaries.

After the resurrection, the disciples were unstoppable. Beginning in Jerusalem, the place of Christ's death and resurrection (and empty tomb), they boldly proclaimed the death and resurrection. They spread the good news from there into the four corners of Rome.

The Temple authorities did everything they could to squelch the Christian movement. They failed. Then the Romans tried in earnest, ten times in particular over the next three centuries to squelch Christianity. But they failed too.

Dr. N. T. Wright of England, once said this when I interviewed him for a television program: "The disciples, at the time of Jesus' crucifixion, were completely devastated. Everybody in their world knew that if you were following a prophet or a Messiah or a leader or whatever and that person got executed by the Roman authorities, then it meant you had backed the wrong horse. Since everybody knew that a crucified Messiah was a failed Messiah, the only thing which explains why they said Jesus was the Messiah is that they really did believe that He had been bodily raised from the dead."

Another recent example of Christian-bashing in our time was when Saturday Night Live crossed a line of respect / disrespect, when they portrayed Jesus vanquishing the Roman Empire through violence. The fascinating thing is that Jesus did vanquish Rome---by love, forgiveness, and non-violent means.

Historian Will Durant wrote a definitive, multivolume survey of world history. Durant commented on the Gospel's success in ancient Rome.

He said, "There is no greater drama in human record than the sight of a few Christians, scorned or oppressed by a succession of emperors, bearing all trials with a fiery tenacity, multiplying quietly, building order while their enemies generated chaos, fighting the sword with the word, brutality with hope, and at last defeating the strongest state that history has ever known. Caesar and Christ had met in the arena, and Christ had won."

You can walk around Rome today and see the ruins of "the strongest state history has ever known," and yet you can walk into a storefront in one of our inner cities and hear the name of Jesus, the risen Lord, being praised. Or in a cathedral, for that matter.

When beautiful American spirituals are performed in church, I'm reminded of how such hymns praising Jesus were written by slaves. These songs of praise are still used today, while the evil system that oppressed those slaves is "gone with the wind."

William F. Buckley, Jr. once introduced a debate between a Christian scholar and a skeptic: "If during the course of the debate, [the skeptic] disappears in a puff of smoke, then rest assured that Jesus up in heaven has just cleared His throat."

The Historical Jesus

3/5/13

Every once in a while, we hear a false charge. A charge that has significance during this Lenten season of 2013.

It's an old lie that seems to keep resurfacing. The accusation is that supposedly there is no historical reliability to Jesus as a person. In other words, we supposedly can't know for sure that He even existed historically.

That is so false. For example, Will Durant, the great historian who wrote the series, *The Story of Civilization*, noted in the volume, *Caesar and Christ*, that if the same criterion by which some philosophers claim Jesus didn't really exist as an historical person, then by that same criterion we'd have to throw out all sorts of historical figures, such as Hammurabi or King David.

Will Durant was not a believer. But even he saw how false this notion was.

This lie that we don't know if Jesus ever existed is even dallied with, and (thankfully) dismissed, by some of the modern bestselling books promoting atheism by Richard Dawkins, Sam Harris, and the late Christopher Hitchens.

I heard a caller on a talk show recently where he was challenging the host and co-host as to Jesus Christ. The caller made the astounding claim that Jesus is only written about in the New Testament, but there were no secular or non-Christian sources writing about Him during those early years.

Unfortunately, the hosts let this comment slide by with some sort of remark like, "You have to take it on faith." But Christianity is well-rooted in history. Jesus is better attested than virtually any figure of antiquity.

Dr. Gary Habermas of Liberty University is the author of *The Historical Jesus*. He tells us that there are multiple non-Christian sources from the first and second centuries that refer to Jesus Christ in one way or another.

These include: Josephus, Tacitus, Thallus, Phlegon, Pliny the Younger, Suetonius, Emperor Trajan, Emperor Hadrian, the Talmud, Lucian, Mara Bar-Serapion, and so on.

In addition, there are multiple sources from Christian writers who are not in the New Testament. They would include Clement of Rome, Diognetus, Aristedes, Papias, Barnabas, Polycarp, Ignatius, Melito of Sardis, Quadratus, Justin Martyr, and so on.

Gary Habermas and Mike Licona, authors of *The Case for the Resurrection of Jesus*, note that there is more documentation for Jesus Christ within 150 years of his life, even from secular sources, than there is for Caesar Tiberius.

That's an astounding observation.

To create an analogy: Imagine if 2000 years from now, there was more documentation on the life of a traveling minister (whose ministry lasted three and a half years) than there was for the President of the United States, during whose term the preacher preached.

Furthermore, Dr. Habermas once told me, "Actually, the life of Jesus is recorded in whole or in part, different segments, in about 20 different non-Christian sources, archaeological or historical, outside the New Testament."

He went on to say, "Now most of these are little snippets, a sentence here, a paragraph there, but you put them all together and there's approximately 60 to 65 facts concerning the life, death, resurrection, teachings of Jesus in the earliest Church. You can get an outline of his life and never touch the New Testament."

If we turn to early Christian sources, including the New Testament, than the recording of Jesus's life is even greater. And there are many early Christian sources writing about Jesus that are beyond the pages of the Bible. Writers such as Clement of Rome, Ignatius, Quadratus, Barnabas, Justin Martyr.

So the next time somebody tries to sell you on the idea that Jesus cannot be documented in history---even secular history, please lovingly but firmly stop them in their tracks…with the facts.

No reputable historian denies the historicity of Jesus.

Passover and Good Friday

3/25/15

There is a great hunger to be forgiven---it is a universal need.

In the classic book by Karl Menninger of the Menninger Clinic, *Whatever Became of Sin?*, he described a situation where a mime on the busy sidewalks of Chicago would point at a total stranger and yell out "Guilty!" Amazingly, the reaction of most of the strangers was to slink away, as if to say, "How did you know?"

We all instinctively know that things are not right between us and the universe. There is a name for that, and it is sin. Sin is what is wrong with this world. But sin has been dealt with in a decisive way. Soon another Good Friday will be upon us. This is the Christian Day of Atonement. This is the Passover to us, just as that original Good Friday coincided with the Passover.

Before a holy God, none of us can stand without condemnation---in our natural state. This is why God sent Jesus, His only begotten Son, to die in our place---to bring salvation for those who believe in Him.

Centuries before Jesus came, God instituted through Moses an elaborate system of sacrifice of animals. From a Christian perspective, all of those sacrifices were foreshadows of Jesus' once-and-for-all sacrifice on Calvary.

One of the great pictures of Christ's redemption is the Passover---because the ancient Hebrews were instructed to take the blood of a lamb without blemish and smear it on the top and two sides of the entrance to their homes---in essence forming the sign of the cross. The angel of death would "pass over" the homes where the blood had been smeared, sparing the occupants. People were either covered by the blood of the lamb or they were not.

Christ is the ultimate Passover Lamb who was slain for our sins. When John the Baptist, the great forerunner of Jesus, who prepared the way for the Lord, first saw Jesus, he famously said, "Behold, the Lamb of God, who takes away the sin of the world!" In Latin, Lamb of God is Agnus Dei.

Often in cathedrals, you can see the image of a lamb with a cross---sometimes that cross is like a flag. That is the Agnus Dei, the Lamb of God.

Years ago I interviewed a Jewish believer in Jesus, Murray Tillis of Atlanta. He came to believe in Jesus as His Jewish Messiah and has founded Light of Messiah Ministries.

He told me, "As I read Psalm 22 [written c. 1000 B.C.] for the very first time as a Jewish person, I was shocked that this writer, David, who is writing long before Jesus ever came and long before crucifixion was ever even a known method or means of execution, he was describing the crucifixion of Jesus." The opening line of this psalm was something Jesus quoted on the cross: "My God, my God, Why hast Thou forsaken Me?"

I asked Murray about Jesus and the Passover. He said, "The meal on the night He was betrayed was a Passover meal. Jesus said to His disciples, 'I earnestly desire to eat this meal with you.'"

That Last Supper, of course, was the celebration of the Passover. Says Murray: "It was within the context of a Passover Seder or Order of Service, where Jesus, sitting around the table with His disciples, was going through the Order of Service that Jewish people were very familiar with then and are very familiar with today---an order that consists of four cups, the cup of blessing, the cup of plagues, the cup of redemption, and then the cup of praise."

Tillis adds, "The cup of redemption comes directly after the meal. In fact, in the New Testament, we read that Jesus took the cup after the meal. That was the cup of redemption...He raised that cup up, He looked at His disciples, and He said, 'This is my blood which is shed for you.'"

And so in one sense, Passover and communion become one. Murray continues: "And then He took the unleavened bread, symbolic of sinlessness or sinless nature, broke it, and said, 'This is my body which is broken for you.'"

Murray Tillis concludes: "And so, within the context of this Passover meal, Jesus was saying to His disciples, 'My blood is going to be shed for you. I am going to be crucified for you. I am the Passover Lamb. And because of that blood, death will pass over you, as well.'"

It is His blood that is the key to forgiveness. It is His blood, received by faith, that washes away guilt. Happy Holy Week.

Easter Hope---Based on Facts of History

4/16/14

Jesus sells. That's why they have cover stories on Him in magazines and TV specials, even if some of them offer strange theories to try to explain away things like the original Easter.

14

I'll never forget the evolution of a famous TV newsman, the late Peter Jennings, the anchor ABC's nightly news broadcasts.

In 2000, Jennings hosted a special, "The Search for Jesus." He never found Him because he relied almost entirely on liberal Bible scholars who dismissed the reliability of the Gospel accounts. The special, though well done, needlessly cast doubt on all the basics about Jesus.

But in 2004, Jennings hosted another ABC special, on Jesus and Paul. This special was fairer, at least they featured an occasional conservative scholar, such as the great Dr. Paul L. Maier.

During that 2004 special, Jennings was walking around Rome, observing that Peter and Paul, two key leaders in the early Church, were absolute nobodies in the first century when they came to that city. They were total outcasts, and both were put to death there as martyrs for their faith. Yet now these two dominate the city. As does, of course, the Jesus they served.

When Jesus walked out of the tomb, He changed history. This is 2014 because Jesus was born circa 2014 years ago. We wouldn't be talking about Him if He had stayed dead.

The famous skeptic David Hume argued that Jesus didn't rise from the dead because dead men don't rise from the dead. True, they normally don't. However, that's what makes Jesus' case so special. Hume employed circular reasoning here. But the Christian does not.

I don't believe that Jesus rose from the dead, only because the Bible says so (which would be circular reasoning). Actually, I believe in the Bible, largely because of the historical evidence that Jesus rose from the dead.

The biggest single reason I believe Jesus walked out of that tomb bodily is because the disciples were so transformed. At Jesus' death, they had been very scared. Peter, their leader, denied three times that he knew Him, just to save his skin.

But then something happened that transformed them and made them unstoppable. They claimed that they saw Him risen from the dead, not just once, but many times. They were not wallowing in credulity. In fact, if you read the Gospels, we see that many of the disciples were the original skeptics of the resurrection. We even have the common phrase "Doubting Thomas" because Thomas didn't believe it---until he saw Jesus alive.

I've had the privilege of interviewing many leading Jesus scholars (both believers and skeptics) on the questions of who is Jesus, are the Gospels reliable, and did He rise from the dead?

All of them, even the most skeptical, agree at least on this: The disciples were convinced that they saw Jesus risen from the dead. The skeptics don't think He arose, but they acknowledge that the disciples absolutely thought so.

How else do you explain their fearless preaching to the ends of the known world (and beyond)? There is historical evidence that ten of the remaining eleven apostles (twelve minus Judas) died a horrible martyr's death. Only John lived to old age, though he was reportedly boiled in hot oil.

None of them denied that Jesus rose from the dead after He died to provide forgiveness for fallen humanity. No, not one. They sealed their testimony in their own blood.

But, you say, people die all the time for what is a lie. Perhaps--- but not *knowingly* so. If the disciples were a part of some supposed "Passover Plot," if they had stolen the body and made up this story, would they have given their lives for what they *knew* was a lie?

Historian Dr. Paul Maier once told me, "Myths do not make martyrs. And if this story had been invented, they would not have gone to death for it. If Peter had invented the account as he's ready to be hoisted up on a cross in Rome, he would've blown the whistle and said, 'Hold it! I'll plea bargain with you. I'll tell you how we did it, if I can come off with my life.'"

The disciples did not abandon their discipleship after Jesus died. Why not? They told us themselves---because He rose from the dead.

Jesus' resurrection on a Sunday changed the day of worship for the church, and established it as a day of rest. Each Sunday through much of the world now serves as a weekly reminder of that resurrection. Thus, even the atheist who sleeps in this Sunday morning will be ironically paying homage to Jesus' walking out of the tomb 2000 years ago. He is risen indeed.

On the Resurrection---Just the Facts, Ma'am
3/24/16

If Jesus Christ walked out of His tomb after His death, then certainly everything He said about Himself---that He is the Lord, the way, the truth, and the life---would all receive a stamp of approval.

Why should we listen to Jesus? Because He was dead, and then He was alive. He showed Himself to be alive by "many infallible proofs" according to Luke the physician, in part two of his New Testament writings---what we call the Acts of the Apostles.

A few weeks ago I got to see the movie, "God's Not Dead 2," which I enjoyed very much. Even a loved one with a skeptical bent enjoyed the movie. It comes out April 1. I recommend it highly.

In the movie there are some cameos from leading Christian apologists, such as Lee Strobel, a former atheist and Chicago Tribune investigative writer, and Dr. Gary Habermas.

Habermas is a leading scholar on the resurrection of Jesus Christ. At Liberty Baptist Theological Seminary, he is a Distinguished Research Professor and the Chair of the Department of Philosophy. He has studied the resurrection for decades now and has written or co-written 21 books specifically on the topic.

In fact, Habermas had a period of doubt for about ten years. But the more he studied the historical resurrection of Jesus, the more convinced he became that Jesus indeed rose from the dead.

One thing is for sure, the Apostle Paul, who staked his life on the resurrection of Jesus, argued that if Christ did not rise from the dead, our faith is in vain and we are to be pitied more than all men. But Christ did rise from the dead, and therefore everything else falls into place.

Habermas takes an approach to the resurrection called the "minimal facts." He wants to see where scholars---even liberal ones---agree on certain basic facts that apply to this issue. It's like Sergeant Friday from *Dragnet*, "Just the facts, Ma'am. Just the facts."

But what about skeptical scholars? Habermas has two rules for assigning something as a "minimal fact."

In a recent radio interview, he told me: "The two rules for minimal facts are 1) I will use not one bit of data which is not attested from several sources. I have several strong reasons to accept these as facts. 2) Because that evidence is so good, that's why the vast majority of critical scholars get on board with these minimal facts and allow them."

He estimates that the following facts about the resurrection of Jesus would be verified by 90% of the *skeptical* Jesus scholars. I would add that they would be accepted by virtually 100% of the conservative ones.

Here are the following minimal facts that the majority of scholars, including skeptics, agree to:

1) Jesus was crucified by the Romans. Habermas said that this is "not an evidence for the resurrection, but it's a pre-requisite."

2) The disciples had experiences that believed were appearances of the risen Christ.

3) Because of their insistence that they saw Him risen from the dead, they totally changed in disposition from being afraid to being bold and unstoppable. They proclaimed, not just any message, they proclaimed the resurrection message and were persecuted for their proclamation. Habermas notes, "A number of them died for their faith. They were totally transformed and willing to die for their faith."

4) This proclamation of the resurrection was there at the very beginning of the Christian movement---it was not some later add-on.

5) One of the earliest to believe in the risen Jesus was the formerly skeptical James, the brother of Jesus.

6) Another skeptic changed by claiming he saw the risen Christ was the Apostle Paul, formerly Saul of Tarsus, the anti-Christian persecutor.

Again, these six facts are generally agreed upon by scholars of early Christianity, both friendly and hostile scholars to the faith.

From these, we see a clear pattern. Jesus died on the cross. Then His disciples, who were scared for their lives, suddenly changed into bold witnesses for the risen Christ. Nobody dies for something they *know* is a lie.

Habermas adds there are other widely accepted facts accepted by many scholars as well, such as:

* The tomb was empty beginning Sunday morning.

* The proclamation of the resurrection began in Jerusalem, which the disciples would not have dared to pursue if it could easily be disproven by procuring His body from the tomb. (This provides much of the tension in another movie I recommend, *Risen*).

* These strict observers of the Sabbath began to worship Jesus on Sunday, since He arose on Sunday.

What is the best explanation for all these facts? He is risen. He is risen indeed. No wonder the world was changed by the events that began on the first Easter morning.

The Alleged "Lost Tomb of Jesus"

9/21/16

Geologist Dr. Aryeh Shimron claims to have found the "lost tomb of Jesus" in Jerusalem, proclaimed the Drudge Report (9/18/16). This is known as the Talpiot Tomb, first discovered in 1980. The implications of this claim, if it were true, are enormous---world-changing.

Writing for *The Sun* (UK), Hannah Farrett notes, "he apparently has proof that Jesus Christ is buried at a site in East Jerusalem. But now Aryeh has done some tests, which he says prove Jesus of Nazareth, his wife Mary Magdalene and SON Judah were laid to rest there."

She adds, "There are nine burial boxes in the tomb, and they all have names with links to the New Testament of the Bible on them....This was highly controversial, given Christians believe Jesus was resurrected....Some people rubbished the claims, saying all the names etched on the boxes were so common at the time there's no way of drawing any conclusions."

It certainly is "highly controversial." But is it true? Short answer: No.

Dr. Paul L. Maier, Harvard-trained retired professor of ancient history at Western Michigan University, is a best-selling author. Most of his books are non-fiction. But he once wrote a novel called, *A Skeleton in God's Closet.*

The book deals with an alleged discovery of Jesus' tomb---providing actual "proof" that Jesus had not risen from the dead---bodily, historically, physically---and that the whole Christian church in all of its manifestations was, therefore, built on a lie. Soon, the whole thing (Christianity) collapsed---as well it should---if Jesus has not indeed risen from the dead.

For this column, I reached out to some leading New Testament scholars for comments.

Dr. Maier emailed me: "It seems that sensationalizing writers about Jesus always try twice to gain public attention with their bizarre claims when their first effort fails....Now Israeli Geologist Aryeh Shimron has done the same thing in the case of the Talpiot

Tomb in Jerusalem. Virtually the same headlines were used now as when the 'discovery' was first announced in 2007. It was junk then, it is junk now. The current warmed-over version will receive the same reception now as nine years ago: Dead on Arrival."

Dr. Michael Licona teaches at Houston Baptist University. The conclusion of his 700-plus page book, *The Resurrection of Jesus: A New Historiographical Approach*, states: "Jesus' resurrection from the dead is the best historical explanation of the relevant historical bedrock" (p. 610).

He adds, "Since it fulfills all five of the criteria for the best explanation and outdistances competing hypotheses by a significant margin in their ability to fulfill the same criteria, the historian is warranted in regarding Jesus' resurrection as an event that occurred in the past."

Responding to this new story, Licona wrote me: "Some things in history are more certain than others. One fact that is virtually certain is Jesus' disciples were convinced their rabbi had risen from the dead and had appeared to them. The data supporting this fact are so secure that virtually 100 percent of all historians of Jesus grant it, whether Jewish, agnostic, or atheist."

And Licona notes, "Moreover, the earliest Christians proclaimed that Jesus had been raised bodily, leaving behind an empty grave. Dr. Shimron must explain how Jesus's corpse went missing, then received an honorable burial without any of His disciples ever learning about it. It seems more likely that Dr. Shimron is engaged in wishful thinking and that his claim to have found the family tomb of Jesus will soon be laid to rest in the graveyard of discarded fanciful hypotheses."

Dr. Gary Habermas of Liberty University is a walking encyclopedia on the resurrection of Jesus and has written on it voluminously. His book, *The Secret of the Talpiot Tomb: Unraveling the Mystery of the Jesus Family Tomb* (2008), shows why the Talpiot Tomb could not possibly contain the tomb of Jesus of Nazareth.

Habermas emailed me, "Thankfully, virtually no scholars support him [Shimron] at all."

Finally, I also received feedback on the alleged "lost tomb of Jesus" from Dr. Darrell Bock, one of the world's leading New Testament scholars. Bock teaches at Dallas Theological Seminary.

He emailed me, "Nothing has changed since this erroneous conclusion was originally proposed. Jesus would not be in a family tomb as his execution as a felon prevented him by Jewish tradition from being buried in a family tomb. In the Mishnah, Sanhedrin 6.5 says, 'And they did not bury [the felon] in the burial grounds of his ancestors.' So no burial with the family."

In short, the claim that the lost tomb of Jesus has been found is just recycled sensationalist rubble. As Maier noted: "I guess there is no end to the way these deluded sensationalists will try to whack a dead horse!" In short, Jesus is risen indeed.

Global Warming or Crucifixion Day?

4/19/11

This Friday marks one of the holiest days in the Christian calendar. To the believer, Good Friday marks the day that Jesus Christ died for sinners. He laid down His life to pay a price He didn't owe, but a price we could never pay.

As noted, to Christians, this is our Day of Atonement and our Passover—all rolled into one on the same day. To put it in religious jargon, the death of the Lamb of God brings forgiveness of sins for those who believe.

In short, Good Friday is the day when we honor the self-sacrifice of Christ on the cross on behalf of sinners.

But wait.

There's something else to commemorate this year's Good Friday, says a group of liberal religious leaders in the Episcopal Church.

We should also honor Mother Earth.

It turns out that Holy Week this year coincides with the celebration of Earth Day. So to these religious liberals, they can spend time not only contemplating the Passion of the Christ, but also the passion of the earth.

The Episcopal Church's office of Economic and Environmental Affairs notes that the faithful should not only remember the crucifixion, but also recycling and the need to combat global warming and the necessity to reduce carbon emissions.

Mike Schut, a Church spokesman, said, "On Good Friday, the day we mark the crucifixion of Christ, God in the flesh, might we suggest that when Earth is degraded, when species go extinct, that another part of God's body experiences yet another sort of crucifixion—that another way of seeing and experiencing God is diminished?"

You can't make this stuff up.

Here we have lip service to a high holy day in Christianity, yet they put the *theory* of man-made global warming essentially on the same level as Jesus on the cross.

Schut called the falling of Earth Day this year within Holy Week, "specifically on Good Friday, a profound coincidence." He added, "To fully honor Earth Day, we need to reclaim the theology that knows Earth is 'very good,' is holy. When we fully recognize that, our actions just may begin to create a more sustainable, compassionate economy and way of life."

So I suppose for some of their followers, they can pay homage to Christ for His ultimate sacrifice or they can reflect on what they can do to recycle more effectively.

Take your pick.

I suppose the one redeeming aspect of this story—no pun intended—is that it does show that for many, global warming has become a type of religion.

This whole thing is also amazing to me because I don't even buy the premise.

Oh, I believe we should be good stewards of the earth. Don't litter, that sort of thing. But man-made global warming? Is it not a bunch of hot air?

It's hard to believe that people still believe in anthropogenic global warming. In late 2009, a big hoax surrounding the subject was uncovered. A multitude of emails were revealed—secret communiqués from scientists that documented that some of the key scientists advocating the theory of man-made global warming were allegedly tinkering with the data.

I spoke recently with Brian Sussman, a TV meteorologist who doesn't believe in man-made global warming. He wrote the book *Climategate: A Veteran Meteorologist Exposes the Global Warming Scam.*

We spoke about these email leaks. They came from the Climate Research Unit at the University of East Anglia in the UK. (Sussman said he thinks they were leaked by someone inside—not hacked by someone on the outside).

In any event, he told me, "in the CRU, we had emails with names attached from people who really made it clear that the temperature record of the earth had been manipulated. They made it very clear that deniers like myself, they were trying to keep out of major scientific publications, we weren't allowed to publish anything in some of these various research journals."

Sussman summarizes the upshot of all this: "We can no longer trust the temperature of the earth. It's being so seriously compromised by people with an agenda."

So to put the celebration of Earth Day with grave concerns over global warming at the same level of Christ crucified seems terribly misguided to me.

However well intentioned some of these Episcopal leaders may be, it seems that they continue to allow themselves to fall prey to an ongoing hoax, while trivializing the commemoration of the greatest act of love in history.

Kyrie Eleison.

Lord, have mercy.

Jesus Is Coming Back---But Not as Saturday Night Live Depicted

3/11/13

The recent tasteless Saturday Night Live (SNL) satirical parody, "DJesus Uncrossed," has many Christians incensed. The American Family Association contacted sponsors of the program who pledged not to allow their ads to air when that segment goes in reruns.

ChristianNews.net reported [2/20/13] that the skit, which portrays Jesus taking vengeance against his enemies with guns and a sword, (He cleaves the head of a Roman soldier and shoots a hole through Judas), "has generated uproar across the country from those who find the dramatization to be blasphemous."

The skit was intended as a spoof of the recent movie by Quentin Tarantino "Django Unchained," which shows the freedman former slave, Django, taking vengeance on the slave owner who tortured and raped his wife and killing as many white men along the way as possible.

According to ChristianNews.net, the SNL skit "plays like a movie trailer. In the two-minute feature, Jesus is seen rolling the stone away from His tomb, and after the final push, declares in a

Terminator-like fashion, 'Guess who's back?'" The narrator relates, "He's risen from the dead, and He's preaching anything but forgiveness."

Those who protest the skit's blasphemy of Christ are right to do so. Nevertheless, it is significant that the writers could think of no cultural icon other than Jesus to use as their foil for their skit.

Who else can we think of who might have cause to come back with a vengeance to wreak havoc and judgment against those who have persecuted and tortured Him? There are other figures in history who likewise have suffered unjustly. But Jesus stands above them all as the most recognizable.

By using Jesus as their foil, SNL played off the one characteristic most people associate with Jesus, His forgiveness. The line, "He's risen from the dead, and He's preaching anything but forgiveness," sets the stage for the behavior that seems incongruous—He walks around taking vengeance upon his enemies with sword and gun. The skit "works" because Jesus is portrayed, in satiric fashion, in a way that is inconsistent with His character.

Or perhaps we should say, that's not how we commonly think of Jesus. We prefer the depiction of "Jesus meek and mild," the one who welcomes sinners and offers us forgiveness regardless of our past foibles, follies, and faults. We'd like to think of Jesus as an unending "fountain of forgiveness" who is sitting waiting for us to come to Him to make us "right with God,"—but on our own schedule and at a time that's convenient to us.

However, this is not all there is to "the Jesus story." Ironically, the "DJesus Uncrossed" skit has pointed to a sober truth that is also found in the Gospels, but which rarely gets much coverage.

The truth is that one day Jesus Christ will return as "King of kings, and Lord of lords" and will judge and administer final justice to those who have failed to live up to God's standard of righteousness. As Matthew 16:27 states, "For the Son of Man will come in the glory of His Father with His angels, and then He will reward each according to his works."

The standard against those works—our works—will be judged is God's moral law, the Ten Commandments, which schools no longer want children to read, and courts have ruled may not be displayed in many public venues. But they remain the standard, nonetheless. And who can say that they have kept every commandment? Who has never lied, or coveted? Who can say that they have no other gods in their life?

Jesus summarized the Ten Commandments in two as recorded in Matthew 22:37-39.

You shall love the Lord your God with all your heart, with all your soul, and with all your mind. This is the first and great commandment. And the second is like it: You shall love your neighbor as yourself.

Who among us can say we have met this standard...perfectly? As Jesus said, "Therefore you shall be perfect, just as your Father in heaven is perfect" (Matthew 5:48).

There is no one who can meet that standard of perfection. But as Colossians 2 tells us, Christ took away the requirement that was against us, and nailed it to His cross. Now we are "unchained"— loosed from the grip of sin and death, and Jesus, by His own death, "disarmed principalities and powers," and "he made a public spectacle of them, triumphing over them in it."

While on earth, Jesus made it clear that when He returns He will not be "chained" in any way. In fact, besides the picture of Jesus "meek and mild" who forgives sins—and He is willing to do that— there is another picture of Jesus the Bible clearly shows.

Stephen saw Him "standing at the right hand of God" in glory. Paul was blinded by His brightness as the Lord Jesus spoke to him on the road to Damascus. As Paul later wrote to the Philippian Christians, "God also has highly exalted him and given him the name which is above every name, that at the name of Jesus every knee should bow, of those in heaven, and of those on earth, and of those under the earth, and that every tongue should confess that Jesus Christ is Lord, to the glory of God the Father."

In the book of Revelation, chapter 19, the Apostle John recorded the vision he was given of Jesus returning as the righteous judge of the nations: "Then I saw heaven opened, and behold, a white horse! The one sitting on it is called Faithful and True, and in righteousness he judges and makes war. His eyes are like a flame of fire, and on his head are many diadems, and he has a name written that no one knows but himself. He is clothed in a robe dipped in blood, and the name by which he is called is The Word of God. And the armies of heaven, arrayed in fine linen, white and pure, were following him on white horses. From his mouth comes a sharp sword with which to strike down the nations, and he will rule them with a rod of iron. He will tread the winepress of the fury of the wrath of God the Almighty. On his robe and on his thigh he has a name written, King of kings and Lord of lords."

Some may mock Jesus now and use Him to get cheap laughs, but when He returns and descends from heaven "with a shout, with the voice of an archangel, and with the trumpet of God" as I Thessalonians 4 tells us, only those who have humbly come to him and received His forgiveness "shall be caught up...to meet the Lord in the air" to "always be with the Lord."

On the other hand, those who have rejected Jesus' offer of forgiveness for their sins and spurned His sacrificial love will be cast into outer darkness where—as is recorded three times in Matthew—there is "weeping and gnashing of teeth."

"And this gospel of the kingdom will be preached in all the world as a witness to all the nations, and then the end will come" (Matthew 24:14).

Judgment Day on May 21?
Let's Talk It Over---on May 22

5/16/11

Oh brother, here we go again.

Another false prophet---dare I say that?---is predicting exactly when Christ is coming again, even though Jesus Himself said that no man knows the hour of His return, including Himself.

From the early days of the Church to the present day, hundreds of millions of Christians have affirmed, "Christ has died. Christ is risen. Christ will come again."

But now a group is trying to fear people into thinking they know when Jesus is coming. May 21, 2011 is the day, supposedly, of Christ's "secret" rapture. (Doesn't sound too secret to me.)

The latest prophets of doom have managed to get their message out in a series of billboards and bus ads. In my humble opinion: What a waste of money and what a mockery they make of people's faith. (If the message said simply Judgment Day is coming---get ready to meet your Maker, then I would whole-heartedly endorse that message. It's the specific date that's the problem.)

Do I think Judgment Day is coming on May 21? Well, let's talk it over, on May 22.

In addition, October 21, 2011, according to these people, is Judgment Day.

Who are "these people"?

The main leader is Harold Camping, who has a network of Christian radio stations. You would think he would be gun shy about setting a date for Christ's return.

He wrote a book about it, predicting that 1994 would be the year. I own a copy of his book explaining the details. It's called *1994*.

Another man predicted that Jesus would return in 1988, and he listed 88 reasons for it.

But you can *always tell* that such predictions are wrong. Why? Because they are specific.

With all due respect, how do I know that these people are always wrong? The fact that they're setting a date in the first place violates what Jesus said.

In Matthew's Gospel, He said about His return: "But about that day or hour no one knows, not even the angels in heaven, nor the Son, but only the Father. As it was in the days of Noah, so it will be at the coming of the Son of Man" (24:36-37).

I'm tempted to say to these people who give a specific date---like May 21, 2011---What part of "no" as in "no man knows the hour" don't you understand?

I even read one such prophet who essentially said—with a straight face: Christ didn't tell us the day or the hour of His return, but that doesn't mean we can't know the year, the month, or the week!

It's tragic to me that the watching world looks at such predictions that come and go and just laugh, justifiably so, at those who think Christ will return one day.

I am as sure of the return of Jesus Christ to planet earth some day, as I am that the sun will rise tomorrow.

But I have no idea when, nor will I engage in speculation based on "jigsaw theology."

Jigsaw theology is when you cobble a Bible verse over here with a Bible verse over there to create some sort of timeline for the Second Coming.

The group that has made the May 21, 2011 prediction says this: "The Bible has opened up its secrets concerning the timeline of history. This information was never previously known because God had closed up His Word blocking any attempt to gain knowledge of the end of the world."

But now *they* know, supposedly.

A friend of mine noted this is like modern day Gnosticism.

The Gnostics were an early Church heresy that got the basics of the faith wrong. They claimed that the way of salvation was not Christ crucified, for sinners died and raised from the dead, but rather some sort of *secret knowledge.*

People have been wrong often throughout Church history as to the return of Christ.

Many were convinced that Jesus would come in AD 1000, so they sold everything and went to Jerusalem and waited. And waited.

Others sold everything they had and waited for Christ to return in America in the 1840s. And waited. The Seventh Day Adventist denomination was born out of that experience.

When Hitler was alive, some people thought he was *the* Anti-Christ. Can you blame them? But they were wrong.

Through the ages, even otherwise-wise servants of Christ have made the mistake of predicting a specific date of the end of the world. Included in this category are Christopher Columbus, Sir Isaac Newton, and Cotton Mather.

How come we keep repeating this same mistake? I'm reminded of the little poem by British poet Steve Turner: "History repeats itself. It has to. No one is listening."

A Challenge to Skeptics: An Easter Message

4/1/15

Have you ever heard of Theudas? How about Judas of Galilee? They were would-be messiahs in the first century. How many followers do these men have today? Zero, zip, nada.

Of course, we've all heard of Jesus Christ. One-third of humanity professes to believe in Him. But I guarantee you we would never have heard of Him had He not risen from the dead.

Whoever you are, whatever you believe, *you* have a vested interest in looking into the issue of Jesus' resurrection from the dead. There are millions today who simply dismiss the message of Christianity out of hand and don't realize the eternal peril they are in by doing so.

On the first Easter, the tomb of Jesus was empty. That is an historical fact. Furthermore, the original skeptics of the resurrection were the disciples themselves. The only explanation for their turn from cowering in fear to boldly proclaiming Christ, though it cost virtually all of them their lives, was that they had encountered the risen Jesus.

The late Chuck Colson worked in the Nixon White House. He said: Compare the Watergate scandal with the resurrection. With Watergate, there was a human conspiracy; but once it began to break, it collapsed completely. And 80 men went to jail---Colson being one of them. But nothing (not even torture, nor martyrdom) could stop the disciples who proclaimed the resurrection of Jesus.

Honest skeptics who have examined the evidence have eventually become believers. Repeatedly.

* General Lew Wallace (1827-1905) was an unbeliever and set out to disprove the faith that he later came to embrace and help to promote. His pro-Christian book, *Ben-Hur: A Tale of the Christ*, became the basis for the 1959 film of the year.

* One of the best known defenders of the Christian faith of today is Josh McDowell, but as a young college student, he was very skeptical about the historicity of Christianity. In fact, he spent some time on study leave at the British Museum specifically to refute the faith.

After a few weeks of intense study, he realized how wrong he was. He realized that the Christian faith is based on the facts of history, available for anyone open-minded enough to discover.

He became a dedicated believer, has written many books, including the best-selling, *Evidence That Demands a Verdict*, and has proclaimed Christ all over the world. Josh McDowell said of the resurrection of Jesus: "It's the most fantastic fact of history."

* C. S. Lewis (1898-1963) was one of the greatest Christian writers of the 20th century. He taught at Oxford and at Cambridge University. But as a young man, he had been an atheist, until he examined Christianity more closely. He describes himself in *Surprised by Joy* as "the most dejected, reluctant convert in all of England . . . drug into the kingdom kicking, struggling, resentful, and darting [my] eyes in every direction for a chance of escape."

* Lee Strobel used to be the legal affairs editor of the *Chicago Tribune*. He graduated Yale Law School and was no intellectual slouch. He also was a confirmed skeptic. But when his wife started attending church, he decided to go on a quest: to use his

investigative skills to examine the claims of Christianity, including the resurrection of Jesus from the dead.

Strobel was honest enough to follow where the evidence would lead him. He became a Christian and now is a leading apologist. He has now written such classics as *The Case for Christ* and *The Case for Faith.*

* Author Dr. Mike Licona, professor at Houston Baptist University, told me that he had serious doubts as a young man: "So, I resolved to do a thorough investigation and go where the evidence led. After years of research, the conclusion was inescapable that Jesus had risen from the dead, and the Christian gospel turns out being true."

Licona's key professor was Dr. Gary Habermas of Liberty University. Habermas is one of the greatest scholars on the resurrection alive. He tells me: "I struggled through many years of religious doubt, for some ten years straight and then more sporadically for many more years beyond that. It dominated my thinking during those years."

He concludes: "Having studied other philosophies and world religions along the way, at one point I thought I was becoming a Buddhist. Throughout my entire search for answers, nothing quieted my toughest questions more thoroughly that did my detailed study of the resurrection of Jesus Christ. This event became my anchor and foundation for faith ever since."

Skeptics are welcome to examine the evidence for themselves. He is risen indeed.

New Theory Tries to Debunk the Original Easter
4/4/12

Every year, like clockwork, there seems to be a new theory that arises to explain away the Easter event, i.e., that Jesus Christ rose from the dead, bodily, and appeared to His apostles and convinced them He was alive.

Historically, it's true that the apostles---so convinced---went out and began to turn the Roman Empire upside down with the message of forgiveness through the cross and resurrection. Now roughly a third of humanity claims to believe this historic message.

In past years, theories to explain away the Easter event have included:

· *Jesus the Man* which presents Him as a divorced father of three, who later remarries.

· *Jesus: A Revolutionary Biography*, which proposes that Jesus didn't rise from the dead because He was never buried in the first place. His corpse was instead eaten by dogs.

· *The Lost Tomb of Jesus* TV special a few years ago declared Jesus did not rise from the dead, but the disciples cleverly stole the body. (I would ask: Why? So then they could go on to the horrible martyr's deaths most of them experienced? What would they gain?)

But now comes a strange new theory to explain away the resurrection of Jesus.

An art historian with ties to Cambridge University, Thomas de Wesselow, has written a book called, *The Sign*. As best I understand this new theory, he believes that the Shroud of Turin is truly the authentic shroud that Jesus was laid in (which I also believe). But he goes on to propose that Jesus didn't really rise from the dead after all. Instead, the apostles simply saw the Shroud with its mysterious image and believed.

Writing about this new book's thesis in the UK *Telegraph* (March 24, 2012), Peter Stanford notes, "Having established – at least for the purposes of argument – the Shroud in first century Israel, it is now time to turn to his potentially even more earth-shaking theory, namely that the Resurrection was a kind of optical illusion."

The illusion, as described by Stanford, is this: "What the apostles were seeing was the image of Jesus on the Shroud, which they then mistook for the real thing. It sounds, I can't help suggesting, as absurd as a scene from a Monty Python film." (And how exactly did that image get on the cloth? And this convinced them to the death?)

Here's some important background information on the world's most scrutinized artifact: The Shroud of Turin, a linen cloth 14 feet by 3 feet, contains the image of a man who was badly scourged, was crucified, wore a crown of thorns, and was stabbed in the chest with a Roman spear.

One of the great experts on this subject is Dr. Alan Whanger, a retired professor from Duke Medical Center who has spent his life studying medicine. Since the late 1970s, he has studied intensely the Shroud of Turin. I've interviewed him many times.

Although the Shroud was dismissed by some as a fake because of the carbon-dating in 1988 of a single specimen (divided into three tiny parts) that was said to date from 1260 to 1390 A.D., Dr. Whanger says that test was not valid because the sample chosen was from a rewoven part of the cloth (which was often displayed during the Middle Ages).

Furthermore, Dr. Whanger notes, "The Shroud is the most intensely studied single object in existence. There are probably 67 different fields of scientific and academic interests that have looked into the Shroud in one way in another. So, there's been a huge amount of research gone in on it. It is our conviction that the Shroud is, indeed, the burial cloth of Jesus of Nazareth. And we feel that we can date it to the spring of 30 A.D. in the Middle East, and that what we see on the Shroud with the various wounds, that this is entirely consistent with the scriptural account of the crucifixion of Jesus. And traditionally, this has been known as the image of Jesus."

We know where the Shroud has been since 1357, when it showed up in the home of a French crusader. Knowing it dates from 1357 or earlier, consider these details:

• The human anatomy represented on the Shroud is 100% correct---far ahead of its time.

• The Shroud's image is a photographic negative---long before photography.

• The faint image on the Shroud was not painted on. It was lightly burned on, through some sort of scorching process. The image is only 5/1000's of an inch thick.

• The blood on the Shroud is real human blood---with all the wounds corresponding with the passion of Jesus in the Gospels. The blood did not see decay---He was sandwiched inside that cloth for less than 72 hours. **Yet the blood was undisturbed, which means He somehow went through the cloth; it was not yanked off Him.** This fact alone would seem to throw de Wesselow's theory out the window.

• In the Middle Ages (and even sometimes today) artistic representations of the crucifixion place the nails in the palms. Yet the Shroud of Turin places the nails in the wrists, which turns out to be the only way a crucified person could be held in place.

• The image of the Shroud is three-dimensional. NASA scientists studied it in 1978. When ordinary photos or paintings are studied through a specific NASA, space-age machine (a "VP 8 Image Analyzer"), the image always becomes distorted. However, the

Shroud has been proven to have three-dimensional properties. It could not have been a painting.

I agree with de Wesselow that the Shroud is authentic, but to me, it points *to* the resurrection, not *away* from it.

In my view, it is one of those reminders that "He is risen." "He is risen indeed!"

The Non-Jesus Religion

11/6/13

The Supreme Court has heard arguments this week about whether prayers at government meetings, for example, a town council, can include the name of Jesus.

The case is *Galloway v. City of Greece* (which is a suburb of Rochester, NY), and it will likely be decided in the summer (or possibly spring) of 2014. The case could potentially have strong ramifications for this nation, especially in light of our extensive Christian heritage.

Jesus told His followers to pray in His name. That's why people pray "in Jesus' name. Amen" Or, as is often heard in the Book of Common Prayer (from the Anglican Church, which was very influential in the founding of America), "through the merits of Jesus Christ our Lord. Amen." George Washington was an avid reader of the Book of Common Prayer.

Different judicial circuits have ruled in ways that contradict each other on this issue. Hence, the Supreme Court's decision to clarify the matter.

One could wonder why there would even be prayers at all (much less prayers in the name of Jesus) at government settings in the first place. But we should keep in mind that, historically, opening legislative sessions or town councils often began in prayer and mostly in Jesus' name.

When the ACLU challenged the notion of chaplains---paid by the state to offer prayers, Christian or otherwise---the case went all the way to the Supreme Court in the 1980s. The prayers won; the ACLU lost. In *Marsh v. Chambers*, the Court, said, We had chaplains before we were a nation.

Our tradition of praying in Jesus' name in public shouldn't surprise us, since at the time of Independence, 99.8% of colonists were professing Christians ("Policy Review," Fall '88, p. 44).

The same Congress that gave us the First Amendment, now used to suppress prayers and other religious expression, were the same men who hired chaplains for the Senate and the House of Representatives. The US Capitol building was used from its beginning until the 1880s for Christian worship services on Sunday. Presidents Jefferson and Madison often attended these.

The first time the Continental Congress met, they wondered if the next day (9/7/1774) they should open their proceedings in prayer. Virtually all were Christian, but different Christian groups can pray in different ways. Samuel Adams said he was no "bigot." He could hear a prayer from a man who loved his God and his country. So they opened with a lengthy Bible-reading (Psalm 35) and fervent prayer in Jesus' name from a local Episcopal minister, Jacob Duché.

George Washington told the Delaware Indian chiefs when they brought their sons to learn the Englishmen's ways, "You do well to wish to learn our arts and ways of life, and above all, the religion of Jesus Christ." (5/12/1779).

Washington went on to say, "Congress will do everything they can to assist you in this wise intention." (John Rhodehamel, ed., *George Washington: Writings* (1997), p. 351.)

Thomas Jefferson, in whose name so much of the cleansing of anything religious----no, anything Christian---from the public square, would be shocked at this. For all his heterodox views later in life, he regularly (perhaps daily) read the teachings of Jesus Christ, for his own edification.

Jefferson said, "Of all the systems of morality, ancient or modern, which have come under my observation, none appear to me so pure as that of Jesus." (To William Canby, 9/18/1813).

My friend, constitutional attorney David Gibbs III of the National Center for Life and Liberty, is fighting in this current case for the government to not censor prayers at the behest of the ACLU.

David told me, "What the ACLU is arguing is that praying in Jesus' name is establishing a religion. The reality is that their goal is to establish a non-Jesus religion." David noted the ACLU is advancing cases only against anybody praying in Jesus' name, not in any other tradition.

David adds, "Do we really want judges deciding what words are okay and what words are not okay, in religious prayers? The ACLU is bullying government officials (by threat of expensive lawsuits) to eliminate traditions that have been happening since our government's founding."

I remember when a liberal lady called a conservative talk show during the HHS-mandate controversy. She advocated that Christians be forced to fund abortions, even though it violates their consciences. She said, "If you don't like it, then go off and start your own country!" Wow, lady, I think we did. And because we began with that Christian base, people of all faiths or no faith are welcome here.

But why should those who continue the tradition to pray in Jesus' name, yes, even in official government meetings, have their prayers censored?

The Answer to Muslim Violence: Jesus

3/30/16

Virtually a week does not go by without some headline of a Muslim attack somewhere in the world. The latest stories involves the alleged crucifixion of a Christian priest on Good Friday, as well as an Easter suicide bombing targeting Christians in Pakistan, which killed 71 at last count.

Some Muslims get disgusted with their fellow Muslims for such attacks. What is the ultimate solution to radical Islam? I believe Jesus is the solution to whatever ails the individual, family, society, the country, and nations.

We have freedom in the West because wise leaders of time past recognized that humanity is best off when religion is not forced on anyone. Thomas Jefferson wrote the Virginia Statute for Religious Freedom in 1777 (passed, 1786). This gave freedom to all in that state, regardless of religion.

Jefferson argues that it violates the principles of Jesus ("the holy author of our religion") to force anyone as to how they believe.

Obviously, professing Christians have sometimes gotten this wrong through the ages---but Jesus, the Prince of Peace, does not operate that way.

So, how is Jesus the answer to the Muslims? I think some clues can be found within the Qur'an *itself*, for those willing to see the truth.

I had the privilege of learning many things about the Qur'an from the late Aril Edvardsen, a follower of Jesus from Norway who was a preacher. In 1998 and 1999, I went with him to Malawi, Africa and to Islamabad, Pakistan.

Aril held open air Gospel meetings for Muslims and Christians in these places, using the Bible and the Qur'an. His goal was for everyone to have a better understanding of who Jesus (Isa bin Miriam, Jesus, Son of Mary) really is.

Here are some things found in the Qur'an worth highlighting:

* The Gospel (injil) is good, according to the Qur'an, but it does not specify what the gospel is.

* The Qur'an uses the term "Jesus Christ." Christ was not the last name of Jesus. It was His title. The Hebrew word is Messiah; in Greek, it is Christ; in English, it means Anointed One.

* The Qur'an calls Jesus "the Word of God." This means God has communicated to us through Jesus.

* The Qur'an teaches Jesus is born of a virgin and was conceived by the Spirt of God. There are liberal "Christians"---including many "Christian" leaders---who do not even believe that.

* The Qur'an references briefly the miracles of Jesus.

* It also says that Jesus will return one day. But Christians and Muslims disagree on the details surrounding that.

So what's the point of all of this? That we all hug and sing Kumbaya? No. The point is that there is One who can be found in the Qur'an itself who can bring personal peace and salvation to those who believe in Him.

But doesn't the Qur'an teach that Jesus was not crucified, but rather Judas in His place? No, but *commentators* on the Qur'an proclaim that. But that is just an interpretation. Who is to say that that interpretation is the correct one?

What the Qur'an actually says is that the Jews *claimed* that they crucified Him, but they crucified Him not. That is technically correct. The Romans took the right to perform capital punishment out of the hands of the Jews in AD 10, and it was they who crucified Jesus.

Meanwhile, the Qur'an teaches two of the most important things about Jesus: that He dies and rises again. Specifically, in Surah 19:33, where Jesus is talking, it is written of Him: "'So peace is on me the day I was born, the day that I die, and the day that I shall be raised up to life (again)'! Such (was) Jesus the son of Mary: (it is) a statement of truth, about which they (vainly) dispute."

Thus, the death and resurrection of Jesus are found in the Qur'an, although commentators dispute that too.

So *why* did Jesus die? When John the Baptist saw Jesus, he declared, "Behold, the Lamb of God who takes away the sins of the world."

Another great prophet, Isaiah, said that all of us like sheep have gone astray. But the Lord has laid on Him the iniquity of us all.

When people come to believe in Jesus and ask Him into their hearts and ask Him to forgive their sins, they are amazed at the peace and positive transformation He brings. Through faith in Him, because of His substitutional death, we can find the removal of our guilt and shame, and find true forgiveness from all our sins. When people truly trust in Him, violence finds no place in their hearts.

As the late Andre Crouch sang, "Jesus is the answer for the world today. Above Him there's no other. Jesus is the way..."

Part 2.

Hollywood and the Media

Is Hollywood Poised to Slander George Washington?
12/4/12

Ever since the 1970s, it seems many of our heroes are being toppled---especially by the media and entertainment industry. This happens whether or not such a toppling is deserved.

We're often scolded, "Don't impose your morality on me," with no thought given to the immorality they might impose on the rest of us.

Now, it looks like Hollywood is ready to impose its immorality on a man who not only doesn't deserve it, but is not here to defend himself. George Washington.

They're working on a TV series---with complete artistic license---showing the father of our country hopping in bed with his best friend's wife. And Hollywood elites wonder why millions of tradition-minded Americans have been avoiding their work for years?

This is not a bio-piece on some politician whose womanizing has been well-documented. But rather, this is a series on a man whose contemporaries praised him endlessly for his character.

If I could write an open-letter to the producers, writers, and bosses, I'd say, "Don't include this. Don't stoop to a scandal-sheet version of George Washington---especially since the facts are not on your side." The true facts about our first commander-in-chief are compelling in themselves.

The facts reveal over and over Washington doing the impossible---leading a rag-tag army of farmers and others, and beating the largest army in the world at the time---defeating the full might of the British Empire---for the sacred cause of liberty.

And Washington himself gave the Lord the credit for the victory. As he said in his First Inaugural Address, "Every step by which [we] have advanced to the character of an independent nation seems to have been distinguished by some token of providential agency...."

But now he is to be depicted as a philanderer. The writer for the upcoming NBC dramatic series is David Seidler, a British gentleman who did a wonderful job for the Oscar-winning film, *The King's Speech*. Ron Chernow wrote the book, *Washington: A Life*, the basis of this new series.

Seidler is quoted by writer Nellie Andreeva (deadline.com, 11/14/2012) as saying: "There's George Washington the national icon, gazing out from the dollar bill with his mouthful of supposedly wooden teeth, and then there's the George Washington who had an adulterous affair with his best friend's wife."

It's bad enough that Hollywood revisionists leave out (for the most part) the importance of Washington's faith. But now they want to make him guilty of adultery. That said, I do applaud the overall excellent HBO series on John Adams, where, for example, they showed Washington being sworn in. And true to the facts, they depicted him with his hand on the Bible, adding the common words for an oath "So help me, God" and leaning over and kissing the sacred text.

I co-wrote a massive book on the true George Washington. The lead author is the president of one of our leading seminaries, Westminster, in Philadelphia. Dr. Peter Lillback compiled research on our first president for about twenty years. We teamed up to produce the 1200-page book, *George Washington's Sacred Fire* (2006), which documents beyond a reasonable doubt that he was a devout 18th century Anglican. Glenn Beck helped it become a bestseller.

In that volume, we address some of the objections to the idea that Washington was a true Christian. Included there are allegations of potential scandals, including a passage on his relationship with Sally Fairfax (pp. 521-528). After looking at the allegation, Peter and I sum up, "We believe there is no evidence of an adulterous affair between George Washington and Sally Fairfax. The charge is baseless. But, may we suggest that Washington may well have wrestled with romantic feelings for Sally in his youthful years?" (p. 524).

When I first heard about NBC's upcoming series, I thought, "Oh no, here they go again, with their historical deconstruction." Fault Washington for a bad temper (at times), but not this.

A few days ago, I shot off an email to Dr. Lillback: "Peter, is there the slightest possibility that GW slept with his best friend's wife?!? Is there a scintilla of evidence anywhere that that might have happened? Hollywood is poised to poison the well on our guy!"

Dr. Lillback wrote back: "Dear Jerry: No way could it have happened, according to the evidence. Alexander Hamilton did have an affair, and it ended in the duel that took his life. GW and his wife and the Fairfaxes remained friends till the latter returned to England.

It is clear that the lonely, single colonial officer had romantic feelings for Sally, however. What's great is that he did the right thing, even though his heart felt otherwise....God bless, Pete."

Perhaps Hollywood producers don't realize there's a distinction between being tempted and giving into temptation. As Martin Luther said: You can't stop a bird from flying overhead (temptation), but you can prevent it from building a nest in your hair (giving in to it).

Here's an appeal to the producers, the writer(s), the board of directors, NBC, etc.: The true story of George Washington is fascinating in and of itself. Don't ruin your series by depicting him engaged in adultery when the evidence suggests he did not. As the saying goes, "We're all entitled to our own opinions. But we're not entitled to our own facts."

I pray a passion for truth will win out at NBC---as opposed to a passion for the sensational. My older brother, Rick, once asked sarcastically, "Why let the truth get in the way of a good story?" Answer: because at the end of the day, truth is all that matters.

Moviegoers Tend Not To Relish Their Values Being Assaulted

9/17/13

For good or ill (often for ill), Hollywood wields enormous influence on the culture. But we the people often fight back when they go too far in their anti-Christian and amoral ways.

The Hollywood Reporter (9/10/13) notes that the next Johnny Depp *Pirates* movie has been postponed. Included in the article was the idea that Disney was potentially skittish about releasing the movie so soon after the major failure of *The Lone Ranger* with Johnny Depp.

So Johnny Depp then is to blame for *The Lone Ranger* doing poorly? Why did the movie fail? One answer is: It was anti-Christian and anti-American---contrary to the popular radio and TV series that propelled the Lone Ranger and Tonto on the national scene.

Dr. Ted Baehr is a missionary to Hollywood. Year after year, his research shows that by-and-large the anti-Christian movies do poorly at the box office, whereas the well done movies with pro-Christian content do very well. (All things being equal.)

Ted Baehr and co-author Tom Snyder note in a recent article: "Year in and year out, the Christian Film & Television

Commission® and Movieguide®'s annual study of the movie box office figures proves that wholesome family-friendly movies and inspiring movies with Christian faith and values, no graphic foul language, sex, or nudity, and strong conservative, patriotic elements make the most money, especially when compared to movies with Anti-Christian, Anti-American, leftist values and abundant foul language or explicit sex and nudity."

They wrote about this film in particular: "Why did the Lone Ranger ride into theaters only to fail miserably at the box office? What went wrong with the beloved hero and role model that multiple generations grew up watching? A few will blame the director, others will blame the marketing team, and some might just believe the competition was too tough. What few are pointing out is the obvious fact that Disney's THE LONE RANGER is not a movie for kids."

They note that, "Only 16 percent of the moviegoers were under the age of 18. Disney shouldn't be surprised at all by these numbers for several reasons. The Lone Ranger character was created to be a role model for children. And even if Disney's version provides some role model material, it's presented in a world that is too gruesome and violent for young children to handle. The fact that THE LONE RANGER garnered a PG-13 rating should have warned Disney of its fate."

When the Lone Ranger and Tonto first appeared on the radio in the 1930s and TV in the 1950s, they were positive role models for children. Good was good, and bad was bad.

In fact, Ted Baehr and Tom Snyder point out that the series producers "even wrote up a creed of what principles their characters stand for":

It reads:

- "I believe...
- "That to have a friend, a man must be one.
- "That all men are created equal, and that everyone has within himself the power to make this a better world.
- "That God put the firewood there, but that every man must gather and light it himself.
- "In being prepared physically, mentally and morally to fight when necessary for what is right.
- "That a man should make the most of what equipment he has.

- "That 'this government of the people, by the people and for the people' shall live always.
- "That men should live by the rule of what is best for the greatest number.
- "That sooner or later. . . somewhere. . . somehow. . . we must settle with the world and make payment for what we have taken.
- "That all things change but truth, and that truth alone, lives on forever.
- "In my Creator, my country, my fellow man."

Theologically, I prefer the Nicene Creed, and politically, the Declaration. But, nonetheless, this extolling of good virtues over bad ones typifies fare from the "the Golden Age of Hollywood." That was a time before the 1960s, when the church abandoned their Hollywood offices, and morals became relative. Good often became evil and vice versa.

Baehr and Snyder add: "If Disney is still wondering why THE LONE RANGER tanked at the box office, it's because they alienated not just a young audience that would enjoy such a character, but a young audience that could be inspired." They also write: "Hollywood forgot that there's a large portion of America that attends church weekly and salutes the American flag."

I would hope that Hollywood would take note at this recent box office failure and not draw the wrong conclusion. Some of the leftists that control so much of the movie-industry want to continue to impose their liberal view of the world on all their products. But as legendary movie mogul Samuel Goldwyn once advised, "If you've got a message, send a telegram."

On the Lighter Side

2/15/12

Why can't modern comedians be clean? They would be funnier if they were.

Recently, I went to support a friend, whom I know from church and lately from our local Toastmasters club, who had the moxie to get up and do an 8-minute or so stand-up comedy routine at an improvisational night. It was gutsy for her to do this. And to her credit, there were no bad words gushing from her lips---as there were from just about every other would-be comic that night.

There was an MC, who was crude. He was so nasty, I was compelled to leave for a while.

Then there were unprofessional would-be comedians, one after another. Many of them going for cheap laughs by titillating the audience with crudities. It was embarrassing. (I understand that some of them brought their own audiences with them---by getting family members and friends to support them.)

Then came to the stage my friend who didn't curse at all. She was a breath of fresh air. And funny too---without resorting to bathroom humor, as did so many before her.

When a comedian is forced to resort to his wit, he is much funnier by being clean. I'm glad W. C. Fields and Groucho Marx were born when they were. If they belonged to a later generation, they could have easily gone the lazy route for cheap laughs. But I guarantee you people wouldn't be watching their movies half a century later (as I do).

I often write about more serious matters, like politics and morals, but I think it's good to reflect on entertainment choices once in a while. Entertainment has a greater influence on our culture than we sometimes realize.

Columnist and author Robert Knight once said this, "If I had my choice to controlling Washington or Hollywood, I'd pick Hollywood in a heartbeat. Hollywood . . . has enormous influence on our culture. Political institutions don't operate in a vacuum, they arise out of culture. I'd rather control the high ground of culture than the political superstructure that grows out of that culture."

That's a fascinating remark coming from him, since he lives in the DC area and has worked in the Beltway for years.

So I commend my brave comedic friend for her willingness to come out of the church cocoon and speak comically before a potentially hostile audience.

As people of good will, meanwhile, we need to choose the good and eschew the bad. Hollywood will still make bad movies, even if we boycotted all the bad ones---because some film-makers have an animus against traditional morality and religion they want to express. But there are many Hollywood producers who are only in it for the money. If family oriented films make the most money (and they generally do, if well done), then they'll make them.

Regardless of the consequences, I think as consumers we need to be sure our entertainment choices match our professed morality and beliefs. Otherwise, we have no reason to complain about Hollywood's products.

Every time you see a movie, you vote---with your ticket purchase---and say, "Yes, Hollywood, make more movies like this."

I must confess---sometimes I give blood just to get the free movie ticket. About a year ago, my wife and I saw a time-waster of a film, and I blurted out at the end, "I want my blood back!"

Thankfully, groups like Ted Baehr's Movieguide.org can provide detailed information on films, so we don't waste our money or time on bad movies.

Of course, these things apply equally to our TV-viewing and radio-listening habits.

And that reminds me of a quip from Woody Allen: The reason Beverly Hills is so clean is that they turn all their garbage into television shows.

Robo-Christ?

7/2/12

Here we go again. Another blasphemous anti-Christian movie is in the works. Moviemaker Paul Verhoeven appears to be on the verge of making a major film that will besmirch Jesus.

The Dutch director who made *Basic Instinct*, *Robocop*, and *Showgirls* has now reportedly found funding and a writer for a movie to be based on his 2010 book, *jesus of nazareth* [sic].

The book asserts the myth that Jesus may have been the product of a rape of the not-so-Virgin Mary by a Roman soldier. That statement alone says all you need about this upcoming movie, if indeed it ever makes the big screen. I pray it will not.

According to the scholars, even ones not friendly to conservative Christianity, there is not a shred of historical evidence for the premise of Verhoeven's proposed film. Thus, the whole thing will help promulgate a lie. As noted, we're entitled to our own opinions, but not our own facts.

Dr. Paul L. Maier, a best-selling author who is a Harvard-trained professor of ancient history at Western Michigan University, sent me an email statement on the idea that Jesus was a product of a rape: "This crude, worthless claim is old and discarded by all serious scholars. The rapist Roman soldier was supposedly a fellow named 'Pantera,' which is a corruption and misunderstanding of 'parthenos,' Greek for 'virgin' and applied to Mary. This is an example of the silly season on sensational Jesus claims."

I also sought a comment from Dr. Darrell L. Bock of Dallas Theological Seminar. He wrote me, "Assuming [the story about the movie] is real, you can simply note this charge is a later effort to slander Christian claims and is not historical."

Dr. Gary Habermas is also a great New Testament scholar. He teaches at Liberty University (founded by Jerry Falwell). He told me: "No early historical sources assert that Mary was raped by a Roman soldier. Leave it to contemporary guesswork to come up with something like this."

Although a filmmaker and not a theologian per se, Mr. Verhoeven has been a part of a radical group of 70+ scholars called the Jesus Seminar. This group sat in judgment on the words of Jesus as found in the four Gospels. They voted---anonymously---that Jesus supposedly only said (for sure) 18% of that which is attributed to Him in the Gospels. Their judgments were not based on any manuscript issues, but rather their own opinions. (They threw out everything Jesus said in the Gospel of John---even though John was an eyewitness of Jesus.)

The late theologian and author, James Montgomery Boice, once said of the Jesus Seminar: "Imagine a group of scholars, now, two thousand years from the time that Jesus lived and whose words were written down by eye witnesses, a group of scholars two thousand years later voting in a meeting on what Jesus really said and what He didn't. That is laughable."

If Verhoeven makes his movie, here's an easy prophecy to make: It will fail spectacularly.

When I first heard about this potential upcoming movie the other week from my favorite missionary to Hollywood, Dr. Ted Baehr, publisher of *Movieguide*, I said to him in an email about these kinds of anti-Christian movies: "We get darned if we do (speak out against it, which supposedly increases the attendance) and darned if we don't."

Ted responded: "Since we do the numbers, I have never ever seen speaking out drive up box office [traffic]. That is an urban myth. We have countered many movies and television [shows]. LAST TEMPTATION cost over $50 million, and made about $8

million. We pulled the teeth on GOLDEN COMPASS. We got
PLAYBOY CLUB and GOOD CHRISTIAN B**** off TV."
I remember well, back in 1988, the controversy surrounding Martin
Scorsese's blasphemous movie, *The Last Temptation of Christ*, that
Ted refers to.

Some of the $8 million dollars or so that it made came because of
movie-goers that wanted to defy the Christian protesters. As a
Jewish friend of mine told me at the time, he went to see the film
because "Jerry Falwell made [him] do it." My friend told me that as
a movie, it was horrible---not that he had any qualms about the bad
theology or bad history. He said that that film belonged only in art
theatres or the like. (No offense to art theatres).

Successfully (and respectfully) translating Jesus to the big screen
is obviously not always easy. Perhaps that's part of the reason for the
old notion that religion is box office poison.

But didn't Mel Gibson prove that wrong? In 2004, knowing that
Hollywood had already shunned him for daring to make *The Passion
of the Christ*, he successfully marketed his movie to the church
crowd.

During Lent 2004, he managed to fill many theatre seats with his
very moving picture. His movie made hundreds of millions of
dollars, even though it totally lacked Hollywood's imprimatur.
Mel Gibson proved that there was a huge potential audience for pro-
faith movies. He crashed through the gates and paved the way for
more faith-friendly box office fare.

I remember shortly after that, Hollywood released *Saved*, a very
anti-Christian movie about religious hypocrites at a Christian school.
The moguls probably figured, "Hey, maybe religion sells after all."
So they released the movie, which bombed---because generally
Christians are not going to see a movie that ridicules their faith and
degrades their Savior.

The difference between *The Passion of the Christ* and Saved,
apart from all the quality differences as to story-telling, was the
difference between showing respect versus denigrating the professed
religion of the majority of Americans. That will be the difference
between *The Passion* and Verhoeven's movie, if it ever makes it to
the silver screen.

Hollywood and the Siren Song of Socialism

6/24/15

Mr. Sanders Goes to Hollywood. And he got a good reception too. That is, super-liberal Bernie Sanders, Democrat from Vermont who believes in socialistic policies, has a message that apparently resonates with the limousine liberals in Tinseltown.

Writing for *Hollywood Reporter* (6/20/15), Tina Daunt notes, "After the glitz and glitter of Barack Obama and Hillary Clinton's fundraising trips to L.A. this week, a cadre of industry super-liberals turned out Saturday to support Sanders."

She adds, "...Sanders — a self-described Democratic socialist — is the candidate who checks all the progressive boxes, earning him a devoted Los Angeles following."

His platform sounds appealing to the naive, until you ask the question how will all this be paid for? And what happens if you don't happen to agree with that particular policy?

Here are a few of the 12 points of his "Agenda for America": Reversing Climate Change...Creating Worker Co-ops...Growing the Trade Union Movement...Raising the Minimum Wage...Making College Affordable for All...Health Care as a Right for All. Most of the points read like socialist pamphlets in the 1930's.

This positive reception from Hollywood of an avowed socialist reminds me of how collectivist thinking gets repackaged and resold as if it's something new and exciting, as we've seen recently with the move for "social justice."

Everywhere the siren song of socialism is received, even with supposedly the best intentions, it fails. I write this with the caveat that I'm not claiming Hollywood types embrace atheistic communism with its bloody track record. But ideas have consequences.

Socialism violates two of God's Ten Commandments. Thou shalt not steal (even the government) and Thou shalt not covet. By definition, socialism covets thy neighbor's goods. And it relies upon the force of government to redistribute those goods.

Furthermore, it contradicts human nature; thus, it always fails. This is not to be confused with Christian charity, which is voluntary and greatly to be encouraged.

Can you name one spot on earth where socialism has ever worked?

Joshua Muravchik was the national chairman of the Young People's Socialist League from 1968 to 1973. But he became disillusioned with socialism. In 2002, he wrote an excellent book on the subject, called *Heaven on Earth: The Rise and Fall of Socialism.*

I had the privilege to interview him for a TV special, *Socialism: A Clear and Present Danger.* He told me, "Socialism has kind of proved itself to be bankrupt, but it's not dying out in the intellectual world."

In his book, he writes, "From New Harmony [Robert Owen's failed experiment of a socialist commune in 19th century Indiana] to Moscow, from Dar es Salaam to London, the story of socialism was the story of a dream unrealized, a word that would not be made flesh."

He concludes, "By no means all socialists were killers or amoral. Many were sincere humanitarians; mostly these were adherents of democratic socialism. But democratic socialism turned out to be a contradiction in terms, for where socialists proceeded democratically, they found themselves on a trajectory that took them further and further from socialism."

He adds, "Only once did democratic socialists manage to create socialism. That was the kibbutz [in Israel]. And after they had experienced it, they chose democratically to abolish it."

Meanwhile, the USSR was among the most ambitious attempts to force socialism on a country. Lenin and Stalin had to crack a few skulls to do this. Quite a few. Of course, they created a government all based on atheism. Under big government schemes, the government is god. So there is no place for other gods. Religious freedom and true socialism don't mix.

Before being disillusioned by Stalin and the failed USSR, many leftists from the West, "fellow travelers," went to the "worker's paradise" to celebrate the breakdown of traditional society--- capitalism and private ownership, the traditional family, and religious influence in society.

This reminds me of Eugene and Elizabeth Fox-Genovese, a husband and wife team who had been Communists, until they became disillusioned with the whole thing.

When the Soviet Union finally imploded in the early 1990s, they wrote: "When it all collapsed, the question was, After seventy years, what do we have to show for it? Especially when it became clear that, even on a basic level, the system didn't deliver the goods, the one thing it was supposed to do. So what we had to show for it was tens of millions of corpses." That may be the extreme, but so also was Mao's China.

Socialism in any form is a bad idea. Everywhere it is tried it brings misery and sometimes death. If Hollywood were more honest, we'd see some epic movies on the failures of life under the socialists and communists. Why would we want to go down this road again, even partially? Been there, done that.

Is Scripture-Quoting a Sign that You're Nuts?

2/19/13

Currently in the theatres is the movie, *Safe Haven*, based on the book by Nicholas Sparks. In the book, the bad guy goes around quoting Scripture.

Is quoting Bible verses indicative of a mental imbalance? To some of our cultural elites it would seem so.

By way of full disclosure, I have neither read the book nor seen the movie. (Nor do I want to vote with my money by buying a ticket for it, saying, "Yes, Hollywood, make more Christian-bashing movies.") However, my wife read the book and said it's a great story about an abused wife, fleeing from her mentally imbalanced Scripture-quoting, husband, who is a bullying cop. I have no idea if the movie has mollified the anti-Christian aspect of the novel; hopefully, it has.

My wife said, "It's such a good story. Why should the horrible husband quote the Bible and base his irrational behavior on what he believes it to say. I'm so upset."

Why is the bad guy---in many a movie and TV show---quoting the Bible? Put it this way, in the vast majority of cases when a character quotes from the Scriptures, is that a cue that he or she is a good character or a bad one, or even just comic relief?

I remember on *Sanford and Sons* from the 1970s a crazy aunt who would tote her Bible around and quote different verses, like, "The truth shall set you free!" She was a whack job.

Do you know anyone like that personally?

One man I used to know who went around quoting Scripture was among the nicest people I've ever known in my whole life. Charlie used to memorize Bible verses and quote them all the time.

He was also one of the happiest people I've ever known. He had the most irrepressible smile.

Charlie used to go to prisons six days a week for ministry, since he retired in 1964 until he died in 1994. By the end of his life, ALS (Lou Gehrig's disease) so disabled him that the prison authorities said he couldn't visit anymore unless he had a volunteer to wheel him around.

Every single day he found a volunteer. I was that volunteer on January 1, 1994. It was the first time in my life I had been in a prison.

Charlie gave out 8 x 10 certificates to inmates for having memorized key Bible verses, 1 John 1:9 on the forgiveness of sins or John 3:16 on God's gift of Jesus to the world, etc. Yes, he went around quoting the Bible all the time. And no, he didn't go around killing people the way Hollywood's Bible-quoters do. He only helped people---everyone without discrimination.

Hollywood and our popular culture have brainwashed millions to think that if someone quotes the Holy Book, then we know he's certifiably insane or worse.

You'd think if someone was filled with Bible references, then he must be mentally unbalanced.

And yet Shakespeare's writings are replete with some 1300 biblical quotes and references.

Even the world's leading atheist, Richard Dawkins, professor at Oxford, and author of the best-selling book, *The God Delusion*, essentially says you're culturally illiterate if you are not familiar with the Bible. In page after page of blasting the Christian faith (and Islam); after saying terrible things about the Scriptures, suddenly, he says positive things about the Bible---as literature.

Dawkins states, "The King James Bible of 1611---the Authorized Version---includes passages of outstanding literary merit in its own right, for example the Song of Songs, and the sublime Ecclesiastes (which I am told is pretty good in the original Hebrew too). But the main reason the English Bible needs to be part of our education is that is a major source book for literary culture."

Dawkins goes on to cite scores and scores of phrases from the Bible that are common in our parlance, such as "Be fruitful and multiply," "East of Eden," "Adam's Rib," etc.

This does not mean he in any way respects the Bible as holy writ or anything close. He concludes this section: "We can give up belief in God while not losing touch with a treasured heritage." That strikes

51

me as a fruitless venture. But I quote it because he refers to the Bible in general, and the 400-year-old King James in particular as a "treasured heritage."

For those who have never taken the time to read it, the Bible contains a great deal of wisdom---teaching such concepts as: As a man thinks in his heart so is he; you reap what you sow; do unto others as you would have them do unto you; love your neighbor as yourself, and so on.

Several years ago, David Van Biema wrote a cover story for *TIME* magazine (April 2, 2007), wherein he said: "Should the Holy Book be on the public menu? Yes. It's the bedrock of Western culture. And it's constitutional---as long as we teach but don't preach it."

He even implies life would be boring without it: "Without the Bible and a few imposing secular sources, we face a numbing horizontality in our culture---blogs, political announcements, ads. The world is flat, sure. But Scripture is among our few means to make it deep."

Sadly, when you see a character on the big screen, if he or she is quoting the Bible, it's almost a sure sign that he's crazy or evil or both. The other characters need to hold on to their wallets and get ready to defend themselves. Thankfully, the reality is far different.

Great New Movie---"God's Not Dead"

3/26/14

There's an old joke in Christian circles that goes like this: Someone had written in graffiti the famous quote from the 19th century atheist philosopher: "God is dead. Signed, Nietzsche." Underneath it, someone else wrote: "Nietzsche is dead. Signed, God."

There's a new movie out called, "God's Not Dead." I hadn't heard about it, except for a word of praise from Ted Baehr, publisher of Movieguide, who provides a biblical critique of films.

My wife and I enjoyed the movie very much. What I found fascinating was the spontaneous applause from the audience. It was unusual. This wasn't in the Bible belt. It was in cosmopolitan Ft. Lauderdale, Florida.

The movie stars Kevin Sorbo, who played Hercules on TV. He plays the antagonist as an atheist college professor who teaches philosophy. He has his 80 students write "God is dead" on a piece of paper which they are to sign and pass in. But one Christian student can't do this.

So the professor decides to force the student to present his case for God convincingly before him and the class in later presentations or suffer a bad grade.

The protagonist is a student named "Josh Wheaton." I couldn't help but feel that the name was a cross between Josh McDowell, a Christian apologist who's worked in campus ministry for years, and Wheaton College (my alma mater, for grad school).

The plot may sound far-fetched. But not far from where I write this, about a year ago, a professor told his students to write the name Jesus on a sheet of paper; then to stand up, put the paper on the ground, and stomp on it. One brave student refused to do it and was threatened with a bad grade. Thankfully, as word got out, the university apologized for the whole assignment.

At the end of "God's Not Dead," during the credits, there is a scroll with brief names of legal case after case, where Christian students stood up to the prevailing indoctrination toward atheism or toward a politically correct view on traditional morality and fought back.

The legal group representing these courageous students was the ADF, the Alliance Defending Freedom, a Phoenix-based group that was founded in the early 1990s by a handful of Christian leaders, including the late D. James Kennedy, my long-time pastor.

It's not foreordained that the university has to belittle faith. After all, it was Christianity that gave birth to the phenomenon of the university in the first place. And virtually all the great universities were founded by Christians for Christian purposes. Just ask Rev. John Harvard.

As we pointed out a decade ago in a documentary, "What If Jesus Had Never Been Born?" hosted by Dr. Kennedy, the university system began c. 1200 in Christian Europe, essentially to reconcile Christian teaching with the newly rediscovered writings of Aristotle.

The University of Paris became the prototype for the university system, as various tutors and lecturers would meet with students. Even the name "university" was coined because of the ad hoc school that was forming in Paris.

Dr. Alexander Murray, retired Oxford history professor, told our viewers, "Paris was like a market where different people were setting up. And, bit by bit, the city authorities, they said, 'Let's treat them not just as this or that school, but as an altogetherness.' 'Universitas' in Latin."

Dr. Paul Maier of Western Michigan University added, "You had students from England, studying in Paris who decided to go to a place where the oxen crossed the river, Oxenford, otherwise known as 'Oxford.' And that gave birth to Cambridge. Cambridge gave birth to John Harvard, coming over to the United States, Harvard University in 1636. That was the background of our state university system, as well as our private university system, and so on to the universities we have today. Direct Christian origin."

But you would never know that today, in most university settings, where the Christian church is viewed as if it has only produced ignorance and superstition.

The movie, "God's Not Dead" is a breath of fresh air in light of the prevailing secular, politically correct atmosphere that seems to dominate the campuses today. My wife Kirsti said that every church youth group in America should show this movie before people go off to college.

Despite its limited screening, the movie ranked 4th for its opening weekend.

After enjoying the movie, I emailed the actor, Kevin Sorbo; and he wrote me back: "Jerry, thanks for the support of GND! The response around the country has been amazing." Deservedly so.

So, Roseanne, You Want to Go Back to the French Revolution?

10/3/11

Have you ever noticed how generous some progressives are--- when it isn't their money to give in the first place?

I was reminded about this from some remarks from Roseanne Barr highlighted this week in the *Drudge Report*.

She was interviewed by *Russia Today*. (The article in "Real Clear Politics" didn't clarify if that meant the TV show of *Russia Today*. If that's the case, then I have been a guest a couple times on their program, "The Alyona Show.")

Anyway, Roseanne, one time a very popular TV star, said "I am in favor of the return of the guillotine and that is for the worst of the worst of the guilty."

The guillotine? What are we back to the French Revolution?

Who are the "guilty" according to Roseanne? Bankers who make more than $100 million.

I suppose in the minds of some, including Roseanne, if someone makes a lot of money, it's because someone else has lost that same amount of money. Money-making becomes a zero sum game, they think. If you're rich, it's because someone else is poor.

Gambling works that way. Someone wins because someone else loses.

But capitalism doesn't have to work that way. Thomas Edison got rich inventing things, and we are all better off because of his contributions to humanity.

Roseanne goes on to pontificate, "I first would allow the guilty bankers to pay, you know, the ability to pay back anything over $100 million [of] personal wealth because I believe in a maximum wage of $100 million."

I'm not sure how many people make more than $100 million. But she continues: "And if they are unable to live on that amount, then they should, you know, go to the reeducation camps and if that doesn't help, then being beheaded."

Reeducation camps?

What are we back to the Chinese Cultural Revolution?

Beheaded? If you make too much money, off with your heads. Liberals are so generous---with other people's money. They are limousine liberals. They are sofa socialists. They always seem willing to take the profits of someone else and spread the wealth around.

I remember seeing a TV segment once on the lifestyle of Fidel Castro and his inner circle. They lived high off the hog, while normal Cubans suffer under the Communism Castro has imposed.

I can't imagine anyone making as much as $100 million. But is such a person necessarily getting it through thievery? Perhaps millions are being enriched through his wealth.

In any event, regardless of what we make, we will all give an account before God for what we get and how we spend it.

I believe generosity is the best way---through private charity.

What's the difference between socialism and charity? Both involve a form of redistribution of wealth.

The answer is force. Government at its basic level is force. Sheer power.

No matter how much I make or how little, I wouldn't want to have to give an account of it to the likes of Roseanne Barr. Nor the like-minded protesters now camping out at Wall Street.

We've all heard of the Daughters of the American Revolution. I nominate Roseanne as a Daughter of the French Revolution.

The French Revolution was the mother of all socialistic type revolutions, including the Russian and Chinese Revolutions of the 20th century, which killed tens of millions of human beings.

I find it interesting that Roseanne' remarks hearken back to the French Revolution. People seem to forget that that was a very anti-religious movement. Not only did they kill people, including many Church leaders, but they desecrated the churches. For example, they seized Notre Dame Cathedral, halted mass there, and placed a half-naked woman atop the altar and worshiped her, calling her "Reason."

Not only did the French Revolutionaries lop off the heads of thousands (in some cases, just for being rich), but they jettisoned themselves off from any Judeo-Christian influence. For example, they abolished the Christian calendar, by declaring 1791 year 1 (of the Republic). They cut themselves off from any Jewish-Christian Sabbath by even changing the week from seven days to ten days.

Napoleon undid all these "reforms" about a decade later.

The French Revolution was no picnic for anybody. Anti-religious types may cheer its secular spirit. But don't forget that that revolution consumed its own.

Meanwhile, Roseanne expressed her anti-religious feelings about fifteen years ago in a statement against pro-lifers, who are mostly Christians: "You know who else I can't stand is them [sic] people that are anti abortion. EXPLETIVE DELETED. I hate them... They're horrible, they're hideous people. They're ugly, old, geeky, hideous men...They just don't want nobody [sic] to have an abortion 'cause they want you to keep spitting out kids so they can EXPLETIVE molest them."

Usually, the proponents of socialism have a strong anti-religious streak. And why not? Essentially, their first commandment is: "Thou shalt not have any other gods beyond the State."

Everywhere it's been tried, socialism has failed. But it always seems to rear its ugly head again and again, even sometimes from a fading TV star.

Oh the Profanity

6/12/13

Do you remember the last time you saw a movie and when it was over, you thought, "That was great, except there wasn't enough swearing?"

You don't? Neither do I.

There may yet be *more* profanity on broadcast television. For now, the FCC, which regulates broadcasting, is listening to "we the people" on the subject of what will be along on television. There's a deadline to voice our opinions by June 19.

Hollie McKay (5/21/13) wrote about this in a Fox News article, "FCC proposed to allow more sex and profanity during kids' television viewing hours."

We have become accustomed to so much profanity that for many t

hey don't even notice it. But there is a link between manners and morals and how civilized we are. If someone thinks, What's the big deal about swearing? You certainly wouldn't try it in a job interview (not with success).

It's an interesting fact that one of the Ten Commandments deals with the issue of profanity. "Thou shalt not take the name of the Lord thy God in vain. I will not hold him guiltless who takes my name in vain." Of course, not all profanity is taking God's name in vain.

Taking God's name in vain, e.g., in profanity, is to make His name of no value. It is to lie about who He is and how great He is--- the One on whom our every breath depends.

We are awash in profanity today. And it's not just offensive. It reveals a limited vocabulary.

Even the recent, otherwise-decent, movie about Lincoln by Steven Spielberg showed the beloved president swearing. But was that historically accurate?

According to *The Hollywood Reporter* (Dec. 5, 2012), "Biographer Doris Kearns Goodwin reviewed the script and tells THR she 'never had a problem with the language,' but another historian who consulted on the movie says it's 'completely unlikely' for the 16th president."

The historian is James McPherson, a Lincoln biographer. He said, "The profanity actually bothered me, especially Lincoln's use of it...It struck me as completely unlikely---a modern injection into Lincoln's rhetoric."

Many great works of art are often spoiled or marred by the use of profanity. It adds nothing to the movie, but it certainly takes away from it.

I enjoyed the movie of the year, "Argo." It was a fascinating, spell-binding movie, but it was needlessly marred by incessant profanity. It added nothing. It certainly detracted.

Hollywood claims to just be about Box Office success, yet they continue to drive away perhaps millions of potential customers through needless swearing.

During the Golden Age of Hollywood, when the church had greater influence in the content of the movies, actors and actresses had to communicate their emotions through good acting. They couldn't resort to cheap laughs or cheap dialogue by swearing.

At the end of the movie, "The Maltese Falcon," the Peter Lorre character blows up and lays into the Sidney Greenstreet character. It is as if he blasts him away in a string of profanities. But it's all done through Lorre's acting: "You imbecile! You bloated idiot! You stupid fathead!"

Millions of Americans avoid the movies today. Why? I think, in part, because they don't want to be insulted by profanity, sex, and violence.

When Mel Gibson made "The *Passion of the Christ*," he managed to attract millions of movie-goers who hadn't gone to a movie theatre in years (in some cases, decades). Obviously, that work was extraordinarily violent, but there was a reason for it.

The late Dr. D. James Kennedy once pointed out that when an actor portrays a murderer, he is not actually sinning, because he's not actually killing. When he portrays someone committing adultery, the actor is only portraying sin, but not actually doing it. Yet when an actor takes God's name in vain, he is sinning per se. He is violating God's law.

When George Washington became Commander-in-Chief of the Continental Army in 1775, one of his first orders included no profanity.

He said (speaking of himself in the third person): "The General most earnestly requires and expects a due observance of those articles of war established for the government of the Army which forbid profane cursing, swearing, and drunkenness" (July 4, 1775).

Washington did not want our fledgling cause to fail because we offended God. He said at another time, "The blessing and protection of Heaven are at all times necessary but especially so in times of public distress and danger."

Many of us pray today for a great national revival. If such a thing were to happen, I know that profanity would lessen and with it some of the crudeness and coarseness of the time.

So, if profanity is on one's lips and about to come out, he ought to heed the words of the historical Lincoln: Better to be thought a fool, then to open your mouth and remove all doubt.

Shocked No More?

1/22/14

Incest as romance and entertainment? Society seems to play a game of "Can you top this?" Or really "How low can you go?" Hollywood often leads the way, but there are many that follow.

It seems that things acceptable today would have been unthinkable a decade ago and not even on the radar screen a half-century ago and a criminal offense 100 years ago, in many cases.

Lifetime television has brought to the small screen, "Flowers in the Attic," dealing with incest apparently as a romance---based on a popular 1979 novel.

This book was made into a movie in the 1980's, but the producers toned down the incestuous relationship. What has changed between then and now?

Why do they feel comfortable including it now? Because of the sexual anarchy our nation seems committed to, things that would not have been considered for television 30 years ago are now too often commonplace.

The reality is, rejection of sexual norms in one area will make rejection in other areas more palatable to us. We are losing our ability to be shocked at things that should shock us, which is an indication of a seared national conscience, as Paul points to in Romans 1.

Writing about this movie for vocativ.com (1/16/14), Elizabeth Kulze opines, "The plot of 'Flowers in the Attic' itself is a delicious assault on family morals..."

She also adds, "Thematically, one could argue that it's a story about child abuse and its devastating effects." The ultimate villain in this movie is the "puritanical grandma," who forces these children into an attic where things get out of hand.

Kulze says that Lifetime hopes it will be such a success that they will make a sequel. Yipes.

Years ago I once asked my long-time pastor, the late Dr. D. James Kennedy, "How do you deal with the argument that [producers] often say, 'Well, we just reflect life as it is?'"

He responded, "I would like to say to them that life consists of more than a toilet and a gutter and a brothel, and there are other parts of life that could be reflected." Obviously, Hollywood produces more than filth, and well done movies promoting positive values tend to do well.

Kennedy used to often quote Alexander Pope's couplet that included the old-fashioned word "mien" (pronounced "mean"), which means "countenance" or appearance.

Said Pope: "Vice is a monster of such horrible mien, / that to be hated needs but to be seen. / But seen too oft, grown familiar with its face, / first we endure, then we embrace."

Isn't this what's happening so often in our time? We see things that repulse us on television or in movies, but over time, we tolerate that which we instinctively find offensive. Eventually, we are worn down and accept it---and even celebrate it. And the taboo is lost.

I remember years ago, Dr. James Dobson was on a video blasting Hollywood producers for making teen-sex movies, where they were celebrating immorality---often without showing the real life consequences of these things. Said an angry Dr. Dobson (something to the effect), "Just to make a buck, these Hollywood producers are damning a whole generation of young people!"

I have seen a book that contains many photos of vases and pieces of art from antiquity, including the ancient Greeks and the Romans. For a lack of a better term, it's pornographic. How correct Solomon was: There's nothing new under the sun.

Artifacts from Pompeii seem particularly smutty. It would be easy to see how someone could say that the eruption of Mt. Vesuvius in

AD 79 that engulfed the city was divine judgment. Scripture is clear that such was the case of Sodom and Gomorrah, which had less than 10 righteous people.

Artifacts from Pompeii seem particularly smutty. Some would argue that the eruption of Mt. Vesuvius in AD 79 which engulfed the city was divine judgment. Scripture is clear that such was the case of Sodom and Gomorrah. Others would argue that those things that happened, e.g., in the Old Testament, happened as a record for the ages.

In any event, it was into such a filthy world as reflected in that picture book that Jesus was born and through His movement ultimately cleaned things up a lot. Over the centuries, as His influence began to spread all over, laws in much of the Western world became based on the New Testament of which He is the central figure and the Old Testament, to which He gave His imprimatur. In short, because of the Judeo-Christian tradition, incest is illegal.

These laws have been good for society. The home has been safe for women and children for centuries because of Judeo-Christian laws. Much of the West has been spared from a lot of mental illness, which comes as a result of inbreeding.

Someone might say, "Who is to say incest is wrong?" My answer to that is: God is.

I agree with President Lincoln, who said on September 7, 1864, when he received a copy of the Holy Bible: "In regard to this great book, I have but to say, it is the best gift God has given to men. All the good the Savior gave to the world was communicated through this book. *But for it we could not know right from wrong.*" [Emphasis mine].

It behooves us to show discernment in what Hollywood products we choose to support. May God have mercy on us. I think our national shock absorbers could use an overhaul.

Fighting Media Bias----and Winning

9/29/15

A shocking new series of videos exposes Planned Parenthood's gruesome practice of harvesting body parts of babies they had aborted. Yet for the most part these videos are not covered by the mainstream media. Around the same time, an American dentist hunts and kills a lion in Africa, and the media has made the animal virtually a household name.

In fact, the Media Research Center (MRC) reports that Cecil the lion had gained 15 times the mention and attention from the network news media, compared to the explosive Planned Parenthood videos by the Center for Media Progress, centerformediaprogress.org.

This is a recent example of the left-wing bias of the mainstream media. That the media is biased is not news. What is news is the progress that has been made in the last few decades to expose that bias. And much of that progress can be credited to one man, Brent Bozell.

Brent Bozell, the founding director of the MRC, based in Northern Virginia, was honored on Saturday (9/26/15) by Tony Perkins and the Family Research Council for the Vision and Leadership Award.

Syndicated columnist Bozell is a nephew of William F. Buckley, Jr., and by way of full disclosure, Brent is my second cousin. But we never met until the early 1990s in my capacity as a TV producer for D. James Kennedy when I went to Brent's office to interview him on media bias. I have interviewed multiple times since.

In 2010 he told our viewers, "There is a mythology about the news media, particularly, in that they say that their job is: A, to report the news, and B, to deliver ratings. In fact, their job is to educate with a message, regardless of what it does to their ratings. In the last 10 years, you have seen the news media spiral into this far left political agenda...regardless of the fact that it is destroying them in the process, where the networks have all lost 50 percent of their audiences, where newspapers are crumbling, where magazines are falling apart, and yet, they continue projecting this agenda, because of their ideology."

Through systematic recording of thousands of hours of news and information programming, they catch the mainstream media in sins of commission, but perhaps the biggest bias is in the sins of omission---what the media chooses not to cover, such as the recent Planned Parenthood scandal.

Saturday's function was the closing banquet of Family Research Council's very successful Values Voters Summit---where even some of the key candidates came to speak, including Donald Trump.

At the award banquet, Bill Walton of On Common Ground radio, said: "Before Brent, we had a sense of it [media bias]. But he set out to prove it."

I got to congratulate Brent before the ceremony and ask him for a statement for this column. He said, "The two things that drove me--- in 1987 [when he started the MRC] only 25 percent of Americans thought the media was biased. The second thing was that it didn't matter what the issue was---whether it was economic, defense or social issues---if you had to go through the filter of the left wing media, you'd never succeed." That was before Brent's campaign.

He added, "We see the success [of our efforts] and now we can't stop." In a discussion with Rush Limbaugh, Brent said his "ultimate goal was to succeed, get out of the business, and get a real job." But Rush said the left-wing bias in the media is so entrenched, that Brent's work will never end: "You can't succeed. This issue will never end."

Brent certainly has made a big dent in this area. The above-mentioned Bill Walton said, "Had Brent not paved the way for the Media Research Center 30 years ago---documenting, exposing liberal bias, who knows where we'd be today? I remember reading his work in the early 1990s, and I was thinking, 'Wow, who is this guy? He has the media nailed.'"

Mark Levin, the syndicated radio host who used to work for the Reagan administration, called Bozell the "Sam Adams of our time." He called him "one of the great heroes of liberty and republicanism in the last quarter century." Sam Adams, of course, was the lightning rod of the American Revolution.

Former US Attorney General Ed Meese noted that the founders intended that a free press "would be a bulwark against political tyranny." But today's media is so biased that they are hurting the republic: "As a result with too few exceptions, the people are not able to get the truth about what is going on in our country, are not able to form accurate judgments. That's why what Brent [Bozell] has been doing is so important."

It's good to honor a man who has *made* news by exposing the left-wing bias of the news.

Is Religion Box Office Poison?

10/28/15

It has been said that "religion is box office poison." Mel Gibson disproved that 11 years ago with *The Passion of the Christ*.

But what about *Noah*? What about *Exodus: God and Kings*? They did badly, but they were not faithful to the Bible---neither in letter nor spirit.

Meanwhile, low budget Christian films made by a church from Georgia show over and over that religion is not box office poison. I refer to the Kendrick brothers, who made the recent independent film success, *War Room*, which I saw recently and enjoyed and found uplifting.

It is *still* in the theatres---nine weekends after its opening on 8/28. *War Room* is an explicitly Christian movie. The title is in reference to one's prayer closet, where true prayer involves true spiritual warfare. The film is the latest product of the Kendrick Brothers, who made, and *Facing the Giants, Fireproof Courageous*, among other films.

The production quality of Christian films is on the rise.

I interviewed Ray Comfort recently, who has made Internet films seen by several million people, including *180 the Movie* (about abortion) and *Evolution vs. God*. His latest movie deals compassionately and well with how to share the gospel with those trapped in homosexuality.

That movie, *Audacity*, has already begun to be widely seen. I mention Comfort because of this statement he made on my radio show: "We used professional actors because I know five minutes of cheesy acting would sink the whole ship. In past years, Christians have put up with some bad acting because [the film's] got the gospel in it, but non-Christians won't. They'll just tune out right away. So we got professional actors, and I think they did a great job."

Alex Kendrick directed and co-wrote *War Room*. His brother Stephen produced and co-wrote it, as with all their films.

War Room became the number two box office film in America the weekend it was released and number one its second week. Not bad for a movie essentially made by a church. That church is Sherwood Church of Albany, George, for which Alex and Stephen have served as associate pastors.

I spoke with Alex Kendrick many years ago, on the eve of his pro-marriage movie, *Fireproof* (with Kirk Cameron). Alex told me: "Sherwood Pictures has been around since 2002....With each project, we enter into a season of prayer, asking God for a God idea not just a good idea."

Sherwood Pictures in some ways a reflection of the pastor's vision to use stories to reach hearts. Kendrick told me, "We were challenged by our pastor, Michael Catt, to think in terms of reaching the world from where we were. And Jesus told parables. He told stories to engage people and then impart truth. This is a modern way of telling stories to engage people and impart truth. So, [using] movies has worked for us. We've loved that avenue since we were young, and it's exciting to use it now to minister to people."

Kendrick continued, "We want stories that impact and engage the culture---stories that will change lives in presenting the Lord's truth."

How did all their movie-making begin? Alex said, "In 2002 I had wanted to make Christians films....We went to our pastor, Michael Catt and said, 'What do you think about this idea?' and he was cautiously optimistic. And he said, 'Well, if the Lord's in it, He'll open doors. Let's begin praying that way."

That led to a straight-to-video release of *Flywheel*, which did exceedingly well. But then their later movies made it to the theatres and have made tens of millions of dollars and have broken records.

Kendrick said, "We are so excited to see what [the Lord] has done with this. In many ways, we feel like the kid with five loaves and two fish, that we give our best to the Lord and watch Him multiply it."

Most satisfying has been impacting people's lives. For example, Kendrick told me *Fireproof* alone has resulted in "people throwing away pornography, people renewing their marriage vows, people rededicating their businesses and their families. That's what we're after, to change our culture for the glory of the Lord."

So far, *War Room* has grossed an astounding $66 million (Box Office Mojo, 10/26/15)---and this during a year where "Huge Flops Hit the Box Office" (*Wall Street Journal*, 10/26/15). This does not surprise Ted Baehr, publisher of *Movieguide.org*, who told me, "...we expected [the success of *War Room*] since we do the most detailed economic analysis of the movie box office and find year after year that movies with Christian faith and values do better at the box office."

To what would the Kendricks attribute their success of all their films, including *War Room*? Their time in their own "war room."

Regal Cinema 16, Ft. Lauderdale, Florida, October 25, 2015.
[Photo by Jerry Newcombe]

The Alternative Media---A Lifeline of Freedom

5/6/15

On Saturday, March 28, 2015, thousands marched in Indianapolis in favor of same-sex marriage rights. On Saturday, April 25, 2015, thousands marched in Washington, D.C. in opposition to same-sex marriage.

Which story did the media cover? Let's put it this way---which rally did you *not* see covered by the news? The answer is obvious, and it underscores the great need for alternative sources of media.

Norway learned the importance of the alternative media 75 years ago when the Nazis took over that small country for five years. It's been fascinating to learn from my Norwegian wife's older relatives how virtually everyone participated in small or big ways to the resistance against the Nazis.

To be clear, my purpose is not to compare anyone here to the Nazis. Rather, my point is about the vital importance of a free and independent-minded media.

In Germany and in all the countries they conquered, the only information that was legally available had to be approved by the state; and, of course, much of it was a lie. Joseph Goebbels, Hitler's master propagandist, controlled the media with an iron fist.

I spoke one time with a woman who grew up in Germany. She always remembered her mom, during the Nazi years, sticking her head in the oven to listen softly to the BBC on the shortwave radio she had hidden in there.

In those days, the BBC would broadcast news of what was really happening---good or bad---instead of endless propaganda.

Once the Nazis took over Norway, they made it a capital crime to own a shortwave radio. You could listen to the Nazi propaganda; but if you wanted to hear the truth, you had to seek it elsewhere. And that was strictly forbidden.

One day, as a young man, my wife's Uncle Leif was at a train station; and he had a short-wave radio in a bag. Suddenly, he saw some German officers walking near. Without them noticing, he tossed the bag into the valley below. It was smashed, but he wasn't caught.

The Norwegian resistance had brave people hiding in the mountains with headphones to listen to the BBC news broadcasts in order to type out notes. Those notes were then duplicated through mimeograph machines and distributed secretly through various channels.

If a family came over for supper, they would leave their boots inside, by the front door. The children of the host family would secretly wad up the mimeograph sheets and hide them inside the soles of the boots for later perusal. Thus, everyone was getting in the act so that truth could quietly be known.

This may be an extreme example. But it underscores the importance of the flow of information.

Even under dire conditions, there is always an alternative media. In the days of the American War for Independence, there were Committees of Correspondence, disseminating information to the 13 colonies contrary to royal-controlled sources. About half of the New Testament is composed of letters that were written and circulated when the authors were in prison for the "crime" of spreading the gospel.

I'm grateful to live at a time where there is readily available an alternative media. I'm sure if some elitists in our culture had their way, they would over-regulate the Internet or talk radio or Christian broadcasting to make them essentially toothless---as sometimes happens in other countries.

The Internet has helped mollify the monopoly of the mainstream media. The alternative media is an extremely important lifeline to the Christian conservative movement.

Joseph Farah, creator of WorldNetDaily (the first Internet-only alternative news organization credentialed to cover the White House and Capitol Hill), told me once, "We live in a brand new media world today. It's as if the old media world had been scrapped and we've got brand new institutions, facilities, and opportunities that lay before us right now. That's what the Internet has meant to us."

But there are some who would like to change that.

Recently George F. Will, quoted in the *Wall Street Journal* (4/21/15), said that one of Hillary Clinton's goals is "to amend the Bill of Rights to make it less protective. It's an astonishing event. She said that she wants to change the First Amendment in order to further empower the political class to regulate the quantity, content and timing of political speech about the political class..."

I thank God we don't live under the type of repression from totalitarian regimes---an extreme example being the Nazis---with their control of the media. But we must always be vigilant. From the Internet to Christian broadcasting to talk radio, we need the alternative media. Without a free press, I don't see how we can remain a free people.

Photos by Jerry Newcombe. In Kristiansand, Norway's Archives. Here's an ordinary stack of firewood or is it?

The alternative media, such as this illegal short-wave radio in a home in Norway during World War II, proved to be a great life-line for those opposed to the Nazis during those dark years.
[Photos by Jerry Newcombe]

Part 3.

The Bible

Are Adam and Eve Just an Allegory?

3/13/13

How is it that the Bible is so controversial? The recent series on the History Channel on the Bible has sparked many water cooler and media conversations on various aspects of the Scriptures. One of them has important implications: Were Adam and Eve real people?

I'm not a scientist, and I don't play one on TV. But I believe they were. Why? Because I believe Jesus was who He said He was---God's only begotten Son, and clearly He believed they were real. I believe Jesus was the Son of God because *historically* He rose from the dead.

Jesus quotes from Genesis 1 and 2 (chapters with Adam and Eve) as the Word of God.

The Apostle Paul said that death came into the world through the first Adam. Jesus was the Second Adam, who came to save those who believe in Him from spiritual death.

John Hancock, John Adams, and Ben Franklin learned their ABCs with the New England Primer, which says for the letter A: "A, In Adam's fall, we sinned all."

In short, the Bible's argument is: No sin of Adam, no need for Jesus. But hasn't science proven there was no Adam?

How are we to understand claims of overwhelming "scientific facts" backing up the theory of evolution? Well, there are minor biological changes in nature. Some people call this "micro-evolution" (if you will)---which simply refers to a limited range variation within a species or kind. In Genesis, God said, "Let the earth bring forth living creatures after their kind." That's why some dogs are poodles and some dogs are great Danes, while both still remain dogs.

Critics note that Darwinists have tried to make a word game by using undisputed microevolution, (if you want to call it that), which can be observed everywhere, and claim it as proof of macroevolution—the theory that one species can change into another and that all life evolved ultimately from a common ancestor.

Dr. Jonathan Wells, Author, *Icons of Evolution*, once told me in a TV interview, "The evidence for microevolution is abundant. We see minor changes within species everywhere we look. The evidence for macroevolution is missing. The interesting thing here is that before Darwin, microevolution wasn't called evolution at all. It's just minor changes within existing species. Darwin didn't call his book, how existing species change over time. He called his book, *The Origin of Species*, and for that, there's just about no good evidence at all."

Why do so many today back off believing Adam and Eve were real people? They assume that evolution (macro-evolution) is proven; therefore, we have to reinterpret that part of the Bible as allegory. (I see nothing in the text of Genesis that would imply it's allegorical.)

In 1912, scientists discovered in England a human skull with a jaw like an ape. They named him Piltdown man. This was, they said, evidence of true evolution in progress---a real ape man. He was in the textbooks, encyclopedias, museums, and even the dictionaries. Finally, the missing link was no longer missing.

But, of course, Piltdown man turned out to be a deliberate hoax. That aspect was discovered in 1953, after four decades of providing alleged evidence for human evolution during a critical time for the theory to gain wider acceptance.

A geologist friend doesn't discount evolution, but he also believes in a real Adam and Eve. He told me, "I am not going to try to change the Bible based on science, and I'm not going to change the science based on the Bible. Someday we'll understand it all. Being truthful is important." I agree with his statement (but not his position).

He once read in an old geology book, "The work of God cannot contradict the Word of God." (That must have been an old book.) He added: "It is believed there were a first man and woman in the sense of human genetics---Mitochondrial Eve and Y-chromosomal Adam. These terms are widely used in scientific papers." I'm sure we'd disagree on many specifics. Regardless of that opinion, millions of intelligent truth-seekers alive today believe in a real Adam and Eve.

The Gods of Egypt

3/2/16

The title of a recently released film caught my attention: *The Gods of Egypt*. This column is not about the film, but rather it addresses God's judgment on the gods of Egypt by way of the ten plagues.

The ten plagues were the systematic judgments of God against Pharaoh and the Egyptians for enslaving the Hebrews for 400 years and refusing to let them go.

"Let My people go," said God through his servants, Moses and his brother Aaron. But Pharaoh refused. So under God's instruction, Moses unleashed ten plagues against Egypt.

In each of these judgments, God spared His people, the Hebrews. He miraculously kept them from experiencing His wrath.

The final judgment, the slaying of the Egyptian's firstborn, involved the very first Passover event. The Hebrew people were instructed by God to take a lamb without blemish, to sacrifice it, and to spread the blood on the top and the two sides of the doorpost, forming a type of cross.

Then the angel of death would pass over the Hebrew households, but would slay the firstborn of the Egyptians. The New Testament says Christ our Passover lamb has been slain for us.

Dr. D. James Kennedy points out that each of the ten plagues was a judgment on one of the gods of Egypt. You can find his commentary on this it in the new *D. James Kennedy Topical Study Bible* in the book of Exodus.

Kennedy notes, "In the Book of Exodus, we see the great confrontation between Moses and Pharaoh. This is the Old Testament counterpart to the confrontation between Christ and Pilate, the representative of the pagan Roman Empire, with Pharaoh being the representative of the pagan empire of Egypt. Here is a classic confrontation between good and evil, Christ and Satan."

Consider the plagues one by one and what Kennedy says about God's judgment on Egypt's false gods:

1)   The Egyptians worshiped the River Nile, the source of their lives. The first plague attacked that idol by turning the water into blood.

2)   The goddess Hekt (Heket, Heqet) had the face of a frog. "You worship frogs," said God in effect, "now see what it's like to have frogs everywhere." In a short time, the Egyptians were sick of frogs.

3)   Plague number three saw lice fill the land. Kennedy notes, "Now one of the gods of the Egyptians was Seb, the earth god...The Egyptians' reverence for the ground having it covered with trillions of fleas or lice would no doubt cool their amorous desires for that earth god Seb."

4)   Swarms of flies comprised the fourth plague. Says Kennedy, "Scholars say they probably were not flies, so much as they were the

beetles common to that area, called the scarabaeus from which we get the word scarab, which is a black beetle."

5) The fifth plague was the judgment on the Egyptian cattle. Apis, the chief god of Memphis, was a sacred bull worshiped by the Egyptians.

6) The sixth plague involved boils. This was a judgment against the god Typhon. This god, notes Kennedy, was "a magical genie that was worshiped in ancient Egypt. Here was a god who was connected with the magicians, which were the priests of the Egyptian religion. We find here that the magicians could not stand before Moses because of the boils, for the boil was upon the magicians and upon all of Egypt. So their power was broken."

7) Then came the plague of hail. Shu was the "god of the atmosphere." As Kennedy points out, "Now it is hard to go out to worship the god of the atmosphere when you are being pounded with large hail stones."

8) Next, locusts swarmed the land. The Egyptians worshiped the god Serapis, defender of the land against locusts.

9) Another major god of the Egyptians was Rah, the sun god. But Plague number nine saw darkness come over the land, even during the day.

10) "And finally in the last plague upon Pharaoh himself who was supposedly descended from the sun god Rah, his first born was killed," writes Kennedy.

He sums it all up this way, "In the ten plagues, God shows the world for all time that He alone deserves our worship."

Tragically, people today worship all sorts of false gods: money, celebrities, football or other sports. Some even worship their own possessions. Each of these will one day be burned up in God's final judgment of this earth, and then all will see that only the Triune God is worthy of worship.

Whether audiences find the new movie, *The Gods of Egypt*, to be an entertaining fantasy adventure or just a high tech stinker, it's good to remember that the ten plagues were God's judgments on human idolatry.

A Great Injustice to the New Testament

5/4/11

There's a terrible injustice that's being done to *the* best attested book of antiquity, the New Testament.

If the same principles of scrutiny were applied to the writings of Cicero, Caesar, and Marcus Aurelius, we would reject virtually all of them as hopelessly unreliable.

Essentially, the collection of 27 books known as the New Testament lately is being lied about as being fraudulent, as lacking integrity and authenticity. But that's based on some unproven assumptions, not actual facts or manuscript or archaeological evidence.

In reality, the accusers---for example, liberal Bible scholars who teach at major universities and appear on network television specials---begin with the premise that miracles are not possible. Based on that unproven construct, they then theorize to debunk the New Testament. There are many qualified conservative Bible scholars and historians who don't buy these theories.

Much of the conflict centers around *when* the New Testament was written.

Most of the liberal scholars assert as *fact* that the Gospels we have in the Bible were written so late that they do not reflect personal memory. They couldn't, since they were supposedly written so late after the events that the reported evangelists would have already died by then. So it's not personal memory found in Matthew, Mark, Luke, and John.

Why do these liberal scholars hold this theory?

Because the fall of Jerusalem was predicted so accurately in the first three Gospels by Jesus that these documents had to have been written after that event---AD 70. Forty years removed from the time of Jesus, in their opinion. By then, many of them would have already died.

But wait. What if there is a God (the New Testament surely assumes there is), and what if that God and His Son, Jesus Christ (clearly the central figure of the New Testament), could do miracles and did know the future?

Then Jesus could perform the miracle of predicting what would happen in the future, i.e., the fall of Jerusalem and the destruction of the temple. Predictions so stunningly accurate that to the modern miracle-denying Bible scholar, these writings *had to have been written before* AD 70. (See Matthew 24, Mark 13, and Luke 21.) Josephus, a first century Jewish historian, wrote in great details about the war between Rome and Israel.

The first great historian of the Christian Church was Eusebius of the 4th century, who wrote the first complete history of the Church. He marveled at how Jesus was able to predict the fall of Jerusalem with such accuracy. He said, "If any one compares the words of our Saviour with the other accounts of the historian [Josephus] concerning the whole war, how can one fail to wonder, and to admit that the foreknowledge and the prophecy of our Saviour were truly divine and marvelously strange."

Here is an important ancient source recognizing the miraculous nature of Christ, who could predict the future. The modern scholar doesn't buy it because he *knows* miracles (including predictive prophecy) cannot happen. But that's just circular reasoning.

But even if a modern scholar thinks there is no such thing as a miracle, it's interesting to note that in the first century, the temple authorities indirectly acknowledged that Jesus was doing miracles--- only they said He was doing them by the power of the devil.

Dr. Paul Maier, professor of ancient history at Western Michigan University and author of *In the Fullness of Time*, has reproduced what was essentially the arrest warrant for Jesus of Nazareth (listed here as Yeshu Hannozri) while He was on earth:

Wanted: Yeshu Hannozri

He shall be stoned because he has practiced sorcery and enticed
Israel to apostasy...Anyone who knows where he is, let him
declare it to the Great Sanhedrin in Jerusalem. (This is based on the
Sanhedrin 43a of the Babylonian Talmud.) (p. 114)

So here we have a source traced back to the first century providing attestation from a hostile source that Jesus Christ did supernatural works (attributed to demonic, not divine, power). Would it be so hard to picture Jesus predicting the future--- something only God can do (with accuracy)?

Because of the late-dating of the Gospels held by these liberal scholars, then all of a sudden virtually everything else in the New Testament becomes suspect---including the writing of James, Peter, John, and half of Paul's letters.

Next thing you know, an iconoclastic scholar and former Christian, like Dr. Bart Ehrman of the University of North Carolina, ends up saying that many of the documents of the New Testament are deliberate forgeries.

But what if we approach the dating issue like historians---not treating the New Testament as guilty until proven innocent?

Scholars tell us that Mark's Gospel was written first. Matthew and Luke clearly had access to and incorporated major portions of Mark's Gospel in theirs. An early Church Father, Papias, tells us that Mark was based on Peter's remembrances.

Luke is the physician who accompanied Paul on some of his missionary travels. He wrote at least two books in the New Testament, the Gospel According to Luke and Acts. They are Part I and Part II of his writings. Acts ends with Paul under house arrest in Rome.

The great fire of Rome has not yet happened. Paul has not yet been executed. By the time Acts (Part II of Luke) ends, Paul is still alive. He died around 65 or 66 AD. Certainly no later than 68, when Nero was deposed. That would be true of Peter also, since tradition holds that these two pillars of the first century Church were both executed in Rome under Nero. (Paul, a Roman citizen was beheaded; Peter was crucified---upside down, by his choice).

In 1 Timothy 5:18, Paul quotes Luke's Gospel as "Scripture." That means that already Luke's Gospel (and, therefore, Mark's) was circulating before Paul's death.

I recognize that because of stylistic concerns, some modern scholars (including Ehrman) allege that Paul didn't write 1 Timothy. But again this is based on assumptions, not actual evidence.

As to Matthew's Gospel, Paul Maier notes that the evangelist repeatedly refers to prophecies Jesus fulfilled. Over and over, Matthew will say how a certain event happened, thus fulfilling what the prophets had foretold.

Dr. Maier told me, "Can you imagine that if Matthew had been written after the fall of Jerusalem? Wild horses couldn't have prevented Matthew from saying, 'And Jesus' prediction was fulfilled when Jerusalem was destroyed.' He doesn't say that, and that's very unlike Matthew."

That leaves John's Gospel. Early Church Father Polycarp was John's direct disciple, and he says that John probably wrote his Gospel in the last decade of the first century.

Even though John was old by then, he recalls the incredible events he personally witnessed as a young man. Events that changed everyone's life. He spent three years in the public ministry of Jesus.

77

With the exception of John---who tradition tells us was boiled in hot oil for not denying Christ, yet it didn't kill him---virtually everyone involved in the Acts Church, including those who wrote the books of the New Testament, died a martyr's death, according to traditional accounts.

They could have saved their skin if they denied Christ. But how could they deny what they themselves saw and heard? They chose faithfulness to Christ, even though it meant a horrible death. In many cases, those deaths were in the arena, with cheering and jeering crowds.

Dr. Sam Lamerson, professor at Knox Theological Seminary, put it all in perspective:

> Those people who died did so knowing that it was going to be painful, knowing that it was going to be embarrassing, knowing that it was going to be terror-filled, and yet they did it anyway as a direct result of the fact that they believed that Jesus Christ was God. And they lived in the 1st century, and we live in the 21st century. And it seems to me that it is the height of arrogance for us to say in the 21st century, "You, all you people who died, you were just foolish, you just didn't know any better. And, we scholars, we know a lot better than you do."

> ....It seems to me, almost absurd to think, that we, in the 21st century can sit in judgment on eyewitnesses who actually saw what it was that Jesus did and said and say, "Well, sorry Matthew, you may have been there, but I'm from the 21st century. I know that didn't happen."

The apostles' testimony is sealed in blood.

Ironically, the very iconoclastic scholars who reject most of the New Testament as supposedly unreliable accept Paul's letter to the Romans as authentic.

Yet if we only had the book of Romans, we would still have the main points of the New Testament teaching needed for salvation: above all, that Jesus Christ is the divine Savior who died for sinners and rose from the dead.

Meanwhile, to reject the bulk of the New Testament because of the anti-miraculous assumptions is to allow one's bias to cloud one's judgment. This approach is along the lines of: "My mind is already made up. Don't confuse me with the facts."

These scholars judge Jesus. But in the end, it is Jesus who will judge us all, including the iconoclastic Jesus-scholars.

Rebuttal to *Newsweek*'s Cover Story on "The Myths of Jesus"

12/26/12

Suppose you were to read an overall negative article about a man who outwardly appeared to be respectable---but then, suppose you found out that, unbeknownst to the readers of the article, it was actually penned by his ex-wife? Wouldn't that make you at least a little suspicious about the article's contents?

So it is with *Newsweek*'s cover story on Jesus (Dec. 17), entitled, "The Myths of Jesus." They show a Nativity scene with bubble quotes asking these questions: "Who Was Jesus?" "How Many Wise Men Were There?" "Did He Have a Wife?" "In a Manger or a Cave?" "Why Bethlehem?" Just in time for Christmas, they choose to stir up baseless doubt.

What the article doesn't tell you is much about the author's (Dr. Bart D. Ehrman) own background. *Newsweek* mentions him as the author of *Did Jesus Exist?* and *Jesus, Interrupted*. But he formerly professed to be an evangelical Christian, who writes best-selling books that purport to debunk the reliability of the New Testament, such as *Forged*, which postulates that much of the New Testament was forged (a charge easily dismissed).

I'm not saying that Dr. Bart D. Ehrman, a respected scholar and professor of religion at the University of North Carolina, Chapel Hill, can't be fair and balanced per se. But the average reader of *Newsweek* isn't told about his biased perspective, nor is it hinted. As could be expected, knowing Dr. Ehrman's life work, the article overall leads one to doubt the historical veracity of the Gospels, at least when it comes to the birth narratives.

After writing about a highly suspicious late document about Jesus (c. A.D. 300+)---a document that conservative and liberal scholars would agree is totally questionable---he asks, "Are the stories about Jesus' birth in the New Testament any less unbelievable?" (p. 27).

Of the census in Luke 2 (the one called by Caesar Augustus where "all the world should be taxed"), Ehrman writes, "This is not a story based on historical fact." (p. 28).

Yet Dr. Paul L. Maier of Western Michigan University once told me in a television interview: "When Augustus died, he had two bronze plaques erected in front of his mausoleum in Rome in which he listed the 36 things for which he most wanted to be remembered. Point No. 8: 'I took a census of the Empire three times.'"

Ehrman also mentions the common problem of the two seemingly contradictory genealogies of Jesus (Matthew 1 vs. Luke 3). It's difficult, but not insurmountable. The short answer is that Matthew tells the nativity story from Joseph's perspective and does the same with the genealogy. Luke tells Mary's story and includes the annunciation and the Magnificat (Mary's song). The genealogy in Luke is believed to be that of Mary.

Generally, the Jews did not list women in the genealogies. In their *Biblical Encyclopedia*, McClintock and Strong observe that when the blood of the grandfather passed to a grandson through a daughter, the name of the daughter was omitted and the daughter's husband was counted as the son of the grandfather. In Matthew 1:16, Jacob is the father of Joseph. Yet in Luke 3:23, Eli (the father of Mary) is listed as the father of Joseph.

The answers to the types of issues Ehrman raises in Newsweek can be answered in standard books like the *Encyclopedia of Bible Difficulties* by the late Dr. Gleason Archer.

The bigger issue Ehrman raises is the view that the Gospels may be fine at communicating religious notions, but don't look to them for *historical* reliability. Of the Gospels in general, Ehrman states: "These are books that meant to declare religious truths, not historical facts." (p. 28). This seems to separate "religious truths" from "historical facts." But Christianity is based on historical facts.

Ehrman asserts, "… these gospel sources, whatever else they are, are not historically reliable descriptions of what really happened when Jesus was born." (p. 28).

A friend of mine is an up-and-coming Jesus scholar named Mike Licona, theology professor at Houston Baptist University. Dr. Licona has debated Dr. Ehrman on occasion. I asked Dr. Licona for a few statements about the historical reliability of the Gospels.

He emailed me: "Ehrman's statement that the Gospels are meant to declare religious truths rather than historical facts is overly simplistic and misleading. Luke 1:1-4 and John 21:24 (cf. 1 John 1:1-3) dispel such a position. One may reject what the Gospels report. But to say the authors did not intend to declare historical facts is terribly naive."

Licona also notes, "This is not to say that everything the Gospels reported was meant to be interpreted in a historical sense. Their authors employed the literary conventions of their day just as modern biographers employ those of today. But Ehrman goes too far, and his understanding of ancient biography appears misguided."

There are details about the birth, life, death and resurrection of Jesus that could never be verified by historians. (How could a historian prove a birth by a virgin?) But there are many details that can be verified, and we see the Gospels proving reliable time and again.

Not to confuse Easter with Christmas, but if Jesus wasn't raised from the dead---in actual history (if that's a "religious truth," but not an "historical fact")---then Christianity is bogus and ought to be explicitly abandoned. But Jesus did walk out of that tomb, and that's why 2,000 years later, a major news magazine ran yet another cover story about Him, albeit a largely negative one.

Is the New Testament Forged?

3/22/11

A new book by a major New Testament scholar is sure to make mincemeat of many people's faith. Needlessly.

The scholar is the iconoclastic Dr. Bart Ehrman, who teaches religion at the University of North Carolina, Chapel Hill.

The book is called *Forged: Why the Bible's Authors Are Not Who We Think They Are*. Ehrman said on a radio broadcast that about 75% of the New Testament documents are supposedly forged. They're frauds.

Dr. Sam Lamerson is a conservative New Testament scholar who teaches at Knox Seminary in Ft. Lauderdale. (By way of full disclosure, I earned a theology degree there). He heard Ehrman on a radio broadcast say words to this effect: "I want to be the scholar that uses the F-word about the Bible. I want people to know that these books were *forged*."

"Forged" is a strong word. Several of the New Testament books claim no authorship at all. Church tradition has attributed them to various writers, but the biblical text itself does not claim authorship for these particular books. For instance, none of the four Gospels (of which tradition names the writers as Matthew, Mark, Luke, and

John) actually have the names of the authors at the beginning of their documents. But writings by the early church fathers identify the authors of the four New Testament Gospels.

But if a document is anonymous, how could it be a forgery?

Dr. Mike Licona has been reading an advanced copy of *Forged*. He told me that the most prolific biographer of antiquity is widely held to be Plutarch (as in *Plutarch's Lives*), yet of all the 50 or so existing manuscripts we have of Plutarch, none of them are signed.

Were they forgeries? By Ehrman's definition, it would seem so. But no serious scholar holds that view.

Dr. Licona, who has debated Ehrman twice, told me, "What we're seeing from Ehrman [in *Forged*] is not new information. It may be new to many readers who aren't used to looking at the academic stuff, but it's not at all new."

Ehrman goes on to assert that many New Testament books that *do* claim authorship within the text, such as Ephesians, Colossians, and the letters of Peter and James, are *not* written by the claimed authors. It should be noted that this is not based on manuscript evidence. It's based largely on the style of the text, and there are many conservative scholars who are not convinced by these arguments. Thus, Ehrman is stating liberal *opinion* as *fact*.

Ironically, Ehrman even states in his own book, "Virtually all of the problems with what I've been calling forgeries can be solved if secretaries were heavily involved in the compositions of the early Christian writings." [p. 134]

But that's exactly what happened.

Conservative scholars note that many of Paul's writings begin with his name...and that of a co-author, such as Timothy, Silas, or Sosthenes.

Lamerson, who interestingly worked his way through seminary by doing magic tricks, knows sleight of hand when he sees it (or in this case, hears it). He said, "Of course, being forged is very different from having a secretary or having someone help you with the text or not knowing who wrote the text because their name simply isn't included."

Ehrman likes to tout that he's a former evangelical, who went to Moody Bible Institute and Wheaton College. (I went to Wheaton Grad School.) Ehrman then went on to Princeton Seminary where he began to have some doubts about his faith. That faith finally shattered when he was teaching at Rutgers University. Now, he's an agnostic.

So why are Bart Ehrman and other liberal scholars even concerning themselves with this stuff if they don't believe it?

Amazingly, Jesus made a warning that fits here (if the Gospel of Matthew is to be believed—and, no, it wasn't forged; it just isn't signed). He admonished those who "shut the kingdom of heaven in men's faces." He said, "You yourselves won't go in, but you prevent others from going in."

I'm concerned that many people will hear Bart Ehrman and think that he speaks for all the scholars. He does not.

Many people might miss the Gospel because they take Ehrman's word as Gospel. It is not.

It is liberal opinion repackaged well for a mass audience.
For anyone needing a scholarly rebuttal to Bart Ehrman's 2011 book, feel free to read Terry L. Wilder's excellent article called "Pseudonymity and the New Testament," which appears in a *2001* book, *Interpreting the New Testament: Essays on Methods and Issues*. (Indeed, Ehrman's arguments aren't new.)

Dr. Paul Maier, a professor of ancient history at Western Michigan University and a first rate scholar of the New Testament and its history, told me, "Both [Ehrman] and his publisher [HarperOne] are guilty of cheap sensationalism with little or no regard for the truth."

Ehrman's book went on sale today (March 22, 2011). Just in time for Easter, he, his publisher, and the lackeys in the media who go for all the anti-faith iconoclasm get another chance to try and cash in. What a friend we have in Jesus.

Time to Give the Gnostics a Rest

4/27/11

Another Easter has passed, and the TV specials and articles on Jesus (some positive, some negative, some hopelessly mixed) have aired and are gone.

Every Easter (and Christmas, for that matter), it seems to be time to bash Jesus or the Gospels or the Church.

Sometimes it's subtle. Sometimes it's not so subtle.

As one writer put it: "You can count on it. Every few years, some 'scholar' will stir up a short-lived sensation by publishing a book that says something outlandish about Jesus....his 'findings' will be treated respectfully as a scholarly work.'"

Was he talking about some recent specials on TV or some articles on the Internet? No, actually, this is from an article by Louis Cassels in *The Detroit News*, from June 1973. It was called, "Debunkers of Jesus Still Trying."

They were trying in 1973, and they're still trying in 2011. Very trying, to borrow a line from Groucho Marx.

Modern day debunkers remind me of the ancient heretics known as the Gnostics. The name comes from the Greek word to know. (An agnostic is one who doesn't know, e.g., if there is a God).

The Gnostics were a stubborn band of heretics rejected by the early Church. Acknowledged but rejected. They wrote many materials in the 2nd, 3rd, and 4th centuries. They wrote "Gospels" in the names of some of the 1st century apostles.

But their "Gospels" are nothing like Matthew, Mark, Luke, and John, which are based on eyewitness material and were written in the 1st century.

The only one of the Gnostic pseudo-"Gospels" that comes even remotely close in time to the biblical Gospels is "The Gospel of Thomas," which consists of 114 sayings, attributed to Jesus.

The early Church rejected the Gnostics and did not perpetuate and circulate their writings. A stash of some ancient codices (book-like manuscripts) were found in 1945 in Nag Hammadi, Egypt.

One of the TV specials on the History Channel called it the most important find of Christian history.

No, it wasn't. If anything, it just showed how correct Irenaeus and other early Church Fathers were in their condemnation of the Gnostic heresies.

The Nag Hammadi find has caused a rebirth of interest in the Gnostics. Finally, there are "alternative Christianities" that liberal scholars can learn about and promote—as if the Gnostics were on the same level as the early Christians. The mega-bestseller, *The DaVinci Code* tried to make the case that the Gnostic Gospels were just as valid as the four we have in the Bible.

As if the Gnostic writings were as important as the writings we have in the New Testament—even though these writings were removed from the subject, in some cases, by centuries.

Liberal scholars seem to swoon over the Gospel of Thomas. Some of them seem to prefer it to the Biblical Four.

Thomas is generally held to be too late to have been written by the Biblical Thomas (although that assertion is not without controversy).

I find it ironic that politically correct Bible scholars, like Elaine Pagels of Princeton or Bart Ehrman of the University of North Carolina, who show up on these TV specials, talk about The Gospel of Thomas as if it's more important than the Biblical Gospels. Yet look at how it ends:

(114) Simeon Peter said to them, "Let Mary leave us, for women are not worthy of life."

Jesus said, "I myself shall lead her in order to make her male, so that she too may become a living spirit resembling you males. For every woman who will make herself male will enter the kingdom of heaven."

That's sexist, to put it mildly. Its overall point does not fit the Judeo-Christian view that God made man (humanity) in His image— male and female He made them. Or the evidence from the true Gospels that Jesus allowed women to play a critical, positive role in His mission.

But it does fit the strange Gnostic worldview, which was anti-creation, anti-matter, and anti-law. I suppose many of today's Gnostics are really just selective Gnostics.

What's more, many of these Nag Hammadi texts are essentially "word salad." They just don't make sense. They are gibberish. No wonder the early Church rejected them. Here's a statement from the Gospel of Philip (again, not written by Philip): "God is a dyer. As the good dyes, which are called 'true,' dissolve with the things dyed in them, so it is with those whom God has dyed. Since his dies are immortal, they become immortal by means of his colors. Now God dips what he dips in water." (James M. Robinson, editor, *The Nag Hammadi Library*, p. 146).

The Gospel of the Egyptians III, 2 and IV,2, has even more meaninglessness, if that were possible: "Domedon Doxomedon came forth, the aeon of the aeons.....

iiiiiiiiiiiiiiiiiii eeeeeeeeeeeeeeeeeeeeeeeeeeeeeeeeeeeeeee

oooooooooooooooooooooooooooooo

uuuuuuuuuuuuuuuuuuuuuuuuuuuuuuuuuuuuu eee eeeeeeeeee

aaaaaaaaa aaaaaaaaaaaaaaaaa ooooooooooo ooooooooooo." (*The Nag Hammadi Library*, p. 210).

These are actual quotes from the Nag Hammadi texts of the Gnostic Scriptures.

And some of today's scholars prefer this kind of stuff to statements from Jesus from the Biblical Gospels, like,

    ·The truth shall set you free.

    ·Do to others what you would have them do to you, for this sums up the law and the prophets.

    ·Those who live by the sword shall die by the sword.

    ·Beware of wolves in sheep's clothing.

I suppose this last warning could apply to some of our politically correct Bible scholars who are re-peddling Gnostic heresies from the 2nd, 3rd, and 4th centuries all over again.

Isn't it time to give the Gnostics a rest?

Prescription for a Truly Happy New Year

12/29/15

Do you want this next year to be happier than the last? A first century letter written in prison by the Apostle Paul to the Philippian Christians has much advice on how to know true joy, and much of it was confirmed in May, 2015 by a major study released by the Mayo Clinic.

The study said that happier people are healthier people. That's why the Mayo Clinic studied the issue of happiness in the first place.

CBSNewYork reported on this study after it was it released: "After decades of studying and working with tens of thousands of patients, researchers at the Mayo Clinic say they've cracked the code to being happy."

And the answer is *what*? More money? Bigger car? More stuff? Fame? Long before he was a presidential candidate, Donald Trump once said, "Whoever says money can't buy happiness doesn't know where to shop."

The article reported: "Psychiatrist John Tamerin says for many people the root of everything we're chasing, a better job, more money or true love, is happiness. But this endless pursuit often backfires. If you lead your life always waiting for a great thing to happen, you probably will be unhappy."

The Mayo Clinic summarizes their findings, which were released:

"People who are happy seem to intuitively know that their happiness is the sum of their life choices, and their lives are built on the following pillars:
- Devoting time to family and friends
- Appreciating what they have
- Maintaining an optimistic outlook
- Feeling a sense of purpose
- Living in the moment."

Paul's letter to the Philippians directly or indirectly addresses all these things. Relationships. An attitude of gratitude. A positive outlook. A sense of purpose. Living now and not letting the past cripple your present or future.

As to purpose for living, Paul says, "For to me to live is Christ and to die is gain."

The Mayo Clinic study on happiness said we need to forget negative things. Paul said as much in Philippians 3: "...this one thing I do, forgetting those things which are behind and reaching forward to those things which are ahead, I press toward the goal to the prize of the high calling of God in Christ Jesus."

Forgetting the things behind us---the past that we cannot undo, but for which we can be forgiven if we would ask God for forgiveness---makes us more resilient and more positive in our outlook.

The study speaks of the importance of gratitude and of not complaining. Paul says, "Do all things without grumbling or disputing." How many people, even professing Christians have allowed murmuring to get the better of them, instead of cultivating a thankful spirit?

The Mayo study tells us to "Invest in relationships." Yet, as I write these words, I see of a new report that some will be seeking companionships---from *robots*.

Indeed, the study reports that self-focus is one of the great obstacles to human happiness. Paul told the Philippians, "in humility value others above yourselves, not looking to your own interests but each of you to the interests of the others. In your relationships with one another, have the same mindset as Christ Jesus..."

The study found that complaining will not make you happy. Paul said, "do everything without grumbling." He also said that he had learned to be content in all circumstances. He added, "I can do all things through Christ who strengthens me."

Isn't it interesting that this study and all the thousands of dollars spent in research, dealing with thousands of clients, finds that if you want to be happy, focus on others, and put their interest before your own---just what Paul told the Philippians---as they strive to follow the example of Jesus.

I have had the privilege of regularly participating in a food distribution ministry. No matter how blue I may possibly be going into it, my feelings are uplifted after helping others in need in the name of Jesus Christ.

The Mayo Clinic study also recommended focusing on positive things. That's just like Philippians 4:8: "Finally, brothers, whatever things are true, whatever things are honest, whatever things are just, whatever things are pure, whatever things are lovely, whatever things are of good report, if there is any virtue, and if there is any praise, think on these things."

In the same chapter, Paul also talks about choosing to give thanks to the Lord. He says, "Rejoice in the Lord, always. Again, I say, rejoice."

In a sense, we could say Philippians is the answer as to how to be happy.

When Jesus said that it is more blessed to give than to receive, who could have realized that that is *literally* true? Forgetting what is behind, thinking on good things, and caring about others are key precepts to a truly happy new year.

The Price Paid to Get the Bible into English
3/18/15

This month, March 2015, marks the 150th anniversary of Lincoln's classic Second Inaugural Address. Historian, author, and college professor Daniel Dreisbach has written a wonderful piece on how the Bible played a key role in that address, which is chiseled in stone on the wall of the Lincoln Memorial. He notes that there are some 45 allusions to the Bible in that one speech, including three complete Bible verses.

Any honest student of American and English history must admit that the English Bible, the King James Version in particular, has played a key role in history. Even the leading atheist in our time, Richard Dawkins, has called it "a treasured heritage."

What people don't realize is the high price that was paid to get the Bible into English. A price paid in blood in some cases. In 1408, a law was passed in England that strictly prohibited the translation of the Bible into English.

Knowing that history, when I visited National Cathedral in Washington, D.C. about half a year ago, I was fascinated to carefully examine the large stone pulpit that stands on the right hand side at the front of the sanctuary.

Since the sermon is delivered from this beautiful pulpit, the designers of the Cathedral, who began its construction in 1907, chose to commemorate the history of the English Bible with four carved statues on the corners of the pulpit and carved bas-reliefs on the sides.

The four statues honor men whose lives are significant in the history of the English Bible. Presumably, Alfred the Great (849-899) is there because of his use of the Bible and its principles in his ruling. Winston Churchill once wrote of him, "King Alfred's Book of Laws...attempted to blend the Mosaic code with Christian principles and old Germanic customs."

There is also a statue of John Wycliffe, a 14th century Oxford professor. He is credited with being the first to translate the Bible into English (the English of 1383) from Jerome's Latin Vulgate.

Wycliffe is often called, "the morning star of the Reformation." Reportedly, he first coined the phrase "government of the people, by the people, for the people"---a concept he saw in the Word of God. For his efforts, Wycliffe's remains were later desecrated by Church officials who opposed the translation of the Bible into English.

The two other statues on the pulpit memorialize Bishop Lancelot Andrewes, the best known of the translators of the King James Version (1611), and Bishop Brooke Westcott, who helped publish the Revised Version of the Bible in the 1880s.

One of the bas-relief depictions on the pupil shows the martyrdom of William Tyndale (c.1494-1536). Underneath this scene are his last words, a prayer: "Lord, open the King of England's eyes." That king was Henry VIII, who later started the Reformation in England by leaving the Roman Catholic Church—but not for noble reasons. He wanted to divorce his wife and marry someone he hoped would give him a son.

Amazingly, just three years after Tyndale prayed, his prayer was answered, King Henry authorized the publishing of a Bible in England---the first time it was legal to do so.

Tyndale played a major role in history, but he is an unsung hero. He was the first major translator of the Bible into English from the original languages. He wanted to see the day when even the "plow boy" would be able to read the Bible for himself.

Although Tyndale was martyred for his efforts, Dr. Harold Rawlings, author of *Trial By Fire: The Struggle to Get the Bible into English*, notes that major portions of Tyndale's Bible ended up in the King James Bible of 1611, thus, insuring wide distribution of Tyndale's work---to this very day.

Tyndale first coined the English words "atonement," "Passover," and "scapegoat," based, of course, on biblical teachings.

Meanwhile, the King James Bible of 1611 is acknowledged as a literary masterpiece, which has had profound and positive influence on the English language and every English speaking culture.

How we got our English Bible is a fascinating story, and for anyone interested in learning more about it, I would recommend Harold Rawlings' book, *Trial by Fire*.

In light of the high cost to get us the Word of God in our own language, it is tragic that some people, even professing Christians, neglect the daily reading of the Good Book.

Today, a vast majority of Americans might read a speech as fine as Lincoln's Second Inaugural Address and have no clue about the Bible's incredible influence on it. Nor would they have any idea of the price paid so that the Bible could become available to everyday folks---plow boys, if you will.

The Lost Art of Bible Meditation

5/18/16

We have lost the great art of Bible meditation today, and we are the poorer for it.

In 1987, newsman Ted Koppel gave a classic commencement speech at Duke, in which he famously said that Moses didn't come down from Mt. Sinai carrying the "Ten Suggestions."

Note what Koppel then said about television and our ability to concentrate: "Look at MTV or Good Morning America and watch the images and ideas flash past in a blur of impressionistic appetizers. No, there is not much room on TV for complexity."

We have been losing concentration power through the constant stimulation of media. And it seems to be getting worse. Now, little children are accessing media at their fingertips, perhaps earlier than their little brains can handle it.

We are becoming so distracted that we have lost the ability to focus. "Oh, look---a squirrel."

In earlier times, some people spent time contemplating God and the Bible. George Washington spent so much time directly with the Bible or with biblical passages found in the 1662 Book of Common Prayer, which he avidly read, that his writings and speeches (public and private) are replete with biblical phrases and allusions.

Is biblical meditation the same as Eastern meditation? No, because in the latter, you empty your mind. In the former, you fill your mind with the things of God. Biblical meditation means to quietly ruminate---turning in your mind over and over, phrase by phrase---the truths of God.

The ability to meditate on Scripture may be a lost art, but it is one that is worth recovering. My long time pastor, the late Dr. D. James Kennedy, noted that Joshua 1:8 is the only place in the Bible where it directly promises success. What is that success contingent upon? Meditating on God's Word.

I was thinking recently about an elderly man I once knew, who was a great model of a life shaped by Bible meditation. I am in debt to his example of living a life focused on Scripture.

Charlie Hainline always had an irrepressible smile on his face. His love for Jesus Christ radiated from him and defined him and made him a great man to be around.

Charlie used to have an old broken-down, dilapidated cassette player, on which he played one song over and over. The gist of the gospel song was that you can't stand on the promises of God unless you know what they are. Charlie constantly talked about the promises of God and our need to access them---like blank checks from heaven.

In 1964, Charlie retired from full time work, but that made him available for full time ministry, until his death in 1994.

He once told me that he had been going to prison for ministry sake since the 1940s to share the gospel with inmates, but that was only on the weekends. After he retired, he was able to go six days a week.

The amazing thing about that feat---of going to prison for ministry, six days a week for thirty years straight---is that in the last year or so of his life, he continued to do so even when he developed Lou Gehrig's disease (ALS).

He could barely walk. The prison officials told him that he could no longer come there unless he was with someone who could wheel him around. So he rounded up volunteers.

I was that volunteer on January 1, 1994. I remember the day because it was my first time in prison.

Charlie would share shared the good news of Christ---how Jesus on the cross paid a price He didn't owe, but it was a price we couldn't pay, and he would have prisoners memorize Bible verses.

One of the key verses Charlie had them inscribe in their hearts was 1 John 1:9, which says, "If we confess our sins, He is faithful and just to forgive us our sins and to cleanse us from all unrighteousness." Charlie called this "the Christian's bar of soap"--- useful for daily spiritual cleansing.

Charlie would give inmates who successfully memorized this verse an unofficial certificate---an 8 ½ by 11 sheet proclaiming their accomplishment. Some of them hung their certificates on their bare walls.

Life wasn't always easy for Charlie, but he found inner strength to overcome. He had a daughter who was kidnapped and killed and her head was found floating in a canal. Yet Charlie forgave the convicted murderer and even shared the gospel with him in prison.

Charlie Hainline exemplified the lost art of meditation and what it has to offer to us. One of his oft-repeated statements brings that home: "Look to others and be distressed. Look to self and be depressed. Look to Jesus and be blessed."

Part 4.

The Church

Would Jesus Side with the Wall Street Protesters?
10/12/11

One of President Obama's chief spiritual advisors is Rev. Jim Wallis of Sojourners, a liberal Christian community in the DC area. He has now likened helping the Occupy Wall Street protesters to siding with Jesus.

The Sojourners organization publishes a magazine that I used to subscribe to for about a year when I was at Wheaton Graduate School in the late 1970s.

Looking back at it, that subscription reminds me of Winston Churchill's maxim that if you're not a liberal in your twenties, you have no heart. But if you're not a conservative by your forties, you have no brain.

A year of the magazine was about all I could take. I realized after a while that they never said anything good about the United States.

Then it dawned on me one day---wow, they never seem to criticize the Soviet Union, which was very much a threat to the whole world in those days.

They were constantly carping against Jimmy Carter, with criticisms from the left. I never bothered to see what they said when Ronald Reagan ascended to the presidency. But I'm sure they went apoplectic.

The strange thing is that every leftwing cause they promoted was done in the name of Jesus Christ.

Now, Rev. Wallis has spoken out about the Occupy Wall Street protesters, saying that they are siding with Jesus on behalf of the poor. Therefore, if you're really going to be a follower of Christ, bring them a casserole or a pizza (which he calls a "peace-za").

Wallis said, "The occupiers' desire for change and willingness to take action to do something about it should be an inspiration to us all."

He views them as standing for the poor and hungry. Therefore, they stand with Jesus. Wallis says, "When they talk about holding banks and corporations accountable, they sound like Jesus and the biblical prophets before him who all spoke about holding the wealthy and powerful accountable."

Certainly, there is no justification for backroom deals---from both sides of the aisle---whereby some Wall Street tycoons have gotten rich (off of we the taxpayers) through crony capitalism.

94

And certainly, the Bible speaks about justice and caring about the underdog.

But is Rev. Wallis watching the same videos I am of these protesters?

They seem to me like adolescents who never grew up. They strike me as parasitical, in the sense that they seem to be unable to make it. They basically derive their substance from the labor of others. Can't our colleges do a better job of preparing young people for the work force these days?

In a fascinating video from the Occupy Atlanta protest, the progressives in the group (which seem to play an elaborate game of "Simon Says," as a form of democracy) essentially bar the liberal Congressman John Lewis, long time civil rights advocate, from speaking to the group. What? Is he too conservative for them?

Then there's the Occupy LA spokesman who was advocating French Revolution- type violence.

On top of that, the Occupy Wall Street movement has a computer-hacker group, which calls itself Anonymous, spurring on the protests. In their Internet threat videos, always with a computer voice, they say near the close, "We are legion."

Anyone familiar with the Gospels knows that Jesus exorcised a demon-possessed man, and when the Lord asked, "What is your name?" the demons replied, "We are legion---for we are many." It's perhaps no coincidence that Anonymous signs off with that phrase.

The Bible certainly teaches an ethic to help the needy, especially the family-less. There's a Scriptural phrase for that: "the widow and the orphan."

The Bible also says that if a man will not provide for his own household, he has denied the faith. It doesn't say if he *cannot*, but if he *will not*. After all, sloth is one of the seven deadly sins (as are greed and envy).

But the group Rev. Wallis claims represents Jesus appears to be comprised of able-bodied misfits or 21st century hippies.

I wonder if many of these protesters have simply given up on looking for jobs.

Granted, it's a tough economy. But there are still jobs to be had for those who seek them. Meanwhile, Christian charities through various churches do a tremendous job to help those in need.

Around 1700, when the Puritans ran things in Massachusetts, there was a man from London who stayed in that colony for several years. He stated: "I have lived in a country where in seven years I never saw a beggar, nor heard an oath [a cuss word], nor looked upon a drunkard."

For all their faults, like the Salem witchcraft hysteria, the Puritans instilled a strong work ethic that in some ways is still with us today.

The historical success of Wall Street is related to the Christian work ethic, to which the Puritans made a great contribution. Based on their applying the Bible to labor, they taught that we should work hard (fulfilling our calling), delay gratification, save, invest, and re-invest, and give to those in need. To see the same principles presented basically without religion, just read Ben Franklin's timeless book of maxims, *Poor Richard's Almanack*.

I agree with Rev. Wallis' point that imitating Jesus includes standing with the poor and needy. But, sorry, I don't see how standing with the Occupy Wall Street folks fits that category.

Church for Atheists?

11/19/13

There's an old joke that says: How do you describe an atheist at his funeral? "All dressed up with no place to go."

Well, now, all jokes aside, there is a place atheists can go on Sundays. There's a new type of atheist church that have begun by a couple in England, and apparently it's taking off.

Writing for the AP (11/11/13), Gillian Flaccus penned an article called, "Atheist 'mega-churches' are now a thing in the U.S as popularity spreads from U.K."

These groups, write Flaccus, are "people bound by their belief in non-belief." They have had large gatherings in Los Angeles, "San Diego, Nashville, New York and other U.S. cities."

The founders are "British duo Sanderson Jones and Pippa Evans," who are on a "tour around the U.S. and Australia to drum up donations and help launch new Sunday Assemblies."

The services consist of singing secular songs, inspirational talks, and times of reflection.

Basically, this equals religion without God.

It's a free country, because of our Judeo-Christian base (and that of England), so the atheists are free to assemble or not, just as anyone else is. Only in nations tied to a Christian base does that freedom exist. (It certainly didn't exist in the Soviet Union, which was based on atheism.)

But why accept a cheap imitation when you can get the real thing, possibly down the street?

These atheist churches meet on Sunday mornings, the traditional day of church. It's a fact that the Jewish sect known as Christianity worshiped Jesus because all the early Christians (who were Jewish--- Peter, Paul, and Mary, and all the apostles) believed Jesus had risen from the dead on "the first day of the week," i.e., Sunday. Right at the very beginning of the Christian movement.

Sorry, Mr. "DaVinci Code," it's a fact that the early Christians, including the apostles, as soon as they could wrap their minds around it, worshiped Jesus as divine.

In about AD 112, Pliny the Younger, a Roman magistrate of Bithynia (in what would be modern day Turkey) wrote a letter to Emperor Trajan.

Dr. Gary Habermas writes of this exchange in his classic book, *The Historical Jesus*: "Pliny found that the Christian influence was so strong that the pagan temples had been nearly deserted...Pliny dealt personally with the Christians who were turned over to him" (p. 198).

If these believers continued in the faith, despite torture, Pliny had them killed.

Pliny tortured some of them to learn of their worship customs, which were on Sundays.

So Pliny the Younger writes of the early Christians: "They were in the habit of meeting on a certain fixed day before it was light, when they sang in alternative verses a hymn to Christ, as to a god, and bound themselves by a solemn oath, not to [do] any wicked deeds, but never to commit any fraud, theft or adultery, never to falsify their word, nor deny a trust when they should be called upon to deliver it up; after which it was their custom to separate, and then reassemble to partake of food—but food of an ordinary and innocent kind."

Note the ancient creed, still repeated in many churches to this day: "Christ has died. Christ is risen. Christ will come again."

The 17th century French mathematician and Christian apologist, Blaise Pascal, said that in every one of us, there's a God-shaped vacuum in every heart, just waiting to be filled.

The Bible says God created us, and we will give an account before Him one day. In the 4th century, St. Augustine wrote in his classic book, *Confessions*, "You have made us for Yourself, Oh God, and our hearts are restless until they find their rest in You."

The shorter catechism from the Westminster Confession of Faith from the 1640s asks: "What is the chief end of man? The chief end of man is to glorify God and enjoy Him forever."

The whole idea of organized atheism (especially the militant, full-time kind) is still interesting to me—Why? Because they spend all their energies fighting that which they claim does not exist.

With Thanksgiving coming soon, and "atheist churches" apparently on the rise, I'm reminded of what G. K. Chesterton once said: "The worst moment for an atheist is when he is really thankful and has no one to thank." He also said, "If there were no God, there would be no atheists."

Where Have All the Bold Pastors Gone?

3/6/12

During this election season, the issue of religion has come up on many occasions. But for the most part, we haven't heard from many pastors---except, for example, from the brave priest from Indiana, with his denunciation against the Obama administration's move to force Catholic agencies to fund contraceptives and abortifacients against their consciences.

Another outspoken minister has been Dr. Robert Jeffress of Dallas, who was castigated about half a year ago for stating he preferred a Christian politician to a Mormon one. He was simply quoting founding father John Jay, first Chief Justice of the United States Supreme Court, who said, "Providence has given to our people the choice of their rulers, and it is the duty, as well as the privilege and interest of our Christian nation to select and prefer Christians for their rulers" (October 12, 1816). First Chief Justice or not, one of only three authors of *The Federalist Papers* or no---that's too politically correct to say nowadays.

Many of the controversial issues of our day, such as abortion and marriage, have become political. But in reality, they are simply moral issues that have changed into political ones.

I think part of the reason we don't hear much from pastors these days is because of a misunderstanding of the law. Some fear---wrongly---that if they say anything viewed as a political statement, then they might lose their tax exempt status. I plan on addressing this point in a subsequent article.

In any event, we should remember that some biblical figures, like Moses and John the Baptist, spoke out against the rulers at the time and paid a price for it. Historically, being faithful to their God sometimes had a high price to it, as seen by those brave Christians fed to the lions in the arena rather than renounce their faith.

There's a great painting at the Art Institute of Chicago showing St. Ambrose rebuking Roman Emperor Theodosius (around the end of the 4th century) for an imperial massacre in Thessalonica. The bishop took his life in his hands by making such a pronouncement against the lord of the whole empire. Thankfully, Theodosius repented.

Thomas More wasn't so fortunate in his stance in refusing to give into King Henry VIII's demand for divine sanction for his divorce. More was beheaded for his courage to go against the king.

The price a bold pastor has to pay in our culture is generally a much smaller one than those sometimes demanded in the past---or even today in some of the world's hot spots, such as in the Middle East. There's an Iranian pastor on death row right now for having converted from Islam. [Editor's note: Thankfully, he is now free].

Historically, in the American context, pastors and the church have often led the way in societal reforms---some of which had political implications. Two-thirds of the members of the abolition society in 1835 were ministers of the gospel. Also, the anti-slavery Underground Railroad was run by churches.

For good or bad, there's no doubt that prohibition was led by ministers, churches, and laywomen.

The civil rights movement was essentially born in the basement of Dexter Avenue Baptist Church in Montgomery, led by their minister, Rev. Martin Luther King, Jr. on December 1, 1955, the night Rosa Parks was arrested for not giving up her seat on the bus after a hard day's work. Watch raw tapes of the civil rights marches, and you'll see many different Christian groups participating.

Before we even became a country, pastors (especially in New England) would preach election day sermons, not necessarily endorsing particular candidates, but explaining biblical civic duties. Georgetown-educated Dr. Donald Lutz, political science professor at the University of Houston, even notes that even the word "election" comes from the Bible and not from politics.

Dr. Donald Lutz told me, "Elections were designed by these Americans in the early era for a virtuous people to help identify who amongst are more virtuous. Who are those who are most likely to be among the elect, those who are most likely to be saved? Elections are an attempt to recognize those who are among the elect, those are more likely to have been saved and going to heaven. Therefore, we, in this country, expect those people who are elected to be virtuous."

Dr. Lutz added, "This drives the Europeans crazy. Why do we expect our president and our representatives to be good and Godly people? It's because this is the habit we got into in the very beginning. It's a Puritan notion, which we Catholics buy into right away. "

The professor notes that it wasn't enough that the candidate simply said that they were decent people. Their actions had to match their words: "And then, we would quiz them very carefully. How did you perform in the past? Were you God-fearing and were you pursuing the common good in the way you voted, the way you behaved, the way you acted? If not, I'm not going to vote for you. And so, we would filter upward men or women of greater virtue to higher office."

We are far removed from our Puritan roots. But I think some of their core principles still apply---especially the idea that the church should not completely abandon the political process.

For years, my pastor was the late Dr. D. James Kennedy, who noted, "Someone said to me, 'Do you think Christians should be involved in politics? That's dirty business.' I said, 'Of course not, you should leave it to the atheists; otherwise, you wouldn't have anything to complain about.' Well, we have got plenty to complain about today, because that is exactly what we've done."

"Go to Church, Live Longer"

4/3/13

The quest to live longer is an old one. Around this time, we celebrate the 500th anniversary of the first known European discovering Florida---Ponce de Leon. This was at Easter time, during which in his native Spain, the cathedrals were filled with flowers to celebrate the Resurrection. Seeing all the flowers in the verdant land, he called it the land of the flower---la Florida.

He heard about the Fountain of Youth, which you can visit to this day in St. Augustine, Florida. There you can see the stone cross he and his men made to mark the year---1513.

The Fountain of Youth supposedly would rejuvenate its drinkers. Local Indians who were in great shape appeared to be the beneficiaries of this Fountain of Youth. It turns out it wasn't the water that made them live better; it was their mating patterns and seafood diet rich in protein.

Solomon the Wise once said, "My son, do not forget my teaching, but keep my commands in your heart, for they will prolong your life many years and bring you peace and prosperity."

The promises in Proverbs are general principles we can apply to our lives. Sometimes God is His wisdom and for His sovereign purposes will take a righteous person home early, while young.

It should also be pointed out that there are exceptions to averages. Have you ever heard of the statistician who drowned in a river, the average depth of which was two feet?

But, meanwhile, as a general principle, those who live godly lives are spared all sorts of hardships in this life and all sorts of problems that the Creator desires to spare us from. His commands are not to restrict us, but for *our* good---much like a loving father who wants his children to obey for *their* safety and well-being.

What's interesting is to see that scientists today are discovering empirical data pointing to a similar conclusion to the principle of long life as a reward for godly living.

For instance, in *www.webmd.com*, under the subheading "Go to Church, Live Longer," they report on one of many studies that have consistently found the same thing. Regular church attendance adds to life's quality and longevity. Of course, it's not the physical act of going to church, but the spiritual act of seeking God that makes the difference.

The researchers reported: "People who attend religious services at least once a week are less likely to die in a given period of time than people who attend services less often."

The study reported: "People who attended religious services at least once a week were 46 percent less likely to die during the six-year study, says lead author Harold G. Koenig, M.D., of Duke University Medical Center in Durham, North Carolina. 'When we controlled for such things as age, race, how sick they were and other health and social factors, there was still a 28 percent reduction in mortality,' he says."

Koenig added that going to church a regular basis is just as good for you as not smoking.

In another study, reported in www.sciencedaily.com, they found the same basic results. Going to church on a regular basis adds years to your life. At the University of Colorado at Boulder, the researchers found "that regular churchgoers live longer than people who seldom or never attend worship services."

www.sciencedaily.com adds: "The research showed that people who never attended services had an 87 percent higher risk of dying during the follow-up period than those who attended more than once a week. The research also revealed that women and blacks can enjoy especially longer lives if they are religiously active."

I once interviewed Dr. Byron Johnson, formerly of the University of Pennsylvania, then later Princeton, and now at Baylor University. He is an excellent social scientist, who studies the scientifically quantifiable effects of faith on people's lives.

He said to me, "We reviewed over 770 studies on religion to see what the impact was. Not just a handful, not hand-selected studies, every study that we could find. And that's when we came up with the conclusion that about 85 percent show a beneficial effect." He summarized his findings in a publication, entitled, *Objective Hope.*

Dr. Johnson said that the studies show that if you go to church on a regular basis, you'll add seven years to your life, if you're white. If you're black, you'll add 14 years to your life.

This reminds me of a classic study from about 15 years ago written up in a major news magazine. The cover story of an issue of *US News & World Report* was entitled "The Faith Factor." The subtitle was: "Can Churches Cure America's Social Ills?"

In that article, they noted this: "What's the surest guarantee that an African-American urban youth will not fall to drugs or crime? Regular church attendance turns out to be a better predictor than family structure or income, according to a study by Harvard University economist Richard Freeman. Call it the 'faith factor.'"

The magazine also reported that "Frequent churchgoers are about 50 percent less likely to report psychological problems and 71 percent are less likely to be alcoholics."

Ponce de Leon thought water from a spring in the land of the flowers might give him longer life. It turns out longer life for most of us might be just as close to us as the neighborhood church.

Martyrdom Comes to America?

June 21, 2010

Recently, two former gang members who had been converted to Christianity went out on a Saturday night, as was their custom, to tell strangers on the street the good news about Jesus Christ.

One of the people they spoke with didn't like what they were saying. Before they could get away, he pulled out a gun and shot them in cold blood. Another evangelist who was with them was able to get away and called the police. Through his help, they were able to catch the killer and learn what happened.

This story didn't happen in Pakistan or in Kenya.

It happened in the United States. In fact, it happened relatively close to where I live, in Boynton Beach, Florida.

Has Christian martyrdom come to the United States? Unfortunately, the answer seems to be yes.

The gunning down of these two men took place in January 2010. But it barely made the news.

Stephen Ocean, 23, and Tite Sufra, 24, had troubled pasts and found salvation as the means for personal transformation. The *Palm Beach Post* reports, "Ocean was arrested in 2003 on robbery charges and in 2004 for violating probation on previous battery and petit theft convictions. He was arrested in 2006 for carrying a concealed firearm and resisting an officer." However, Sufra had no adult arrest record.

Because of their transformation, Sufra and Ocean were active in spreading the Word of the Lord. The year before the incident, they had even been ordained by their church. Ocean's sister said: "They go around and minister to boys and say where they came from...They did that all day and all night."

On January 30, 2010, they were out in the streets of Boynton Beach in Palm Beach County when they encountered 18-year old Jeriah Woody. The *Post* reports that they preached to him for a quarter of an hour, until his cell phone rang, and he told them he had to leave. The three were walking away when Woody reportedly ran back to them and shot Sufra dead. He shot Ocean once, and then to shoot him a second time---in the head---execution style.

Woody later turned himself in. He now awaits trial.

I suppose somebody could say it was just another murder on the mean streets of urban America.

And it was. But if they hadn't been out sharing the gospel that night, they would be alive.

Besides, could you imagine if they had been promoters of some sort of protected speech and then gunned down like this in cold blood? Surely, the story of the murders would have then made it beyond the local news.

For instance, Dr. Gary Cass of the Christian Anti-Defamation Commission based in San Diego, who came to South Florida in May and organized a prayer vigil to honor the two men, asked this poignant question: Could you imagine if this slaying had happened to two Muslims preaching the way of Allah and they were killed by an "Islamaphobe"? Or what if these were two gay men promoting their lifestyle who were killed by "a homophobe"? In short, we're so used to anti-Christian bias that disturbing news of anti-Christian bias doesn't seem to faze us anymore.

My wife and I attended that prayer vigil that Dr. Cass and also Rev. Pat Mahoney organized. The memorial service included prayers, speeches, and songs from some of the survivor's families. The climax of the service was when the 50 or so participants were each handed a long-stem flower, and then crossed the street to the very places where Ocean and Sufra had been slain. Each person laid a flower at the spot, and prayers were offered up. Ocean's mother melted into tears at this most gut-wrenching part of the service.

I hope martyrdom has not come to America. I hope this is an isolated incident. But if given the choice: Deny Christ or die, to me there is only one genuine option. It's the one chosen by Stephen Ocean and Tite Sufra. Long live their memories.

Church---Antidote to Loneliness?

2/19/14

I've often wondered why the studies show consistently that going to church lengthens your life and even the quality of your life.

One time I had the privilege of interviewing a sociology professor and author, Dr. Byron Johnson. When I spoke with him, he was teaching at the University of Pennsylvania. He went on from there to Princeton and is now at Baylor. He has made a lifetime of studying the impact of religion on society, on health, mental and physical.

He told me something I've never forgotten. As noted before, if you're white and you go to church regularly, you will live---on average---an extra seven years. If you're an African-American and you go to church on a regular basis---on average---you will gain an extra 14 years.

These are averages. Obviously, there are exceptions but this statistically significant increase must be reckoned with.

Another study released many years ago was conducted with 5000 people from Alameda, CA over a span of 28 years to determine the long term benefits of attending church. The [Ft. Lauderdale] *Sun-Sentinel* summarized the findings with this phrase, "Go to church, live longer."

What factors contribute to this consistent finding? One of them, I believe, is the effect of fellowship. We are designed by God to be social creatures, but we now live in perhaps the most disconnected society in history. Loneliness is the inevitable result--- a new study even finds that loneliness can kill.

Steve Connor wrote an article: "Extreme loneliness worse for health than obesity and can lead to an early grave, scientists say," which is published in the Independent (UK, 2/16/14).

Connor notes: "Chronic loneliness has been shown to increase the chances of an early grave by 14 per cent, which is as bad as being overweight and almost as bad as poverty in undermining a person's long-term wellbeing, a study has found."

The article quotes Professor John Cacioppo, a University of Chicago psychologist, who says, "Retiring to Florida to live in a warmer climate among strangers isn't necessarily a good idea if it means you are disconnected from the people who mean the most to you."

Connor also notes: "Research has shown that at any given time between 20 and 40 percent of older adults feel lonely."

So what does this have to do with active church membership? Quite a bit. Getting involved in a good church can be a real antidote to loneliness. Becoming a Christian actually means joining the largest family in the whole world.

Contrary to the image in the Beatles' song "Eleanor Rigby," implying that church people are lonely, the opposite is usually the case. In fact, there are brothers and sisters all over the world in Christ, from all sorts of tribes and tongues.

I've seen this first hand in marrying a woman from another country---Norway, in her home church, in a bilingual service. (We said, "Ja, I do.") She and her family are all in Christ. When I first met her, our Christian faith was the starting point of our relationship. Before we became family through marriage, despite the language barriers, we were already family.

My daughter has found the same thing. She married a Christian whose family left Egypt in the early 1990s, knowing that their sons (one of whom is now my son-in-law) would have no future as persecuted Christians under a Muslim majority there. His family and mine are one in Christ.

I know sometimes people can go to church and may experience an unfriendly situation. But it's like anything in life: What you get out often tends to correlate with what you put in.

Some people might attend a church just on Sunday morning but not get involved in other ways. They are still better off than if they didn't attend at all. But better yet is to plug in. To find some avenue of service to others, to be a part of an accountability group. For example, joining a weekly Bible study with friends can be a real life-changer and can help overcome loneliness.

To have a friend, be a friend. As Jesus put it, treat others as you would want to be treated. Applying that statement alone helps explain how active churchgoing can lead to longer life.

When the Bible says we should not forsake "assembling" with each other, who knew that such a command was good for our health as well?

More Jesus, Less Crime

1/13/16

One of America's greatest liabilities is crime, not only in the cost of property loss and damage but the lives impacted by lawless acts. The best solution for America's crime problem can be seen when a criminal is transformed through faith in Jesus. In fact, it does quite often, usually under the radar.

Case in point: Hillary Jones of Marysville, California---about two hours north of San Francisco---used to steal. She used to be a heroin addict and was homeless.

Then she became pregnant. Determined to have an abortion, she contacted Planned Parenthood. First, she had to prove she was pregnant. She told me, "as far as Planned Parenthood goes, if you don't have money or insurance, they won't see you. I needed the verification to get insurance for the abortion."

So she knowingly went into A Woman's Friend clinic, a pro-life center, assuming she could stop up her ears, not hear what they were saying---and walk out with a certificate proving her pregnancy. But once she saw her unborn son on the sonogram, she was sold on giving him life.

The kindness Hillary experienced at A Woman's Friend changed her life in all ways. They really cared about her, and she knew it.

Even after she was arrested when her crimes caught up with her, volunteers from A Woman's Friend kept in touch with her.

If a picture is worth a thousand words, then consider the before and after pictures of Hillary Jones---taken within about two years of each other.

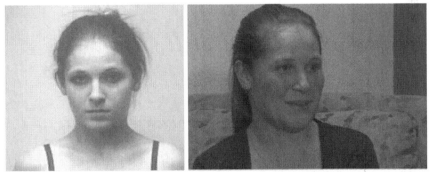

Hillary Jones---before and after Christ

Today Hillary is no longer homeless. She lives with her mother with whom she has reconciled.

When she walked into the pregnancy care center, she was an atheist. Today she is a believer in Jesus Christ.

When she came there, she was determined to abort. Today she is so grateful she gave her one-year old son Adam life. He is the joy of her life. She told me, "I don't even know where I'd be right now without him. I love him so much and he gives me this motivation that I never had and he has changed my life and God has just blessed me with my beautiful boy."

She said, "I know several women, who have been in my situation, and they chose abortion and they regret that now. They go through their lives sad."

Hillary used to be a liability to society. Today she is an asset and on her way toward a career, hopefully, in nursing. The loving, Christian counsel from A Woman's Friend changed her in all ways.

Hillary's story is representative of the fact that Jesus changes sinners. By redeeming them, He sets them on a new path. And we all benefit, even the unbelievers.

Dr. Rodney Stark's book, *America's Blessings: How Religion Benefits Everyone, Including Atheists* (Templeton Press, 2012), documents the positive impact of religion (for the most part, Christianity) on society. Stark teaches at Baylor University. His colleague at Baylor, Byron Johnson, wrote the book, *More God, Less Crime*. Stark observes, "At all ages, religious people are much less likely to commit crimes."

Stark writes: "Americans benefit immensely from being an unusually religious people---blessings that not only fall upon believers but also on those Americans who most oppose religion. In America, militant atheists are far less likely to have their homes broken into or to be robbed on their way to work than they would be in an irreligious society, because of the powerful deterrent effects of religion on crime."

He said that because of the bias of academics and the media, the benefits of Christianity on society are not well known or articulated. But they are there.

For instance, Stark notes, "those who attend church are less likely to have shoplifted....As for 'violent America,' the assault rate in [irreligious] Sweden is about three-and-a-half-times that of the United States..."

And he adds, "All Americans are safer and their property more secure because this is such a religious nation....the higher the church membership of a city, the lower its crime rates."

The amazing thing is that Stark even quantifies the blessings of religion at the end of the book. He attempts to put a price tag on it. The biggest savings are in the realms of crime prevention and reduction.

He writes, "Even if individual religiousness contributes more than $2.6 trillion in savings to the United States every year. I suggest that the intangible blessings on American life provided by our unusually high level of religiousness are worth far more."

Hillary is a living reminder that if anyone is in Christ, he or she is a new creation. "The old has passed away. Behold, all things are made new."

How Christianity Benefits Even "Angry Humanists"
1/20/16

Why has America been blessed in many ways in the past? At its core, the answer has to do with the Judeo-Christian tradition. We are living off of the residue of that great heritage.

As one author put it, "one of our nation's primary advantages over many others lies in the greater strength of religion in American life."

That author is the previously cited Dr. Rodney Stark. Last week I mentioned a remarkable book he wrote that I feel did not get the attention it deserves. It's called *America's Blessings: How Religion Benefits Everyone, Including Atheists* (2012).

Recently I read Stark's book carefully and took copious notes. Here are some of Stark's findings, in addition to the ones related to the reduction and prevention of crime, which I pointed out last week.

Stark observes that "America is an unusually religious nation. Nearly all Americans say they believe in God, about 80 percent believe in heaven, about 70 percent believe in hell, and half pray at least once a day (32 percent pray more than once)."

He notes that religion benefits everyone, even the non-religious, who feel the residual effect.

Those who attend church more often tend to donate much more often. For example, he writes, "...religious people dominate the ranks of blood donors, to whom even some angry humanists owe their lives."

Stark provides a bullet list of many benefits:

*"Religious Americans are far more likely to contribute even to secular charities, to volunteer their times to socially beneficial programs, and to be active in civic affairs.

*"Religious Americans enjoy superior mental health---they are happier, less neurotic, and far less likely to commit suicide.

*"Religious Americans also enjoy superior physical health, having an average life expectancy more than seven years

longer than that of the irreligious. A very substantial difference remains even after the effects of 'clean living' are removed.

*"Religious people are more apt to marry and less likely to divorce, and they express higher degrees of satisfaction with their spouses. They also are more likely to have children.

*"Religious husbands are substantially less likely to abuse their wives or children.

*"Religious American couples enjoy their sex lives more and are far less likely to have extramarital affairs.

*"Religious students perform better on standardized achievement tests.

*"Religious Americans are far less likely to have dropped out of school, which is especially true for African Americans and Hispanics.

*"Religious Americans are more successful, obtaining better jobs and far less subject to being on unemployment or welfare; this is true not only for whites but for African Americans.

*"Although often portrayed as ignorant philistines, religious Americans are more likely to consume and sustain 'high culture.'"

When Stark is talking about religion in America, it would appear that he is primarily talking about those in the Judeo-Christian tradition.

One area we don't think about normally is this: Christians tend to enjoy greater birth replacement rates than their secularist counterparts. That is important to society because if we don't replace ourselves, we'll eventually die off. This is where secular Europe and religious America can be contrasted.

Stark points out that secularists rightfully blame Christianity for upholding higher fertility rates. But that's good because the Bible tells humanity that we should "be fruitful and multiply."

Stark notes that the current TFR, that is, the "total fertility rate" needed for any nation is "about 2.05 per female---one child to replace the mother, one to replace the father, and an occasional child to offset infant mortality."

Secular Europe is not doing well on this front. Facing what some sociologists call a "demographic winter," they've thrown open the doors to immigrants---even those with values contrary to Western ones---partially to grow their lagging economies. They need people to replace those that are not procreating.

Stark says, "Europe's lack of fertility is directly attributable to its lack of religiousness.....

In both Europe and America, fertility is highly related to church attendance."

Stark cites Eric Kaufmann of the University of London, author of the book *Shall the Religious Inherit the Earth* (2010), and summarizes Kaufmann's message: "only the irreligious sector of Europe's population is declining, while the religious sector is growing."

Stark adds, "Translated into comparisons with Western European nations, we enjoy far lower crime rates, much higher levels of charitable giving, better health, stronger marriages, and less suicide, to note only a few of our benefits from being an unusually religious nation. Quite aside from the social and personal benefits of these religious effects, they add up to many hundreds of billions of dollars a year in financial benefits."

Four Myths about Church to Avoid, Lest They Become Self-Fulfilling Prophecies

1/6/16

Are our churches dying? Are young people leaving the church in droves? Is evangelicalism in America all but dead? At the start of a new year, it's good to take honest stock of where we are, so we can adjust accordingly.

I had the privilege recently of interviewing for Christian television a leading church statistician of our time---Dr. Ed Stetzer, head of research for LifeWay (Nashville) of the Southern Baptist Convention. He also teaches part-time at Wheaton College and Trinity Evangelical Divinity School.

I asked Dr. Stetzer about the poll on American Christianity released about a half a year ago by Pew Research. Some people mistakenly interpreted the poll's findings to indicate that the church in America is in a virtual free fall.

Dr. Stetzer told our viewers: "The sky is not falling statistically. Now the ground is shifting. America is becoming much more secular, but the percentage of people who regularly attend church has actually not shifted drastically."

Here are four myths Dr. Stetzer addressed during our conversation:

1) **The church in America is dying.** Dr. Stetzer told me, "The American church isn't dying, and no real researcher anywhere thinks that, though you might think that from of all the books and articles, often by evangelical authors saying, 'We gotta fix things,' so they overstate the situation....But the perception of the church as dying is, I think, unhelpful....facts are our friends and math is hard, but it matters."

The real loss of faith in America is with the nominal Christian---Christians in name only. Millions in this category are abandoning the label "Christian" and identify themselves as having no religion. On a survey, they would mark "none" as to their religion. Even so, notes Stetzer, the number of self-identifying "atheists" is still in the single digits.

2) **No one goes to church any more, except maybe in Three Forks, Idaho.** But actually, Stetzer notes, our rates of church attendance are as they were in the 1940s. They got higher in the 1950s and 1980s and 1990s. Stetzer says, "I don't think most people think of the '40s as a time when the church was dead."

3) **Children reared in evangelical homes are leaving the church in droves.** The statement that 86% of children from evangelical homes leave the faith when they go off to college, never to return, is a myth.

Stetzer refers to a study by two authors for the University of Southern California, published in an Oxford University Press book, "and they say that evangelicals are actually one of the groups that do pretty well keeping their next generation."

Dr. Stetzer said that evangelicals have about 62 percent success rate of their children keeping the faith. That said, there is the challenging fact that those who identify themselves as "none"---i.e., no religion, are a growing group, particularly among the young.

Stetzer says we should face that as a challenge, but not overstate it. He told me, "The reality is, most people get religious as they get older, right? The religiosity grows---they have kids, they often go back to church."

4) Evangelicals are losing the faith in record numbers. About ten years ago, Michael Spencer who called himself "the Internet Monk" predicted "the "Coming of the Evangelical Collapse."

Stetzer describes Spencer's prediction this way: "The next decade of evangelicalism will be a ghost town. The institutions will be empty. The churches will be emptying out. And it got a lot of attention, and it sort of began this narrative that evangelicalism was dying."

But the reality is that evangelicals are holding their own for the most part. The number of evangelicals has actually grown from 2007 to 2014---however, that growth is offset by the fact that it did not quite keep up with the per capita growth of the population during that same time.

Meanwhile, what is often said about the evangelicals is true about the liberal denominations. They continue to hemorrhage members. The Episcopal Church, the Presbyterian Church in the U.S. (the more liberal branch, which is certainly the largest group), the Methodists, and so on.

Many of the leaders in the "mainline" denominations no longer believe in Jesus Christ. The late Dr. D. James Kennedy, a conservative Presbyterian minister, once said of these liberal denominations: "Their churches are withering away---for their congregations instinctively know that there is nothing there but froth, and they will not tolerate being deceived. If Christ was not bodily raised from the dead in human history, Christianity would cease to exist."

Dr. Stetzer summarizes the take home message of all this: "The devout are remaining faithful but we're going to have to learn to live in a different world to engage in fresh new ways for the cause of Christ."

Is the Atheist Population Skyrocketing?

5/20/15

Will the last true Christian in America please turn out the lights on the way out? A recent study on religion and America that has received much attention has been interpreted by some to indicate that Christianity is on its virtual deathbed.

But as the saying goes, "The good news is the bad news is wrong."

The study comes from the respected Pew Research Center: "America's Changing Religious Landscape" (5/12/15). The subtitle is: "Christians Decline Sharply as Share of Population; Unaffiliated and Other Faiths Continue to Grow."

They note that as recently as 2007, nearly eight in 10 Americans identify themselves as Christians; whereas today, that number is down to about seven in 10. Liberal mainline Protestants are losing the largest numbers; the number of self-identifying Catholics has also shrunk somewhat. Evangelicals are basically holding their own. Certainly, the church in all its branches has its work cut out for it.

But the biggest shocker is what we could call the rise of the "nones": "Over the same period, the percentage of Americans who are religiously unaffiliated---describing themselves as atheist, agnostic or 'nothing in particular'---has jumped more than six points, from 16.1% to 22.8%." This includes many young people who are part of the "nones."

Dr. Byron Johnson, a great researcher who often works with Gallup on the subject of religion in America, cautions us on the interpretation of the data. The author of the book, *More God, Less Crime*, Johnson teaches at Baylor and has taught at the University of Pennsylvania and Princeton.

I asked Dr. Johnson about the new study, especially about the rise of the "nones." He said, "Don't be fooled, Jerry. We have some of the world's top religion scholars doing social science research. We publish books and scientific articles in peer-reviewed journals---the other side doesn't do either."

In a recent radio interview I did with him, Dr. Johnson made some fascinating remarks on the perceived decline of Christianity in America and the rise of the "nones."

He said, "There are these ongoing reports by the media that indicates religion is declining. Most of the secular media is looking for something that shows that religion is declining...so that's why you hear all these reports about the growth of atheism."

For example, says Johnson: "In one of their recent studies, Pew found that 44 percent of Americans are not affiliated with the religious tradition/denomination in which they were raised. That finding was interpreted to mean that 44 percent of Americans had abandoned the faith. But this simply acknowledges that Americans shop around in a highly competitive religious economy---looking for the best product. It's a sign of religion's vitality not a sign of leaving faith behind. "

He added, "Much to the chagrin of most of the media, atheism has remained flat for over seven decades. Four percent of Americans fall into that category. It hasn't changed. If atheism were on the rise, it would be such a phenomenal story. But instead, since it isn't, they have to do what they can to make us believe that it is."

But he cautioned, "You'd be blind not to know we have a secular society. But the reality is we have a religious society as well. It's very vibrant."

I asked him about the "nones" and their significant growth in recent times.

He answered: "There are a number of people who would mark 'none,' n-o-n-e, on a survey, and two or three questions later will give you the name and address of a place [house of worship] they regularly attend, and guess what? Almost all of these are non-denominational, evangelical churches. I'm not saying all of the 'nones' are evangelical." But many of them are.

Here's the rub: Are all the "nones" (or even a majority of them) atheists? No, says Johnson: "The 'nones' have been equated with atheism. That's what's really going on here. The number of 'nones' is growing, and it is true. But what I'm saying to you is that when you unpackage it, it looks completely different."

In other words, the recently released report is being interpreted by some to indicate that America is becoming more atheistic because of the increase of those who list no religious identification. He said that's where interpreters of the Pew study are in error.

Meanwhile, how many evangelicals are in the country at present? Using a three-fold criterion to define an evangelical (i.e., one who has accepted Jesus as Savior, believes in the authority of the Bible, and shares the faith), Johnson says based on years of his surveying, there are about 100 million. "That's a huge, huge category."

All this reminds me of the Mark Twain line: "The rumors of my death have been greatly exaggerated."

Will NYC Implement the ABC Principle--- Anything But Christ?

1/23/12

A terrible decision in New York City could have a chilling impact on religious liberty. If it spread to other cities, it could be devastating.

Because of a court's ruling against one particular small church of the Bronx, Mayor Michael Bloomberg has now decreed that come February 12, 2012, all churches and fellowships meeting in public schools have to be evicted. This will impact 160 churches, congregations, and fellowships.

These churches generally have great relationships with the community. Many of them offer important services to the needy, and they even provide revenue for the city. But it seems that among some today, the ABC principle trumps other considerations. ABC as in Anything But Christ.

This case goes back several years. In the name of "the separation of church and state," the educational establishment of New York City decided that churches could not meet in schools for worship. They could meet in schools for discussions or sports events, but not divine services.

So one small church, the Bronx Household of Faith, filed suit with the help of the Alliance Defense Fund, a legal group that fights against anti-religious bigotry in the courts and beyond. As long as the litigation continued, that church (and other churches) have been able to meet in schools.

Greg Baylor an attorney with the Alliance Defense Fund said recently, "Unfortunately, even though they had a temporary injunction that allowed them to meet in the public schools, the New York City education officials kept fighting them in the courts. They were insistent upon their objective of keeping out the churches. And they eventually persuaded the U.S. Court of Appeals for the 2nd Circuit, which is headquartered in New York City, to say 'Yes, you school districts can keep out churches who want to engage in religious worship services.'"

After the Appeals Court decision, the ADF appealed the case to the Supreme Court, which declined to take the case.

The Supreme Court receives thousands of requests every year. (I remember hearing in a recent year, it was about 8,000.) But they turn down the vast majority of requests, only agreeing to a small number of cases (about 80-100). That means they turn down about 99.9% of the requests for appeals. Therefore, no one should read too much into the Supreme Court's refusal to take on any case. It's not on the same level as an out-and-out Supreme Court ruling on a particular issue.

Mayor Bloomberg is reading way too much into the Supreme Court's decision to not hear the appeal.

So here we are in a country founded for religious freedom---where residents of our largest city are about to lose theirs.

George Washington said, "If I could have entertained the slightest apprehension that the Constitution framed by the Convention, where I had the honor to preside, might possibly endanger the religious rights of any ecclesiastical Society, certainly I would never have placed my signature to it." So George Washington would not agree with Mayor Bloomberg's decision.

John Adams said, "Our Constitution was made only for a moral and religious people. It is wholly inadequate to the government of any other." So John Adams would not agree with Mayor Bloomberg's decision.

As president, Thomas Jefferson attended church every week at the U. S. Capitol. Clearly, he had no problem with government buildings being allowed for worship. So Thomas Jefferson would not agree with Mayor Bloomberg's decision.

Clearly the mayor's decision does not fit with our history or traditions or law. (The church had even won at the District Court level.)

Some of the congregations are so small and limited in their resources that they might end up folding if this decision goes through.

Imagine the net impact if this terrible decision doesn't get overturned. Today, New York. Tomorrow, California. Next day, perhaps your town. Cultural trends often spread from New York City to the rest of the country. Think of all the churches in our land that meet in schools. The church I happen to be a part of meets in a school.

Thankfully, the legislative body for the state of New York is considering an emergency bill that would address the issue statewide, thus overruling the mayor's decision. New Yorkers for Constitutional Freedom have been pushing for this.

Even if the mayor's edict goes into full effect (heaven forbid), the kingdom of God will continue---after all, we're talking about the religion of the catacombs. But it's just so ironic that this kind of thing could seriously be considered in a nation whose motto is still "In God We Trust."

Part 5.

Christian-bashing

Can Your Pro-Life Bumper Sticker Actually Get You in Trouble?

9/26/12

When George W. Bush was running for re-election in 2004, someone I know who lives in the greater Los Angeles area put a bumper sticker with the president's name on his vehicle. When he returned to his car one day, someone who didn't share his enthusiasm for Bush had smashed the bumper where the sticker was with a hammer, causing lots of damage.

I knew Bush was unpopular in some circles, but that seemed a bit much.

Writer Tim Brown recently (9/21/2012) posted an article on FreedomOutpost.com entitled, "DOJ: Your Bumper Sticker May Indicate You're A Terrorist."

Brown writes, "The Department of Justice funded a training manual used in the State and Local Anti-terrorism Training (SLATT) program for law enforcement. Apparently certain political bumper stickers can put you on the 'could be a terrorist' list, including opposition to the United Nations and support for the Constitution and the Bill of Rights." Included in that list are those who oppose abortion.

This seems to fit with a fascist pattern: Free speech for me, but not for thee. What is free speech if it isn't really free?

This kind of thing would never pass constitutional muster. Twenty years ago, the High Court caused quite a controversy when they declared that burning a U.S. flag is protected free speech.

If that is the case, then how much more should bumper stickers be considered free speech?

Here's the verbatim wording found on two of the pages of the DOJ training manual:

Terrorism Training for Law Enforcement

Special-Interest/Single Issue Terrorism

·Extremists who seek to force the government or population to alter a specific aspect within the country

·Usually do not seek to overthrow or greatly alter the government

·Often represent a fairly popular point of view

p. 13 of BJA- SLATT Program Law Enforcement Sensitive

Special-Interest/Single Issue Terrorism (continued)
·Most common areas of concern are
·Animal rights
·Antigenetic engineering
·Antiabortion
p. 14 of BJA- SLATT Program Law Enforcement Sensitive

"Anti-abortion"? "Often represent a fairly popular point of view"? It's disturbing when the views of ordinary Americans could be categorized as dangerous to society.

This reminds me of the report from April 2009, under the direction of Janet Napolitano, the head of the Department of Homeland Security, entitled: "Rightwing Extremism: Current Economic and Political Climate Fueling Resurgence in Radicalization and Recruitment."

A footnote on p. 2 of this document states: "Rightwing extremism in the United States can be broadly divided into those groups, movements, and adherents that are primarily hate-oriented (based on hatred of particular religious, racial or ethnic groups), and those that are mainly antigovernment, rejecting federal authority in favor of state or local authority, or rejecting government authority entirely. It may include groups and individuals that are dedicated to a single issue, such as opposition to abortion or immigration."

Since abortion comes up as an issue in both of these government documents, I think it worthy of addressing. The people who are pro-life tend to be consistently pro-life. For example, they do not sanction the killing of abortion doctors or personnel.

When I read the leading atheist's book of our day, Richard Dawkins' *The God Delusion*, I was intrigued by a phrase he occasionally used, "the American Taliban." Who was he referring to? Finally, I realized he was talking about those who kill abortion-related personnel.

But you can count on one hand people who fit in that category. They are not in the mainstream of the pro-life movement. Only one or two that I know of were even professing Christians. That's not the way of Christ. It never has been and it never will be.

Suppose someone had killed the late Dr. Bernard Nathanson before he had repented and became pro-life? Dr. Nathanson had presided over 60,000 abortions. The same applies for Carol Everett, who was partly responsible for 35,000 abortions, as a part owner of a few abortion clinics in the Dallas area. Today she is staunchly pro-life. And no, she's not a terrorist.

In a day where your bumper sticker might get you in trouble, we should remember that tolerance should apply to all—even to those who hold politically incorrect views. True tolerance, which means respect for those with whom we disagree, seems to be disappearing in our time. I believe it's because of the disappearance of Christian influence in public discourse.

Above all, it's disturbing when government documents display intolerance of those with differing views than the policy makers. Such is the way of political correctness. But if that's the case---so be it. Those of us in favor of life should not be intimidated, even in what messages we may choose to put on the bumpers of our cars.

Do Christians Want "Jews to Die" to Hasten the Second Coming?

9/10/12

This seems like a preposterous statement, that Christians want Jews to die. But it was uttered just last week by someone of rank in one of our two major political parties.

The Chairman of the Palm Beach County Democratic Party, Mark Alan Siegel, told PatrioticUpdate.com at the DNC: "The Christians just want us [Jews] to be there so we can be slaughtered and converted and bring on the second coming of Jesus Christ...They're not our friends. They want Israel to pursue policies that are antithetical with its security and existence."

But Siegel said, "The worst possible allies for the Jewish state are the fundamentalist Christians who want Jews to die and convert so they can bring on the second coming of their Lord. It is a false friendship. They are seeking their own ends and not ours."

On 9/7/12, Florida Democratic Party Chairman Rod Smith condemned Siegel's remarks, stating they do not reflect the Party's views: "Today I asked for Mark Alan Siegel's resignation. He has declined. He is embarrassed and humiliated by his inappropriate comments and has requested an indefinite leave of absence, which I have granted." By 9/8, Siegel had resigned.

Siegel also issued an apology: "...I apologize to all Christians, Jews and other people of faith for any embarrassment or anger my remarks may have caused. Throughout my life I have practiced religious tolerance among all people of faith....I alone am responsible for my remarks and I pray that they are not taken as the position of the Palm Beach County Democratic Party."

It's all ironic in light of the fact that support for Israel is stronger from Christians than any other non-Jewish group. Michael Medved, a Jewish conservative, quotes Zev Chafets, author of *A Match Made in Heaven* (on evangelicals and Israel): "The dislike and contempt for evangelical Christians that is so integral to American Jewish cultural and political thinking is almost wholly absent in Israel... The average Israeli—even the average anticlerical secular Israeli like me—appreciates evangelical support" (commentarymagazine.com, May 2012).

For the record, there is no part of the New Testament that says that those of the Jewish faith must be slaughtered first before Jesus will return to planet earth: SILENCE. It's not there. There is nothing in either the Old or New Testaments that makes such an outrageous claim.

There is no part from any creed of historic Christianity in all of its branches---Catholic, Orthodox, or Protestant---that says that those of the Jewish faith must be slaughtered before the Second Coming. SILENCE. It's not there.

Perhaps some strange interpretations of Revelation could possibly be distorted to reach this kind of view. But G. K. Chesterton once said: "Though St. John the Evangelist saw many strange monsters in his vision, he saw no creatures so wild as one of his own commentators."

Did "Christians" do bad things to Jews through the centuries? Absolutely. Inexcusably. Dr. Michael Brown, a Jewish believer in Jesus Christ, wrote a book chronicling such things: *Our Hands Are Stained with Blood: The Tragic Story of the "Church" and the Jewish People.*

They're inexcusable and at total odds with what Jesus Himself and the apostles taught.

Some commentators try to link the Nazis with Christianity. But that is not accurate. The Nazis were anti-Christian.

While many church leaders and laypeople did cave to Hitler, there was still a faithful remnant. *TIME* magazine (12/23/1940) reported this in an article entitled "Religion: German Martyrs."

Not you, Herr Hitler, but God is my Führer. These defiant words of Pastor Martin Niemoller were echoed by millions of Germans. And Hitler raged: "It is Niemoller or I."

So this second Christmas of Hitler's war finds Niemoller and upwards of 200,000 other Christians (some estimates run as high as 800,000) behind the barbed wire of the frozen Nazi concentration camps. Here men bear mute witness that the Christ—whose birth the outside world celebrates unthinkingly at Christmas—can still inspire a living faith for which men and women even now endure imprisonment, torture and death as bravely as in centuries past.

Adolf Hitler once declared: "The heaviest blow that ever struck humanity was the coming of Christianity. Bolshevism is Christianity's illegitimate child. Both are inventions of the Jew."

After the Nazis surrendered, the Draft for the War Crimes Staff (7/6/1945) noted: "Throughout the period of National Socialist rule (of Germany), religious liberties in Germany were seriously impaired. The various Christian Churches were systematically cut off from effective communication with the people...Under the pretext that the Churches themselves were interfering in political and state matters, they would deprive the Churches, step by step, of all opportunity to affect German public life."

Rabbi Daniel Lapin, an Orthodox Jew, has pointed out that modern America is not the same as Medieval Europe: "No country in the last two thousand years has provided the same haven of tranquility and prosperity for Jews as had the United States of America. And, this is not in spite of Americans being Christian; it is because of it. You might say that America's Bible belt is the Jewish communities' safety belt."

I'm thankful for Siegel's apology, and I hope he will understand that true Christians love Jews.

Shooting at FRC: Overcoming Hate with Love
8/16/12

Has a new threshold in the culture wars been crossed? On Wednesday, August 15th, 2012, reports indicate that a man entered the lobby of the Family Research Council building in Washington, DC, declaring, "I don't like your politics." In his attempt to go further into the building, he shot the security guard in the arm. The guard was able to pin him down.

Certainly, the security guard, Leo Johnson, is a hero for his courage and quick action. He prevented further bloodshed. Our thoughts and prayers go out to him and his family in the face of this tragic incident.

The reports indicate that the alleged shooter was a 28-year old Virginia man, who had been volunteering at the DC Center for the LGBT Community.

Thankfully, a coalition of 25 gay rights groups spoke out loudly and clearly that they eschew violence, and they don't agree at all with the actions of the alleged shooter. I'm reminded of when there have been occasional acts of violence against abortion-providers, pro-life leaders cannot get to a microphone fast enough to denounce the violence.

The day after the shooting, FRC president, Tony Perkins, said, "We're not going anywhere. We're not backing up, we're not shutting up. We have been called to speak the truth. We will not be intimidated. We will not be silenced" (AP, 8/16/12).

I've been to that building many times, conducting interviews for Christian television, including with Tony Perkins, as well as with some ex-gays, among others.

Hopefully, Wednesday's shooting incident is not the beginning of some new trend. But historically, persecution often follows effective Gospel work. How are we to respond?

"A Mighty Fortress," Martin Luther's hymn, reminds us "The body they may kill. God's truth abideth still." There is a wider sense in which the Kingdom of Christ will prevail in our world---if we show love even in the face of hatred

Dr. Martin Luther King, Jr. said in his wonderful letter from the Birmingham Jail (May 1963): "We must meet hate with creative love....Let us hope there will be no more violence. But if the streets must flow with blood, let it flow with our blood in the spirit of Jesus Christ on the cross" Obviously, he was dealing with much more difficult circumstances than we are today.

Love is the key to overcoming hate. Christians are commanded to love even our enemies. How can we creatively love those who resort to violence against us, while still taking common sense measures to protect the innocent, just as the security guard did?

When a deranged killer murdered several Amish children a few years ago, the Amish community showed amazing love by reaching out to the widow and family of the killer. If you get a chance, watch the made-for-TV movie, based on this incident, *Amish Grace*. It's very touching.

Rev. Rob Schenck of Faith and Action in Washington, DC, actually saw firsthand some of the love the Amish poured out to the shooter's family. He once told me, "the Amish emissaries, the elders of the Amish community, arrived at that home, while I was there, to offer their forgiveness in Christ to that family...And that extension of Christian love and forgiveness was so powerful."

Look at the example of Norma McCorvey, the "Roe" of *Roe v. Wade*, the infamous Supreme Court decision of 1973 that legalized abortion on demand. When her identity was revealed in the late 1980s, she became a hated woman in some circles.

But Roe now agrees with Wade, in her opposition to abortion. How so? She was "won by love" through the active transforming power of love on the part of some pro-life demonstrators. She even wrote a book, chronicling her story, with that very title, *Won By Love*.

We live in a time where, ironically, normal God-fearing people who are just trying to rear their families in peace, are often accused of being "haters." I wrote about this recently---that we are "living in Orwellian times," when right is called wrong and vice versa.

In modern America, we're generally so removed from violent persecution it's hard to picture it. Yet Cardinal Francis George of Chicago said in 2010, "I expect to die in bed, my successor will die in prison and his successor will die a martyr in the public square."

History tells us that all the apostles except John died a martyr's death. They didn't seek it, but they didn't shrink back, when the time came. They chose the next life by holding on to their integrity, rather than choosing this life by denying the Lord.

Through love, Jesus defeated the Roman Empire, which pulled out all the stops to defeat His movement. In the end, Rome became, at least outwardly, Christian.

It turns out that the way to overcome hate is with the love of Jesus Christ.

A New Low in the War on Christmas

12/16/14

The depths of anti-Christian depravity found among some of the intelligentsia in our post-Christian culture has reached a new low. As if that were possible.

Just in time for Christmas, a season of joy and giving spawned by the birth of Christ, one can now buy a gold necklace fashioned by a fancy designer, celebrating male genitalia, in the form of a cross.

Can you imagine a gold crescent mocking Islam in some sort of perverted way or the same for a star of David? Neither can I. But those in our culture's elite who are ever sensitive to not offend in any politically incorrect way seem to have no compunctions at mocking Jesus.

But it's always Jesus and only Jesus. Why is that? Do they all know deep down that it is to Him that shall all give an account for our lives one day?

I have traveled in many parts of the world---including India, Pakistan, Africa, and Europe. I find that besides the names "God" and "Lord," the main name used in profanity is "Jesus" or "Christ." You don't hear people say, "Oh Buddha!"

But you do hear people take the name of Jesus in vain. You don't hear people swear, "Oh Allah!" or "Oh Mohammed!" But you do hear the name of Christ as blasphemy. Could this be a backhanded commentary on His deity? I have heard fallen-away Hindus in Allahabad, India say, "Jesus Christ" in profanity. Not so the name of Brahma or Vishnu or Krishna.

There's something awfully powerful about the name of Jesus. And His cross.

Mockery of Christ Himself is not new. When working on a TV special on the cross of Jesus for what is now called D. James Kennedy Ministries, I remember being struck by the notion that historically it is possible that the earliest image we have of Jesus is one of a mocking nature.

Dr. Michael Haykin, professor at Southern Theological Seminary of Louisville, noted in that special, "There is an example of graffiti found in what was once the stable of the imperial pageboys in the palace in Rome, in which it's late 2nd century, in which you have a stick figure on a cross with a donkey's head, and under it scratched the words, 'Alexamenos worships his God.'"

The reality is that the cross was a symbol of shame. I once spoke with Dr. Edwin Yamauchi, retired professor of Miami University (in

Ohio), who specialized in ancient history. He contrasted the Christian movement with those of other would-be-messiahs that died out after their leaders were killed.

Said Dr. Yamauchi: "Christians, on the other hand, in spite of the fact that they were persecuted, continued to flourish and expand, and eventually conquer the Roman Empire. Now, the fact that their leader was someone who was crucified was a great stumbling block, as even Paul recognized in I Corinthians 1."

Yamauchi added, "...many Christians were embarrassed by this fact [that Jesus was crucified], because in art we don't have Jesus represented on the cross until the Byzantine Period. Now, how can you explain the expansion of this religion that exalted a Man who suffered the ignominious death, the worst possible death reserved for criminals and slaves, crucifixion, how can you explain the growth and expansion of this religion without the resurrection? You cannot. Now, some scholars have tried to do that, but they do not offer any convincing explanation."

This is not a mere battle over symbols. The cross and resurrection of Jesus is the difference between life and death.

In this last half year, I have just personally experienced three deaths of close relatives. That they were all in Christ gives me hope that I will see them again.

The "fashionable world" may mock Christ all they want. But they should recognize one thing---there is a day when His grace will no longer be extended. And then comes the judgment.

There's a popular Christian song, "In Christ Alone" (words and Music by Keith Getty & Stuart Townend) that says: "In Christ alone, Who took on flesh, / Fullness of God in helpless babe! / This gift of love and righteousness, / Scorned by the ones He came to save. / Till on that cross as Jesus died, / The wrath of God was satisfied..."

"Scorned by the ones He came to save." That's what the war on Christmas boils down to.

As Franklin Graham noted, "Unfortunately, the United States in the last few decades has witnessed increased hostility toward the sacred nature of Christmas, erupting into what has become a blatant war on Christmas. That's because at its root and core the war on Christmas isn't really about Christmas---it's about the Son of God. The war on Christmas is a war on Christ and His followers. It's the hatred of our culture for the exclusive claims that Christ made."

Dr. Gary Cass of defendchristians.org says of our anti-Christian culture today: "Like a spoiled child who reaches up to slap his own mother, so rebellious man who exists and is sustained only by God's common grace, arrogantly defies God and His Christ.

"The Advent of Controversy"

12/2/14

Another Christmas season begins. Get ready to read the headlines of the new lawsuits by the "civil libertarians" ready to throw the baby-in-the-manger out with the bathwater. I remember years ago when somebody called the Christmas season, "The Advent of Controversy."

Why is Christmas such a big deal? Let's put it this way---why do groups like the ACLU, the Freedom From Religion Foundation, Americans United for Separation of Church and State invest time, money, and energy to fight any vestige of religious meaning to the holiday?

I remember what Christian commentator Janice Crouse, formerly with Concerned Women for America, told our listeners when I interviewed her for a TV special hosted by the late Dr. D. James Kennedy. The special was "What If Jesus Had Never Been Born?," based on our book.

Crouse said, "When you see the atheist attack manger scenes, you might think, 'This is an innocuous kind of thing. What do they have against a manger scene for crying out loud?' It gives you some idea of how powerful Jesus Christ is. If He were not powerful, what would they care?"

For the last generation or so, there has been a fascination with UFOs and with speculations of life out there on some other planet. But what if ours is what J. B. Phillips once called "the visited planet"? That is, what if at one time God Himself visited our planet---beginning as a baby?

That's precisely what the controversy over Christmas is all about. We believe, as Paul said to the Galatians, in the fullness of time, God sent His one and only Son. He came to die for our offenses against a holy God. He died so we don't have to. Those who knowingly reject Him will be punished for their own sins. Their pride blinds them to their need for the Savior who came.

This baby in the manger was fully God and yet fully human. As the Nicene Creed (325 AD) declares about Jesus: that He is "God from God, Light from Light, True God from True God, Begotten not made, One in being with the Father..."

For a father to be a father, he has to have a child. Christians believe God the Father---the eternal Father---has always been the Father of Jesus Christ---the eternal Son. And the Spirit is divine.

If Christ were not divine, how could He be our Savior? But how so also if He were not human?

Jesus is God? A few years ago, millions of Americans read the novel by Dan Brown, *The DaVinci Code*. The novel made some rather novel claims about who Jesus was. That book tries to make the claim that Christ's divinity was not held by the early church until decreed by the Council of Nicea because of the Roman emperor Constantine---and at that, it was a close vote.

Here are some quotes from the book: "'My dear,' Teabing declared, 'until that moment in history, Jesus was viewed by his followers as a mortal prophet...a great and powerful man, but a man nonetheless. A mortal.'"

The character goes on to say: "Jesus's establishment as 'the Son of God' was officially proposed and voted on by the Council of Nicaea....A relatively close vote at that."

And he adds: "Nonetheless, establishing Christ's divinity was critical to the further unification of the Roman empire and to the new Vatican power base. By officially endorsing Jesus as the Son of God, Constantine turned Jesus into a deity who existed beyond the scope of the human world, an entity whose power was unchallengeable."

There are so many historical errors here that it's amazing. Let me adjust one or two. First of all, that vote wasn't close at all. The vote was 318 to 2. Secondly, Christians were worshiping Jesus as God from the very beginning. The New Testament, completed before 100 AD, is full of instances that reveal the divinity of Christ.

One of them comes from the opening of John's Gospel, which declares, "In the beginning was the Word, and the Word was with God, and the Word was God." It says He was the Co-Creator.

From secular history, we can also see Jesus was worshiped as divine. Here's just one example. As noted, Pliny the Younger, a Roman administrator in an area in what is now Turkey, wrote to the Emperor Trajan around the year 115 and explained how he had gotten some information about the Christians by torturing a couple of deaconesses.

Pliny found out that the Christians worshiped on the first day of the week (Sunday), that they made a commitment to obey the Ten Commandments, and that they sang hymns and worshiped Christ as God. So it's totally inaccurate to say this was just created by the Nicene Council.

The third point is in reference to Constantine. He gets a bad rap these days---even from Christians. Let me just say that when he became a Christian, it was a God-send to the Christian Church. After centuries of persecution, he gave the Christians freedom. It was a later emperor (Theodosius) who declared the empire "Christian," while it still contained many pagans.

If Jesus were divine, is it hard to believe He could turn water into wine, walk on water, and rise from the dead? We're still talking about these things 2000 years later.

Former skeptic and Oxford/Cambridge professor C. S. Lewis said: "The central miracle asserted by Christians is the Incarnation. They say that God became Man. Every other miracle prepares for this, or exhibits this, or results from this....In the Christian story God descends to re-ascend. He comes down; down from the heights of absolute being into TIME and space, down into humanity...down to the very roots and sea-bed of the Nature He has created."

So why the opposition to Jesus, at Christmastime or otherwise? Jesus summed it up in one sentence: "Light has come into the world, but men prefer darkness because their deeds are evil."

Is Christianity Really to Blame for Much of What is Wrong in our World?

5/10/16

Last month in Philadelphia, there was the 17th annual "White Privilege Conference," which a friend describes as a "liberal confab devoted to self-abnegation."

According to Derek Welch's post at worldreligionnews.com (4/23/16), one of the speakers, Paul Kivel, seemed to blame Christianity as the root of some crises we face in our world today. Kivel is the co-founder of the Oakland Men's Project and founder of "the Challenging Christian Hegemony Project."

Is Christianity really to blame for many of the world's crises? Consider some of the under-appreciated blessings of the Christian church.

Was Kivel born in a hospital or treated in one? Kivel can thank Jesus Christ who inspired His followers to create such an institution. St. Basil of Caesarea who lived in the 4th century is credited with creating the first hospital in the history of the world.

Even to this day, many hospitals bear Christian names, as they were founded to show forth Christian love. I was born in St. Francis Hospital---as in St. Francis of Assisi.

Speaking of St. Francis, he is the name sake of the city across the bridge from Oakland, San Francisco. Father Junipero Sero of the 18th century created a network of 21 Catholic missions---essentially a one-day horseback ride away from each other---from San Diego to Sonoma, essentially establishing California's cities.

Did Kivel go to school? Education for the elite has always existed. Education for the masses was a gift of Christianity to the world. This is especially true after the Reformation. The Reformers knew for their message to stick, people would have to read the Bible for themselves.

The first law for education in America was the "Old Deluder Satan Act" in Boston of 1642. The goal was to teach boys and girls how to read for themselves so that they could read the Bible---thus, thwarting the attempts of that "old deluder Satan," who works hard to keep people from reading God's Word. He is quite effective in our times, but not primarily through illiteracy.

Did Kivel go to college? Again, he can thank the Christian church for that. Scholars say the university was created by the church during the Middle Ages around 1200, with the University of Paris being the prototype. One of the main goals was to reconcile Christian theology with the newly rediscovered teachings of Aristotle.

Most of the greatest universities the world over were founded by Christians for Christian purposes...Oxford, Cambridge, Harvard, Yale, Dartmouth, Princeton, and so on.

Kivel blames Christianity for the wars in the Middle East. It's all the missionaries' fault. Huh? I don't suppose Islam has anything to do with the wars in the Middle East. Enough said.

Did Kivel use a microphone to blast the Christian church? Did he have a lightbulb by which he could see his speech? Christianity played a major role in the development of modern science, which led to all these things.

While the ancient Greeks helped pave the way, modern science was born in the late Middle Ages by Christian experimenters who were, in the words of Johannes Kepler, "thinking God's thoughts after Him." They believed a rational God had created a rational universe, and it was their role, said Kepler, as "priests of the most high God" to discover those laws.

As D. James Kennedy and I point out in our book, *What If Jesus Had Never Been Born?*, the founders of all the major branches of science were professed believers in Jesus.

Another irony about this story can be seen in one of the headlines about this story: "KIVEL SAYS CHRISTIAN LEADERSHIP IS THE REASON FOR THE WORLD'S PROBLEMS."

Presumably, a conference dumping on "white privilege" might pay homage to Dr. Martin Luther King, Jr., the greatest of the civil rights champions.

King was the president of the "Southern *Christian* Leadership Conference." The church was the key launching pad for the whole civil rights movement. King was a Baptist minister.

The classic "I have a dream" speech by King was essentially a sermon by a Baptist minister, in which he quotes Isaiah. "I have a dream that one day every valley shall be exalted, every hill and mountain shall be made low." In short, the humble shall be exalted; the proud shall be humbled.

Who is out there feeding many of the down and out of our society? The Christian church through one agency or another. They are showing the love of Jesus in action.

One thing Kivel did say is correct: Christianity does not teach that the earth is to be worshiped. To the contrary, the Creator of the earth is alone to be worshiped. But humans are stewards of the earth---not to abuse it but to subdue the earth.

Kivel apparently wants a world without Christian influence. Humanity has done that before. It was called the Soviet Union. It was called Pol Pot's Cambodia. They brought hell on earth. To paraphrase C.S. Lewis, if Jesus had never come, it would be "always winter, but never Christmas."

The Blessings of "Christian Hegemony"

5/11/16

Recently, I wrote an article about a presentation at the White Privilege Conference in Philadelphia last month. In response to that piece, I was accused of setting up a straw man and then attacking same.

The speaker in question, Paul Kivel, is the founder of "the Challenging Christian Hegemony Project."

While Kivel in his talk apparently issued a wide-ranging indictment of Christianity's influence, perhaps it was an overstatement to say that he "blamed Christianity for everything bad in the world"—although he indeed blames institutional Christianity for much of it.

I certainly fault myself for not putting down the sources for my article, as I usually do. You can see them and judge for yourself here and here.

Subsequently, after the criticism, I found a video of Kivel himself, where he says that Christian hegemony *is* the ultimate source of three major problems in the world today. I'll address those in a moment.

First, what is "hegemony"? Webster's calls it "the influence of one state over others." After He rose from the dead, Jesus told His disciples that all authority in heaven and *on earth* has been given to Him. Therefore, He commanded them to go and make disciples of all nations.

In this sense, the idea of "Christian hegemony" gets back to Jesus Himself. After all, Christianity *is* Christ.

Kivel says there are three major crises in the world today, all of which can be traced back to Christianity.

> 1) The threat to world peace. Kivel says, "The first is militarism and war---the unending war on axes of evil and terrorists that is justified by concepts of Manifest Destiny and American exceptionalism." Later, he also blames Christianity for Islamophobia.

Well, it is certainly true that in times past, professing Christians picked up the sword for the advance of the faith. But that "Medieval mistake" did not comport with the way of the Master. Jesus said, "He who lives by the sword will die by the sword." He even told His followers we are to love our enemies and pray for them.

Meanwhile, Western nations, through Judeo-Christian influence, have indeed opposed "axes of evil"---all the "-isms" that arise to deprive others of life and liberty. Such as Nazism, Communism, and today, Islamism. We only oppose those Muslims who want to impose their Islam on us---"convert or die." If that's "Islamophobia," count us in.

> 2) The weak economy is due to Christianity, says Kivel. He blames Christianity for stressing a free market economy, "rewarding the greedy and punishing those who have little."

Implied is a criticism of capitalism. The world can *thank* Christianity for capitalism. Baylor professor Rodney Stark wrote *The Victory of Reason*, tracing this connection. Capitalism has helped lift hundreds of millions of people out of poverty.

But capitalism is not always fair, and the Christian church does a great deal of work to help the down-and-out the world over. As to greed, it is one of the 7 Deadly Sins that Christians oppose.

> 3) "The basic Christian concept is that humans are given dominion over the earth. We can't solve our environmental problem without understanding we are interdependent with all life. And that we have to live in balance and in harmony with the plants and animals and the earth itself," according to Kivel.

Yes, the Bible does say that God has given humankind the role of steward of the earth, and it also says, "Woe to those who destroy the earth." Use is one thing; abuse is another.

Meanwhile, the theory of man-made global warming is a myth. For example, the worldwide average temperature has not risen in the last 18 years. So the theorists changed the name to "climate change." Well, to borrow a line from Marco Rubio, there's always climate change---it's called "the weather."

Because Jesus bodily rose from the dead, He has proven His divinity. Every breath we take is courtesy of Jesus Christ, who is seated at the right hand of God. And one day, He'll call it quits for us and then comes the accountability before Him.

One day every knee will bow and every tongue will confess that Jesus is Lord to the glory of God the Father. And today that message is spread through peaceful proclamation of the gospel.

If opposition to "Christian hegemony" refers to opposing every abuse in the name of Christ, then it is the Christian thing to likewise oppose such abuse. But if by "Christian hegemony," one refers to opposition to the ultimate reign of Christ, then such opposition is destined to fail. The day will come, as the Hallelujah Chorus reminds us, when "the kingdoms of this world have become the kingdoms of our Lord and of His Christ. And He shall reign forever and ever."

The War on the Cross

4/20/16

There is a war being waged against a major symbol of Christianity---the cross.

In 1925, a large cross was erected in Bladensburg, Maryland to honor fallen soldiers of World War I. But now that cross is being challenged by a lawsuit from the American Humanist Association. They lost their 2014 lawsuit against it, but they are appealing the case.

Last week, there was a bipartisan effort among members of Congress to save the Bladensburg cross. They filed a friend of the court brief to support this memorial.

First Liberty Institute is instrumental in the fight to save the cross from being demolished. They have been leading the charge in fighting these kinds of cases.

Their founder and president is Kelly Shackelford, who said, "In a time when America is divided over many issues, there is one thing members of the House and Senate, both Democratic and Republican, have agreed on, along with 90% of the American public---our veterans memorials should be protected. We must always strive to honor the selfless sacrifice of our fallen heroes."

Jeremy Dys is an attorney with First Liberty, and I spoke with him about the case on my radio show recently.

Jeremy told me, "There seems to be a general allergy to religion any time any religious symbol appears in public." He noted this applies to Christian symbols in particular and stars of David.

Dys said, "What we're attempting to do in all these cases is to allow these veterans who erect these monuments to honor their comrades who have fallen in arms."

He noted, "In the case of the Bladensburg Veterans Memorial outside of Washington, DC, that was actually even erected by the mothers of these fallen soldiers from World War I."

Dys added, "When you have these moms who scraped together dimes and nickels in order to be able to erect this memorial, and you still have children and grandchildren and probably great-grandchildren now that gather around that memorial on Armistice Day, it's remarkable that someone would have the gall to try to knock down what one mother called 'the tombstone of her son that she could actually visit,' instead of the one that's listed in Flanders Field."

The American Humanist Association sued to have this cross removed because they believe it violates the separation of church and state, because the cross supposedly establishes religion.

The Constitution does not mention the "separation of church and state." Instead, the First Amendment begins, "Congress shall make no law respecting an establishment of religion or prohibiting the free exercise thereof…"

Historically, it was understood in America that "establishing religion" was the creation of a national church, such as the Church of England, which was "by law established." When we became a free country, this was no longer to be the case---that we would have a state church at the national level "by law established."

At the time of the adoption of the Constitution and the First Amendment, even some of the individual states had state churches. That was not ideal, and they withered away of their own volition.

But to say that having a memorial cross to honor the fallen "establishes religion" distorts the founders' words.

These groups that sue against crosses in the public square attempt to jettison America from our true history.

It was the founders of this nation that systematically hired chaplains for the military and legislatures. For the first two hundred years or so of our national existence, most of their prayers were Christian ones.

The founders declared national days of thanksgiving to God. Jefferson did that on the state level, but refused to do that on the national level because he thought it was the province of the states.

Our nation's first Commander-in-Chief was, of course, George Washington. I've visited his tomb at Mount Vernon and written in stone above his sarcophagus are the words of Jesus Christ from John 11---promising that those who believe in Him will live, even after they die. Do those words need to be sandblasted away?

Of course, ultimately the cross is controversial because it points to Jesus' voluntary sacrifice to forgive sinners who believe.

Meanwhile, if we don't defend the memorial crosses now, we could go the way of China where it is reported that the Communist government is now undertaking a systematic removal of *thousands* of crosses in that country, including those atop churches.

This war on the cross by anti-Christian legal groups reminds me of the movie portrayal of Count Dracula who flinches and becomes powerless at even the sight of a cross. I pray they will not succeed in their efforts to tear down these memorial crosses to honor the fallen.

Part 6.

Christmas, the Most Wonderful Time of the Year

This Christmas, Defy the Atheists---Worship the Truth
12/10/14

In years past, atheists have put up billboards in places like New York City to discourage people from attending church at Christmas time (or any time, for that matter). Now they're bringing their campaign to the Bible belt.

A report from their own source (news.atheists.org, 12/1, 2014 years after the reported birth of Jesus) notes: "The billboards feature a young girl writing a letter to Santa; her letter reads, 'Dear Santa, All I want for Christmas is to skip church! I'm too old for fairy tales.' The billboards are located in Memphis; Nashville, St. Louis; and Ft. Smith, Arkansas."

Of course, the premise of this whole campaign is that Christianity is supposedly a "fairy tale." But, in fact, Jesus is "the Truth." Here I'll focus only on prophecies fulfilled by Jesus. Only God knows the future. Only God could have written the Bible.

I teach an adult Sunday school class of about 60 or so in a Presbyterian church in South Florida. Months before the beginning of the new year (2014), I asked my class to take a moment and write down one prediction for the new year. I also wrote down my own "prophecy."

These were not to be fortune cookie type statements, such as "You will soon meet somebody interesting." Instead, these were to be some sort of prediction of the future. In our class, how many of us made a correct prediction? There was none---no, not one. (You try it sometime.)

Yet in the Scriptures, we can see some 350 prophecies foretelling the coming of Jesus---including His ancestors, His place of birth, His ministry, His death, and His resurrection.

One could argue that He fulfilled some of His prophecies on His own. (This is the essence of the skeptical book, *The Passover Plot*). But try choosing your own parents. As to His horrible death, David wrote 1000 BC, "they have pierced my hands and my feet." That was a few hundred years before the Syro-Phonecians invented crucifixion. The Romans later perfected it.

Christ is not the last name of Jesus, but His title. It comes from the Greek word, "Christos," from the Hebrew word, "Meshiach," (Messiah). The English translation is: "Anointed One."

Jesus is the Anointed One described in Psalm 2, where it says that the kings of this world declare war against the Lord and against His Anointed One. (Even the war on Christmas was foretold.)

The Old Testament was written between c.1400-c.400 BC, and it gives us a picture of Jesus from the Hebrew prophets.

Consider just a few facts---of Christ in the Old Testament:

* "...in you [Abraham] all the families of the earth shall be blessed" (Genesis 12:3, c. 1400 BC). "The scepter will not depart from Judah, nor the ruler's staff from between his feet, until he comes to whom it belongs" (Genesis 49:10, c. 1400 BC). The Messiah will come from the line of Abraham, Isaac, Jacob, and Judah.

* "I [i.e., God] will raise up your offspring after you [David], who shall come from your body, and I will establish his kingdom. He shall build a house for my name, and I will establish the throne of his kingdom forever" (2 Samuel 7:12-13, c.1000 BC).

* "The LORD said to me, "You are my Son; today I have begotten you" (Psalm 2:7, c. 1000 BC).

* "Behold, the virgin shall conceive and bear a son, and shall call his name Immanuel [God with us]" (Isaiah 7:14, c. 750 BC).

* "But you, O Bethlehem Ephrathah, who are too little to be among the clans of Judah, from you shall come forth for me one who is to be ruler in Israel, whose origin is from of old, from ancient days" (Micah 5:2, c. 720 BC).

* "For to us a child is born, to us a son is given; and the government shall be upon his shoulder, and his name shall be called Wonderful Counselor, Mighty God, Everlasting Father, Prince of Peace" (Isaiah 9:6, c. 750 BC).

* He will have a forerunner (John the Baptist): "A voice cries: 'In the wilderness prepare the way of the LORD; make straight in the desert a highway for our God'" (Isaiah 40:3-4, c. 750 BC).

* "Behold, your God...will come and save you. Then the eyes of the blind shall be opened, and the ears of the deaf unstopped; then shall the lame man leap like a deer, and the tongue of the mute sing for joy" (Isaiah 35:4-6, c. 750 BC).

* "My God, my God, why have you forsaken me?.... All who see me mock me...they wag their heads; 'He trusts in the LORD; let him deliver him; let him rescue him, for he delights in him!' my strength is dried up like a potsherd, and my tongue sticks to my jaws; you lay

me in the dust of death. For dogs encompass me; a company of evildoers encircles me; they have pierced my hands and feet---I can count all my bones--they stare and gloat over me; they divide my garments among them, and for my clothing they cast lots" (Psalm 22:1, 7-8, 15-18, c. 1000 BC).

Two chapters of the Old Testament are worth mentioning. Psalm 22 (written 1000 BC) has more facts about the crucifixion of Jesus than any one single Gospel. (Of course, if you combine the facts of the crucifixion found in the four Gospels, that exceeds the number of facts of Psalm 22.) Isaiah 53 (c. 750 BC) clearly talks about the crucifixion (for our sins) and resurrection of Jesus.

So, this Christmas, defy the atheist---by going to church to celebrate the Truth. Better yet, invite the atheist, so he too might learn of Him whose coming was foretold long before His birth.

Prophecies Jesus Fulfilled in His First Coming

12/6/14

The following passage is based on the book: D. James Kennedy, Ph.D. and Jerry Newcombe, D.Min., *The Real Messiah: Prophecies Fulfilled* (Boca Raton: D. James Kennedy Foundation, 2008). All verses are in ESV (English Standard Version, unless otherwise noted).

Truths about the Messiah from the Old Testament (c. 1400-c.400 BC). Note: even skeptical scholars acknowledge the Septuagint translation from Hebrew into Greek—dated c. 270-c.160 BC): He will come from the lineage of Abraham, Isaac, Jacob, and Judah.[i] He will come from the house of Jesse, from the house of David. Through this son of David, God will build an everlasting kingdom.[ii] A virgin shall conceive and bear a son, who will be God with us.[iii] This son of David, who will be begotten (begotten, not made),[iv] will be born in Bethlehem.[v] He will be called Wonderful Counselor, Mighty God, Everlasting Father, Prince of Peace.[vi] He will have a forerunner who will prepare the way of the LORD.[vii] The Messiah will be the Prophet predicted by Moses. We are to listen to Him.[viii] His light will shine on the people in Galilee.[ix] God will give the One, whom He calls "the Son of Man," authority over the nations. People from every tongue and tribe will worship Him, whose kingdom will last forever.[x] He will give sight to the blind and will heal the lame.[xi] He will teach in parables.[xii] But He will be rejected by men; He will be a man of sorrows.[xiii] He will come to Jerusalem with great fanfare, riding on a young donkey never ridden before.[xiv] He will come into the LORD's temple in judgment.[xv] He will be betrayed by a close friend[xvi] for 30 pieces of silver—money which will instead be used to buy a potters' field (a graveyard for poor people who can't afford graves).[xvii] By His stripes we are healed.[xviii] He will be forsaken by God, while His hands and feet are pierced, as a band of evildoers surrounds Him. They divide His garments among them and cast lots for His clothing.[xix] He will be the seed of the woman who crushes the Devil's head, even as the Devil strikes His foot.[xx] He dies for our sins[xxi] and commits His Spirit into God's hands.[xxii] Like the Passover Lamb, none of His bones will be broken.[xxiii] Then they will look at Him whom they have pierced, and they will mourn for Him as one mourns for an only child.[xxiv] By His death, many will be justified.[xxv] He dies among the violent, but is buried among the rich.[xxvi] He will rise from the dead.[xxvii] He is a priest in the line of Melchizedek, who gives us bread and wine.[xxviii] He is the stone that the builders rejected, but which has become the cornerstone.[xxix] God is making His enemies a footstool for His feet.[xxx] God will give to His Son the nations as His inheritance. We should revere the Son of God, lest He be angry and we die. All those who trust in Him will be blessed.[xxxi]

Have you ever had 10 people in a room try to order a couple pizzas, and no one seems to agree on the order? (Thanks to Jim Thomas for that illustration).

Yet, God, knowing the future, inspired the authors of the Old Testament to foretell the coming of His Son, who came in the fullness of time.

A mathematician, Peter Stoner, had his graduate students calculate what the odds would be of any one person fulfilling just eight of these prophecies. He found the chance was one in 10^{17}—one in 100,000,000,000,000,000.

Stoner gives an analogy to this. Suppose that we: "take 10^{17} silver dollars and lay them on the face of Texas. They will cover all of the state two feet deep. Now mark one of these silver dollars and stir the whole mass thoroughly, all over the state. Blindfold a man and tell him that he can travel as far as he wishes, but he must pick up one silver dollar and say that this is the right one. What chance would he have of getting the right one? Just the same chance that the prophets would have had of writing these eight prophecies and having them all come true in any one man, from their day to the present time."

If that isn't amazing enough, Stoner had his graduate stu-dents calculate the odds that any one person would fulfill 48 of these prophecies. The odds in that case were one in 10^{157}. And again, we're talking about 350 prophecies fulfilled in Jesus.

Canon Dyson Hague once put it this way: "Who could draw a picture of a man not yet born? Surely God, and God alone. Nobody knew over 500 years ago that Shakespeare was going to be born; or over 250 years ago that Napoleon was to be born. Yet here in the Bible we have the most striking and unmistakable likeness of a Man portrayed, not by one, but by twenty or twenty-five artists, none of whom had ever seen the Man they were painting."

See a list of prophecies fulfilled by Jesus in His first coming at: http://accordingtothescriptures.org/prophecy/353prophecies.html

[i] "...in you [Abraham] all the families of the earth shall be blessed" (Genesis 12:3, c. 1400 BC). "The scepter will not depart from Judah, nor the ruler's staff from between his feet, until he comes to who it belongs" (Genesis 49:10, NIV, c. 1400 BC).

[ii] "There shall come forth a shoot from the stump of Jesse, and a branch from his roots shall bear fruit. And the Spirit of the LORD shall rest upon him, the Spirit of wisdom and understanding'"" (Isaiah 11:1-2, 750 BC). "I will raise up your offspring after you [David], who shall come from your body, and I will establish his kingdom. He shall build a house for my name, and I will establish the throne of his kingdom forever" (2 Samuel 7:12-13, 1000 BC).

[iii] "Behold, the virgin shall conceive and bear a son, and shall call his name Immanuel [God with us]" (Isaiah 7:14, c. 750 BC).

[iv] "The LORD said to me, "You are my Son; today I have begotten you" (Psalm 2:7, c. 1000 BC).

[v] "But you, O Bethlehem Ephrathah, who are too little to be among the clans of Judah, from you shall come forth for me one who is to be ruler in Israel, whose origin is from of old, from ancient days" (Micah 5:2, c. 720 BC).

[vi] "For to us a child is born, to us a son is given; and the government shall be upon his shoulder, and his name shall be called Wonderful Counselor, Mighty God, Everlasting Father, Prince of Peace" (Isaiah 9:6, c. 750 BC).

[vii] "Behold, I send my messenger and he will prepare the way before me" (Malachi 3:1, c. 425 BC). "A voice cries: 'In the wilderness prepare the way of the LORD; make straight in the desert a highway for our God'" (Isaiah 40:3-4, c. 750 BC).

[viii] "The LORD your God will raise up for you a prophet like me [Moses] from among you, from your brothers–it is to him you shall listen" (Deuteronomy 18:15, c. 1400 BC).

[ix] "The people [of Galilee of the nations] who walked in darkness have seen a great light; those who dwelt in a land of deep darkness, on them has light shined" (Isaiah 9:2, c. 750 BC).

[x] "In my vision at night I looked, and there before me was one like a son of man, coming with the clouds of heaven. He approached the Ancient of Days and was led into his presence. He was given authority, glory and sovereign power; all peoples, nations and men of every language worshiped him. His dominion is an everlasting dominion that will not pass away, and his kingdom is one that will never be destroyed" (Daniel 7:13-14, c. 550 BC, NIV).

[xi] "Behold, your God...will come and save you. Then the eyes of the blind shall be opened, and the ears of the deaf unstopped; then shall the lame man leap like a deer, and the tongue of the mute sing for joy" (Isaiah 35:4-6, c. 750 BC).

[xii] "I will open my mouth in a parable; I will utter dark sayings from of old, things that we have heard and known, that our fathers have told us" (Psalm 78:3-4, c. 1000 BC).

[xiii] "Who has believed what they heard from us? And to whom has the arm of the LORD been revealed? For he grew up before him like a young plant, and like a root out of dry ground; he had no form or majesty that we should look at him, and no beauty that we should desire him. He was despised and rejected by men; a man of sorrows, and acquainted with grief; and as one from whom men hide their faces he was despised, and we esteemed him not" (Isaiah 53:1-3, c. 750 BC).

[xiv] "Rejoice greatly, O daughter of Zion! Should aloud, O daughter of Jerusalem! Behold your king is coming to you; righteous and having salvation is he, humble and mounted on a donkey, on a colt, the foal of a donkey" (Zechariah 9:9, c. BC, 500 BC).

[xv] "And the Lord whom you seek will suddenly come to his temple; and the messenger of the covenant in whom you delight, behold, he is coming, says the LORD of hosts. But who can endure

the day of his coming, and who can stand when he appears? For he is like a refiner's fire" (Malachi 3:1-2. c. 425 BC).

[xvi] "Even my close friend in whom I trusted, who ate my bread, has lifted his heel against me" (Psalm 41:9, c. 1000 BC).

[xvii] "And they weighed out as my wages thirty pieces of silver. Then the LORD said to me, 'Throw it to the potter—the lordly price at which I was priced by them. so I took the thirty pieces of silver and threw them into the house of the LORD, to the potter" (Zechariah 11:12-12, c. 500 BC).

[xviii] "Surely he has borne our griefs and carried our sorrows; yet we esteemed him stricken, smitten by God, and afflicted. But he was wounded for our transgressions; he was crushed for our iniquities; upon him was the chastisement that brought us peace, and with his stripes we are healed" (Isaiah 53:4-5, c. 750 BC).

[xix] "My God, my God, why have you forsaken me?.... All who see me mock me...they wag their heads; 'He trusts in the LORD; let him deliver him; let him rescue him, for he delights in him!' my strength is dried up like a potsherd, and my tongue sticks to my jaws; you lay me in the dust of death. For dogs encompass me; a company of evildoers encircles me; they have pierced my hands and feet—I can count all my bones–they stare and gloat over me; they divide my garments among them, and for my clothing they cast lots" (Psalm 22:1, 7-8, 15-18, c. 1000 BC).

[xx] "And I will put enmity between you and the woman, and between your offspring and hers; he will crush your head, and you will strike his heel." (Gen. 3:15, NIV, c. 1400 c. 4000 BC).

[xxi] "All we like sheep have gone astray; we have turned every one to his own way; and the LORD has laid on him the iniquity of us all. He was oppressed, and he was afflicted, yet he opened not his mouth; like a lamb that is led to the slaughter, and like a sheep that before its shearers is silent, so he opened not his mouth....Yet it was the will of the LORD to crush him;" (Isaiah 53:6-7, 10, c. 750 BC).

[xxii] "Into your hand I commit my spirit" (Psalm 31:5, c. 1000 BC).

[xxiii] "...you shall not break any of its [the Passover Lamb's] bones." (Exodus 12:46, c. 1400 BC).

[xxiv] "...when they look on me, on him whom they have pierced, they shall mourn for him, as one mourns for an only child" (Zecharaiah 12:10, c. 500 BC).

[xxv] "Out of the anguish of his soul he shall see and be satisfied; by his knowledge shall the righteous one, my servant, make many to be accounted righteous, and he shall bear their iniquities. Therefore I will divide him a portion with the many, and he shall divide the spoil with the strong, because he poured out his soul to death and was numbered with the transgressors; yet he bore the sin of many, and makes intercession for the transgressors" (Isaiah 53:10, 11-12, c. 750 BC).

[xxvi] "And they made his grave with the wicked and with a rich man in his death, although he had done no violence, and there was no deceit in his mouth" (Isaiah 53:9, c. 750 BC).

[xxvii] "For you will not abandon my soul to Sheol, or let your holy one see corruption" (Psalm 16:10, c. 1000 BC).

[xxviii] "The LORD has sworn and will not change his mind, 'You are a priest forever after the order of Melchizedek'" (Psalm 110:4, c. 1000 BC). "And Melchizedek king of Salem brought out bread and wine. (He was priest of God Most High.) Genesis 14:18, c. 1400 BC).

[xxix] "The stone that the builders rejected has become the cornerstone. This is the LORD's doing; it is marvelous in our eyes" (Psalm 118:22-23, c. 1000 BC).

[xxx] "The LORD says to my Lord: 'Sit at my right hand, until I make your enemies your footstool'" (Psalm 110:1, c. 1000 BC).

[xxxi] "Ask of me, and I will make the nations your heritage, and the ends of the earth your possession. You shall break them with a rod of iron and dash them in pieces like a potter's vessel. Now therefore, O kings, be wise; be warned, O rulers of the earth. Serve the LORD with fear, and rejoice with trembling. Kiss the Son, lest he be angry, and you perish in the way, for his wrath is quickly kindled. Blessed are all who take refuge in him" (Psalm 2:8-12, c. 1000 BC).

'Tis the Season to Attack the Gospels?

12/4/13

Every year at Christmastime, like clockwork, you can expect the mainstream media to come out with some sort of "fresh" perspective on Jesus. We see this on TV specials and in magazines and reports. Since December has just begun, I thought I'd be pro-active in answering the critics.

The basic questions are these: Can we trust the Bible? Can we trust the Gospels? If they were put on trial, as in a court case, how would they hold up?

One man who contributed significantly to Christian apologetics was one of America's great legal leaders. Simon Greenleaf (1783-1853) was a professor at Harvard Law School (1833-1848). He contributed a great deal to the school, expanding it, including its library.

Greenleaf wrote a major textbook used widely, *A Treatise on the Law of Evidence*.

Contrary to some accounts (even found extensively on the Internet, to this day), Greenleaf was not an atheist or agnostic converted to Christianity by the evidence for the resurrection. He was livelong, active member of the Episcopal Church. In 1847, Greenleaf applied his expertise as a pioneer in the area of trial evidence to the Gospels in a landmark book.

Greenleaf wrote *The Testimony of the Evangelists: The Gospel Examined by the Rules of Evidence*. The evangelists, of course, are Matthew, Mark, Luke, and John. As he applied the rules of evidence to the Gospels, he found them reliable.

Greenleaf says, "The foundation of our religion is a basis of fact---the fact of the birth, ministry, miracles, death, resurrection by the Evangelists as having actually occurred, within their own personal knowledge. Our religion, then, rests on the credit due to these witnesses. Are they worthy of implicit belief, in the matters which they relate? This is the question, in all human tribunals, in regard to persons testifying before them; and we propose to test the veracity of these witnesses, by the same rules and means which are there employed..." He answers, Yes.

He goes on from there to highlight the four Gospel writers:

* Matthew (also called Levi), the tax-collector and one of the twelve, an eyewitness of the Gospel events. Writes Greenleaf: "Matthew was himself a native Jew, familiar with the opinions, ceremonies, and customs of his countrymen; that he was conversant with the Sacred Writings..."

* Mark (also known as John Mark) was essentially Peter's scribe in his Gospel---from the early Church comes the consistent report that Peter's recollection of the Gospel events are found in the second

Gospel. Mark went on to preach the gospel in Egypt, where he was martyred.

* Luke, believed to be a physician, traveled with Paul. Says Greenleaf, "If...Luke's Gospel were to be regarded only as the work of a contemporary historian, it would be entitled to our confidence. But it is more than this. It is the result of careful science, intelligence and education, concerning subjects which he was perfectly competent to peculiarly skilled, they being cases of the cure of maladies."

* John was a fisherman of Bethsaida, on the Sea of Galilee. Greenleaf says he wrote his Gospel after the other three, recognizing their truthfulness, and added things not found in the others.

Greenleaf notes a great unfairness shown the Evangelists in modern scholarship: They are somehow guilty until proven innocent. They are viewed as untrustworthy for no cause, until they can somehow be corroborated by some outside secular source. (If it was true in Greenleaf's day, how much more is it true in ours---despite the wealth we have of additional archaeological and manuscript evidence in favor of the Gospels' veracity.)

Says Greenleaf: "But the Christian writer seems, by the usual course of the argument, to have been deprived of the common presumption of charity in his favor; and reversing the ordinary rule of administering justice in human tribunals, his testimony is unjustly presumed to be false, until it is proved to be true."

Greenleaf adds, "It is time that this injustice should cease; that the testimony of the evangelists should be admitted to be true, until it can be disproved by those who would impugn it; that the silence of one sacred writer on any point, should no more detract from his own veracity or that of the other historians, than the like circumstance is permitted to do among profane writers; and that the Four Evangelists should be admitted in corroboration of each other, as readily as Josephus and Tacitus, or Polybius and Livy."

He affirms: "their honesty...ability... the consistency of their testimony...the conformity of their testimony with experience...the coincidence of their testimony with collateral circumstances. Let the evangelists be tried by these tests." He does and finds them trustworthy. He also answers common objections, such as the miraculous elements found in the Gospels.

149

So, be prepared, when you see the TV specials coming up about "the true story of Christmas" or the like, when they attack the Gospels. The Gospels have been put on trial, and they have passed the test. Don't take my word for it---take that of the legendary professor at Harvard Law School.

It's Time to Call it "Black-eye Friday"

11/26/12

Another Black Friday has come and gone in these United States. And I think it's time to rename one of the busiest shopping days of the year. How about "Black-eye Friday"?

Just look at the headlines, for example, as seen on the Drudge Report (11/24/12):

- 'Gang fight' at Black Friday sale...
- Man Punched in Face Pulls Gun On Line-Cutting Shopper...
- Shots fired outside WALMART...
- Shoppers smash through door at URBAN OUTFITTERS...
- Customers run over in parking lot...
- Woman busted after throwing merchandise...
- Thousands storm VICTORIA'S SECRET...
- VIDEO: Insane battle over phones...
- Mayhem at Nebraska mall where 9 murdered in 2007...
- Shoplifter tries to mace security guards...
- Men Steal Boy's Shopping Bag Outside BED, BATH & BEYOND...
- Heckler calls them zombies...
- Manhattan cop busted for shoplifting...
- Shopper Robbed At Gunpoint Outside BEST BUY...

Later there were reports of a "mall brawl" over a pair of shoes. Then there was the alleged shopper who died after being subdued by the employees of a popular retailer. And on it goes.

The irony of all this is that Christmas is theoretically all about the birth of Jesus. The first Christmas gift was the gift of God's Son. This is ultimately the only Christmas gift that counts.

This is the gift that keeps on giving. For example, the late Mother Teresa worked for decades helping the poorest of the poor in India. She said: "Today God has sent us into the world as he sent Jesus, to show God's love to the world. And we must sacrifice to show that love, just as Jesus made the greatest sacrifice of all."

The next Christmas gifts, and the tradition of getting Christmas gifts for others, gets back to the Wise Men (Magi, from which we get the word magic) from the East (Persia/Iraq), who came from afar to worship the Christ child, bearing Gold, Frankincense, and Myrrh.

And, in one sense, Christians have been giving gifts ever since. Even many others have joined in the festivities, without really understanding the essential message.

Even the mythical character of Santa Claus ultimately points back to the babe in the manger. Although he often regrettably upstages Christ at Christmastime, St. Nick unquestionably arose within the Christian tradition; and the legend is symbolic of the spirit of giving that marks the coming of Christ.

According to *The New International Dictionary of the Christian Church*, we know very little about the real St. Nicholas (from whose name we get Santa Claus). He lived in Myra in the fourth century and was reported to have given gifts to some children on his feast day, December 6. No Jesus, no Santa Claus.

One minister from Denver feels called to try and get more people in the church to practice greater generosity. Rev. Brian Kluth, who has three children, decided to put generosity into practice in his own family a few years ago.

As Christmas approached, and they bought plenty of gifts for themselves, he asked his children, "Whose birthday is it anyway?"

He said to them, "Well, who should get the biggest presents, and they said 'Jesus, but He's not here.' And I said, the Bible says, 'When we [give] to the least of these, we've done it unto Him.'"

So, in addition to Christmas gifts for his children, he gave each of them an envelope with $1,000 respectively, for them to give to whatever charity they desired. They gave some of the money to orphanages, and they also bought some things for a nearby family (with children), whose mother was dying of cancer.

It was their most meaningful Christmas, and it underscored what Jesus said, when He noted, "It is more blessed to give than to receive."

There's plenty of gifts to go around, and what a joy to participate in such a festive holiday by remembering the less fortunate as well.

In the hustle and bustle of getting our Christmas shopping done, I hope we don't forget what the holiday (the holy-day) is really about.

It sure seems like some of those participating in Black-eye Friday did.

Away With the Manger?

12/21/11

There's a controversy brewing in Broward County, Florida, where I live.

You may recall, this is the same county that caused our state to be called "Flori-duh" in the 2000 Gore vs. Bush election, when "dimpled chads" and "hanging chads" suddenly became household words.

The controversy now revolves around one father, Jorge Egues, a parent of four children who attend a local elementary school.

A few years ago, in December, he noticed how the school decorations had secular symbols of the holiday and even a Menorah, but no manger scene. He commended the principal for the Menorah, but she claimed to not realize it was a religious symbol.

He also offered to provide a manger scene for the school at his expense. She said, No, thank you. No religious symbols were to be allowed.

Jump ahead to November 2011, when Jorge had a discussion with his now-10-year old son.

Jorge says, "I was discussing the importance of education with him and stated that knowledge without the principles taught by God is incomplete in developing a person's character. His response was, 'Well Dad you can't talk about God in the Public Schools; that would be illegal.' I explained to him that the First Amendment of the Constitution supports our rights of religious expression."

Then he met with the principal in the same month, and she said that such a message as his son had picked up was not intended. He quotes her as saying, "Where would he get that idea? We don't say that here."

Jorge also pointed out that when Hispanics say Merry Christmas, they refer directly to the nativity---Happy Nativity (Feliz Navidad).

When he respectfully re-asked the principal about the possibility of a manger scene to fit with the other multi-cultural symbols of the holiday, she again declined and added that someone from the School Advisory Council would get back to him.

152

No one did. He later learned that their next meeting would be after Christmas anyway; so by then it would be a moot point, at least for this year.

So he contacted the Thomas More Law Center, a religious legal rights group, if they could help. So they wrote a very polite letter to the principal, which commended the display of the Menorah and added, "… the addition of a Nativity scene, which represents the historic basis for Christmas, a national holiday, would enhance this important cultural and historical education of the holiday season."

The school responded by removing *all* symbols of the winter season. Gone were the Menorah, the tiny Christmas tree, the snowflakes, whatever.

A week later, they re-allowed decorations, but no Menorah--- presumably because they assumed that the price of having a Menorah was also to have a nativity scene---a price to high. To me, this reminds me of the ABC principle. Anything but Christ.

In this kind of environment, it's easy to see how a ten year old could conclude that God is indeed illegal in the public schools.

Around this time, I had Jorge on my radio show to discuss all this and also invited the principal to get her side, but she "gracefully declined."

To Jorge Egues, who is of Cuban descent, this battle over the acknowledgement of God in the public realm is personal. Cubans have suffered the price of extreme anti-God measures.

Jorge's own parents left Cuba shortly before Castro and his forces turned the Caribbean island into a godless wasteland. But other family members stayed.

In forcing Communism on Cuba, Castro was of course forcing atheism on the population, even if that meant sometimes resorting to violence.

This doesn't mean I'm calling those who would squelch God in the public arena (certainly not in America) Communists. Thankfully, the war against God in America has never been violent.

But certainly the secular forces that banish God from any public institution are out of step with Supreme Court decisions, which allow for manger scenes in public if surrounded by other symbols of the holiday. They also allow for Christmas carols at a school celebration, if secular songs are included.

The anti-God in the public arena crusade is even more out of step with the founders of America and their stated intentions.

Our Declaration of Independence (our national birth certificate) says our rights come from God. George Washington said religion and morality are indispensable supports to our political prosperity.

The founders who gave us the first amendment (which is sometimes abused today to banish God from public places)---the very same men---also passed the Northwest Ordinance, which provides a template for new states that join the Union to follow.

In Article III of that key document, they said "Religion, morality, and knowledge, being necessary for good government and the happiness of mankind, schools and the means of education shall forever be encouraged."

The purpose of schools according to the founders? To teach religion (in a nation at the time that was more than 98% professing Christian), morality, and knowledge.

Besides all this, education for the masses was a Christian invention. Certainly that was true in America.

The first act for public education came from the Puritans in Boston in the 1640s. It was called the Old Deluder Satan Act. The act says because that "Old Deluder Satan" keeps people in darkness by keeping them from the Word of God, they need to be able to read the Bible for themselves. Therefore, they need to be able to read--- period. Therefore, schools shall be established.

Now, we're at a place where the Bible and its message, including the birth of Christ, are subject to censorship.

Maybe, it takes the son of immigrants from a godless country (which once was Christian) to wake us up from our apathy.

So, I'll pass on the Merry Unmentionable, and say, Merry Christmas to all.

'Tis the Season to Jettison Reason?

12/2/10

For the last couple decades, Senator Jim Inhofe has ridden a horse in the Tulsa Christmas parade, year after year. And he has loved it. With a twinkle in his eyes, he proudly says, "There are only two things I do well. Ride horses and fly planes." He was all set to ride in the parade last year for the nth time, when he found out that they had dropped "Christmas" from the name of the parade. Now it's just the "holiday" parade. He hadn't realized it until he showed up last year. So he said then (and he says now), "I'm not riding in this."

I had the privilege of interviewing Sen. Inhofe the other day for a religious television program on a variety of issues, when he happened to mention his recent decision to boycott the parade because of the name change---which is just one more example of what's been called the war on Christmas. Said the Senator, "Now they're making a big issue in Tulsa, Oklahoma that I'm refusing to ride, as I've done for decades in the Christmas parade because they took Jesus out of the Christmas parade. Well, if He goes, I go."

If more people were courageous like Sen. Inhofe, we'd probably not see the further secularization of the Christmas season. Perhaps, I should say "holiday season." An interesting irony of the anti-Christmas forces that use the word holiday is the origin of the word....holiday is a contraction of holy day---that's why there's only one l in holiday. Gee, I wonder what holy day that would be referring to?

Every year like clockwork, the Grinches come out of the woodwork in their war against Christmas.

For example, a group of atheists in New York City have paid for a billboard ad with an anti-Christmas message in the wording. (If you didn't speak English, you would assume the ad was a pro-Christmas message, as it shows the wise men going to worship the baby Jesus in the distance, under the Bethlehem star.) But the billboard declares "You know it's a myth. This season celebrate reason." Well, I celebrate both Christmas and reason, and I know plenty of intellectuals who do as well. Just try struggling through one page of St. Thomas Aquinas' *Summa Theologica* and tell me that faith and reason are incompatible. The great appeal of Christmas is that the message is simple enough to satisfy people with all levels of IQ.

It is strange when you consider how threatening a manger scene is to some in our society today. It represents a baby, for heaven's sake. A baby that escaped the clutches of King Herod. A baby that inspires acts of mercy and love all over the world. A baby that received gifts from the wise men which has inspired the annual season of gift-giving. Frankly, I think all the retailers in this country should assemble on December 26 each year, hold hands, and sing, "What a friend we have in Jesus."

And yet the war on Christmas goes on unabated. It's as if He is not invited to His own birthday party. A few years ago, children at the Ridgeway Elementary School in Dodgeville, Wisconsin, performing in a "winter program," were to sing the melody of "Silent Night" but with the words, "Cold in the night, no one in sight, winter winds whirl and bite, how I wish I were happy and warm, safe with my family out of the storm." The school officials didn't dare offend anyone with the original words of the classic carol.

But at the end of the day, nothing can stop Christmas. After all, we're talking about the religion of the catacombs.

Even the Grinch in the classic tale couldn't stop Christmas. Nor can the "holiday parade" organizers of Tulsa, Oklahoma. It's just too bad that we find that now the war on Christmas reaching even into a place like Tulsa. New York City I can understand, but Tulsa? With each passing year, it seems that the only principle getting stronger in our culture is the ABC principle. Anything But Christ.

Hopefully, the town officials in Tulsa will not jettison reason, but come to their senses and relent, so that the good senator will be able to saddle up once again to celebrate Christmas this year, as in times past.

The Birth of a Classic: Handel's Messiah

12/14/11

One of my favorite "viral videos" that circulates around the world through the Internet takes place in a food court in a mall, presumably in Canada.

As people are eating and resting from the hustle and bustle of Christmas shopping, suddenly a woman with a scarf on, who appears as an ordinary shopper, stands up and starts singing the "Hallelujah Chorus."

Clearly, this is a professional musician, who is soon joined in by another professional musician singing a different counterpart to the first soloist.

Then comes other singers, one after another.

These are high quality musicians, and the whole act is well choreographed (and well shot too). What throws off the average viewer is the inconspicuous appearance of the singers. They fit right in with the frazzled shoppers.

This beautiful video, recorded in November 2010, has now had more than 35 million views.

I have heard that the opening lines of the Hallelujah Chorus are the most recognizable piece of music the world over.

Of course, the Hallelujah Chorus comes from *Messiah*, an oratorio (a sacred opera) by George Frederick Handel. The whole work is heavenly, and its highlight is the Hallelujah Chorus. (Sometimes, I view *Messiah* as the zenith of Western civilization.)

I remember when the millennium change-over first hit on January 1, 2000 (although geeks like to say technically the first day of the millennium was January 1, 2001). In one far eastern country's time zone after another, people the world over were celebrating the new year, the new century, the new millennium.

As I recall watching television of the celebration, the one song that I heard more than any other on that day, from various countries, was the Hallelujah Chorus. It is universally loved.

Within months of the Berlin Wall coming down, Pepsi had a beautiful TV commercial celebrating the historic event. The piece they chose for that spot was the Hallelujah Chorus. It worked perfectly.

There's something deeply touching about that piece of music.

In his book, *Spiritual Lives of the Great Composers*, Patrick Kavanaugh tells how Handel barely ate during the 24 days he wrote *Messiah*. At one point, the composer had tears in his eyes and cried out to his servant, "I did think I did see all Heaven before me, and the great God Himself." He had just finished writing the Hallelujah Chorus.

Amazingly, *Messiah* came at a time in his life where the 56-year old Handel was facing bankruptcy and complete failure. He also had serious health problems. Also, some Church of England authorities were apparently critical of him and his work.

He seemed all washed up---with his future behind him. But writing *Messiah* proved to be the positive turning point in his life.

Handel was born in Germany. His father wanted him to study law, but George Frederick had an aptitude for music, which was clear early on. His mother bought him a harpsichord, which they kept up in the attic, secret from his father.

By the time he was twelve, Handel wrote his first work.

Later, after his father's death, he tried to study law, but he had no interest. So he studied music at the University of Halle.

In 1712, Handel moved to England and never returned to Germany.

While he experienced various successes through various compositions, including operas and sacred operas (oratorios, based on biblical themes), Kavanaugh notes that his failures threatened to overwhelm Handel: "His occasional commercial successes soon met with financial disaster…He drove himself relentlessly to recover from one failure after another, and finally his health began to fail. By 1741 he was swimming in debt. It seemed certain he would land in debtor's prison."

But 1741 proved to be the turning point. On the one hand, he gave what he feared was his farewell concert. On the other hand, a friend of his, Charles Jennens, gave him a libretto (a text) for a sacred work. It was essentially seventy-three Bible verses, focused on the Messiah, both from the Hebrew and the Christian Bible. Furthermore, a charity in Dublin paid him money to write something for a charity performance.

Messiah was the result, and it was very successful.

It's interesting to note in this year, 2011, the 400th anniversary of the King James Version of the Bible, that Handel's work was impacted by that literary masterpiece. Every word of *Messiah* comes from that book.

Oxford professor Alister E. McGrath wrote, "Without the King James Bible, there would have been no *Paradise Lost, no Pilgrim's Progress*, no Handel's *Messiah*, no Negro spirituals, and no Gettysburg Address. These, and innumerable other works were inspired by the language of this Bible."

Charles Jennens' role in this masterpiece is often lost, even on fans of *Messiah*. He is the one who carefully gleaned through the King James Bible and assembled the verses about the Christ that Handel so brilliantly set to music.

I count that forty-two of the verses come from the Old Testament, including many passages from the Psalms and Isaiah. Thirty-one come from the New Testament.

Messiah was first performed in Dublin in 1742. It was a benefit concert for charity. According to one source, proceeds freed 142 men from debtors' prison.

A year later, King George II was present at the first performance of *Messiah* in London. Is it said that the monarch fell asleep, and at the opening of the Hallelujah Chorus, he rose to his feet, thinking it was his cue. Whatever the reason, he stood, and that has been the custom ever since---to stand during the Hallelujah Chorus.

About 100 years later, even the aged Queen Victoria, who sat in her wheelchair as the chorus began, struggled to her feet as the choir sang, "King of kings and Lord of lords." She said, "No way will I sit in the presence of the King of kings."

So out of one genius's pain and low point in his life came a work of beauty that continues to uplift millions of people the world over. Kavanaugh notes the secret of Handel's success, "He was a relentless optimist whose faith in God sustained him through every difficulty."

Are We Winning or Losing?

12/23/13

Imagine two men engaged in a conversation on an international flight. These two men, presumably businessmen, are strangers to each other. As they talked with each other, it was revealed that one was a businessman. The second man was a representative of a worldwide organization with franchises in every country.

"Really?" asked the first. "You must work for Coca Cola."

"No," replied the second, "We have far more field representatives than they'll ever have! We have more employees and more customers, if you can call them that."

Now, the first man was definitely intrigued. "Microsoft?"

"No---infinitely bigger."

"The U.N.?"

"Again, much bigger."

"Well, then I can't imagine who you work for. Tell me."

The second man looked him straight in the eye and replied that he was a minister in the Church of Jesus Christ.

Think about it. The largest institution on the planet, the kingdom that contains more citizens than any country on earth, the association that has the most members, the world's biggest most diverse family, is the Church of Jesus Christ.

Not any one denomination within Christendom, but the collective body that professes to believe in the Son of God comprises the largest group of people on the globe.

Christ's Church contains members from every country and every race, speaking a vast multitude of languages, from every socio-economic stratum. There's simply no other group, institution, or fellowship even remotely similar. That's true diversity.

Dr. Paul L. Maier is a great scholar and professor of ancient history. He has a very sharp understanding of the big picture of the human story.

He once told me in an interview, "Well, there's no question that the Christian Church is the most successful phenomenon, even statistically considered, of anything that has ever happened on this planet."

He gave these statistics as an example: "...there are two billion, 250 million Christians across the globe and nobody has statistics like that. The nearest competitor would be Islam with about a billion, 100 thousand adherents."

Dr. Maier added, "So there's no other religion, there's no other faith, way of life, institution, governmental group, ethnic group---you name it---that has that number....There's hardly an area of the world that Christianity has not touched. And in many ways it's a remarkable fulfillment of the command that Jesus made in Matthew 28 when he sent out His disciples to conquer the world for His message."

Sometimes it's easy to get discouraged. Sometimes it's terrible to read about the regress of the Church in parts of the world---including our part. We're reminded of that virtually every day.

> * Christians have lost many aspects of the culture war in the West.
> * Formerly Christian institutions (like Harvard) now often promote the opposite message.
> * There's unprecedented slaughter of Christians in some parts of the Muslim world.

Yet as Dion DiMucci sang years ago in his song "I Believe (Sweet Lord Jesus)": "When kids run laughing by on Sunday mornings / You can hear the distant church bells chime / You see how we've survived the thousand decades / Don't you know he helped us through that time?"

Every Christmas is a reminder that the King of kings, seated at the right hand of God the Father, is slowly building His Church in virtually every nation on earth---even in places where it is extraordinarily dangerous to be a Christian. The future belongs to Him.

Considering all this began so modestly 2000 years ago in Bethlehem, where a visitor could easily have been repulsed at the smells of the original Christmas---as the Son of God was laid in a manger….not a bed for baby Jesus, but a feeding trough for animals.

But these were simply the humble roots of the most successful enterprise in the history of humanity. As has been said, Despise not small beginnings.

Disputing the Pagan Roots of Christmas
12/23/15

If Jesus had never been born, to borrow a phrase from C. S. Lewis, it would be "always winter, but never Christmas."

But some Christians, even today, think of the celebration of Christmas as a pagan holiday. When the Pilgrims and the Puritans had the opportunity to assert their influence, they did not celebrate Christmas. I agree with the Pilgrims and the Puritans on many things, but this is not one of them.

One of the main points is that Christmas is often celebrated in ways that exalt pagan revelry. I agree that it should not be, but that is guilt by association. It is also argued that Christmas is the appropriation of a pagan holiday.

Why is December 25th the day that we celebrate as Jesus' birthday? Sometimes if you look this up, sources will say things to the effect that in the 300s, there was a pope who took the pagan worship, Saturnalia, around the time of the winter solstice, and he baptized it and brought it into Christianity.

My rebuttal would be, actually there is some historical evidence that Jesus was born in the winter time of 5-4 BC. And it's possible that the actual day was December 25.

Dr. Jack Kinneer, professor of Reformed Presbyterian Theological Seminary of Pittsburgh, once explained to my radio audience that when Zecharaiah, the father of John the Baptist, was in the temple in Jerusalem, and the angel appeared to him and foretold him of the birth of his son, John the Baptist, who would be the forerunner of the Lord, this was at the time of the Day of Atonement in September. Zechariah then goes home to be with his formerly barren wife, Elizabeth.

When John has been in utero for six months, Mary receives the word from the angel that she will conceive through the power of the Holy Spirit. Mary and Elizabeth, who are cousins, have a joyous reunion at that time, presumably in late March. This is described in the first chapter of Luke's Gospel.

Do the math. When Mary, who was just at the beginning of her pregnancy with Jesus, visits her cousin Elizabeth, the latter was about 6 months pregnant. Nine months later brings us to late December. So December 25 is a plausible date for the birth of Christ.

This would be in the winter of 5-4 B.C.. That is based on the death of Herod the Great, which was in the spring, 4 B.C. Christmas is not as pagan in origins as some want to make it out to be.

Furthermore, Dr. Kinneer points out that there is a list of feast days of martyrs, the anniversaries of their deaths, and included in that list from the early church is that December 25 is the day honored as Jesus' birthday. That list is from the 300s. By ancient standards, that too is plausible.

Some have said that shepherds to whom the angels declared His birth on the evening of His birth would not have been in the fields at winter time. But other theologians have countered that the shepherds were watching the flocks in Bethlehem that were slated to be sacrificed in nearby Jerusalem.

That being the case, how fitting that at the moment of Jesus' birth, we would be reminded of the reason He came. He was born to die--- to offer Himself up as the ultimate Lamb of God, the ultimate sacrifice who would take away the sins of the world.

Furthermore, the wise men came with three gifts listed---gold, frankincense, and myrrh. The last one was a spice used for burial. Jesus was born that He might die, that we might truly live.

In his book, *There Really is a Santa Claus: The History of Saint Nicholas & Christmas Holiday Traditions*, Bill Federer notes that in 567, the Council of Tours attempted to reconcile the Western celebration of Christmas on December 25 with the Eastern Church's celebration of same on January 6---Epiphany, the feast of the visit of the Wise Men.

No agreement was made, but a compromise of 12 holy days between Christmas and Epiphany---otherwise known as the 12 Days of Christmas. So, even the Twelve Days of Christmas has Christian origins.

Regardless of the actual *date* of Christ's birth, what really counts is that the *fact* of it. He was born, so that He could fulfill the plan to save those who believe in Him from their sins. He has become the focal point of all history. And it all began on that first Christmas.

As C. S. Lewis once put it, "The central miracle asserted by Christians is the Incarnation. They say that God became Man. Every other miracle prepares for this, or exhibits this, or results from this."

Which Side of History Are You On?

12/24/14

I saw a recent hand-held sign from a protester on television with the words: "Which side of history are you on?"

With another Christmas approaching, I can't overstate how relevant that notion is when it comes to Christ's kingdom, which began 2000 years ago and will one day see its wider fulfillment.

Christmas is a special time of year, by anybody's reckoning. It isn't because it's winter solstice. It isn't because it's "sparkle day" as some secularists now want to re-label Christmas. It's because of the birth of a baby. A very special Baby.

I noticed the other week that attendance at the gym I visit was much lower than normal. It dawned on me that this was indirectly related to His birthday. People are traveling, running around shopping, getting ready for Christmas Day.

Retail-wise, the merchants have much to be grateful for Jesus' birth. Doesn't the celebration of His birthday, explicitly or implicitly, drive up sales and save their businesses---year after year? The late D. James Kennedy once quipped that all the merchants should gather together on December 26, hold hands, and sing "What a Friend We Have in Jesus."

Philosophically, how would we know what God is like and who He is, unless He revealed Himself first? Christians believe that is exactly who Jesus is---God revealing Himself in a Man.

Half a millennium before Jesus came, the Hebrew prophet Daniel foretold of a "Son of Man." Christians believe that this son of man was Jesus---the name He used of Himself the most.

Here's what Daniel said, "In my vision at night I looked, and there before me was one like a son of man, coming with the clouds of heaven. He approached the Ancient of Days and was led into his presence. He was given authority, glory and sovereign power; all nations and peoples of every language worshiped him. His dominion is an everlasting dominion that will not pass away, and his kingdom is one that will never be destroyed" (NIV).

To anyone familiar with Judaism, this is an astounding prophecy. A figure "like a son of man" was led into the presence of the Almighty God, described here as "the Ancient of Days," as one existing forever.

This son of man was given the kingdom, power, and glory. Things reserved for God alone. And He was given something else reserved for only God---worship, from those around the world.

How can these things be? Jesus is not "a god," as the Jehovah's Witnesses say, He is *the* God. The second person of the Triune God. Furthermore, when He came in a corner of the Roman Empire 2,000 years ago, He established a kingdom that will never be destroyed. Beginning with 12 men---one of whom turned out to be a traitor--- Jesus established a kingdom that continues to this day. It now claims the professed allegiance of about one-third of humanity.

I view the "Hallelujah Chorus" from Handel's *Messiah* as one of the high points of Western civilization. Based on Revelation, we hear these words: "The kingdoms of this world have become the kingdoms of our Lord and of His Christ...and He shall reign forever and ever."

The elites of our culture today assume that the future does not belong to "religion," as some prominent unbelievers have smugly said. I would counter that the past, present, and the future belong to Jesus Christ. Even our reckoning of time centers around His first coming (dividing into B.C., "Before Christ," and A.D., "Anno Domini," i.e., "in the year of our Lord"). Our future marches toward one climax: His return some day.

When George Washington was a young man, he wrote in his own handwriting a Christmas poem that he copied from a 1743 London Magazine. Here are some of the lines from that:

> Assist me Muse divine to sing the morn,
> On which the Saviour of mankind was born....
> Incarnate God our nature should embrace!
> That Deity should stoop to our disguise!....
> Oh never let my soul this Day forget,
> But pay in grateful praise her annual debt....

What is Christmas? An "annual debt" of thanksgiving to God for sending His one and only Son.

Napoleon once said, "I know men; and I tell you that Jesus Christ is no mere man. Between Him and every person in the world there is no possible term of comparison. Alexander, Caesar, Charlemagne, and I have founded empires. But on what did we rest the creations of our genius? Upon force. Jesus Christ founded His empire upon love; and at this hour millions of men would die for him."

And he also said, "I search in vain in history to find the similar to Jesus Christ, or anything which can approach the gospel....Nations pass away, thrones crumble, but the Church remains."

Despite apparent regress in the West, His kingdom still marches forward worldwide.

So the question is: Which side of history are *you* on? As a bumper sticker once noted, "Wise men still seek Him." Merry Christmas.

Part 7.

Christian History

Love, Commitment, and Valentine's Day

2/13/13

There's nothing very romantic about a man being beheaded because of his politically incorrect views. But February 14 marks the 1744th anniversary when tradition tells us that St. Valentine was executed in the Roman Empire for practicing his Christianity.

This was under a persecution of Emperor Claudius II, who banned his soldiers from marrying because he thought that single men could serve as better warriors.

He also forced the emperor-worship of a predecessor, Gallienus, upon the empire. This was something practicing Jews and Christians could not do---they worshiped God alone.

Author Bill Federer notes the consequences of Claudius' actions on an Italian bishop (or priest?) named Valentine: "When the Emperor demanded the Church violate its conscience and worship pagan idols, Bishop Valentine refused to comply."

Not only did Valentine not worship the emperor, he also surreptitiously married young couples.

Federer notes, "Saint Valentine was arrested, dragged before the Prefect of Rome, who condemned him to be beaten to death with clubs and then have his head cut off on February 14, 269 AD."

Before he was beheaded, tradition tells us he prayed for the warden's ill child, and she got better. The bishop wrote her a small note and said it was "from your Valentine."

As Paul Harvey used to say, "And now you know, the *rest* of the story."

Valentine's Day is a great time to remember the importance of love in marriage. Something that seems to be often lacking these days. I just learned this week is National Marriage Week USA.

I gave a speech at my wedding in 1980 in my wife's church in Norway on "The Ten C's of a Happy Marriage." I don't remember everything I said, but here a few key points I made.

The first "C" of a happy marriage for us is Christ, the foundation of our marriage. When we made Him #1 in our lives, everything else worked out, come what may.

About twenty years ago, I was on the road around Valentine's Day. I called a florist to request flowers to be sent to my wife, and I dictated this message to accompany the flowers:

Roses are red,

Violets are blue.

I love you the most,

Except for you know who.

The florist didn't understand and was reluctant to even write it up that way. "Are you sure?"

"Yes, I'm sure." My wife, Kirsti, picked up the message right away, as to the "you know who."

I remember another "C" was commitment. If you're committed to each other, then you'll work things out, even if hard. This is not the same as romantic feelings. It's rock solid commitment. Feelings come and feelings go. Then feelings come back, and they go. But commitment slogs on.

I remember a man who got married before I did. He also got divorced before I got married. I asked what happened. They got into a fight. OK, that happens to virtually everyone.

And then he said, "Don't you love me anymore?" And she hesitated and said, "I'm not sure."

He shouted, "That's it. It's over." And it was off to the divorce court.

But feelings of love are one thing, and commitment to each other in love is a different thing. Millions of couples today think that that if they fall in love with the right person, then the feelings of love will continue. But, again, feelings come and go. Commitment remains the same.

My wife and I made an agreement that before we got married, we could freely talk about divorce. But after we got married, we wouldn't even joke about it, since divorce is not an option.

I used to laugh at the late Mrs. Billy Graham's joke, when she was asked if she ever considered divorce. "Divorce? No. Murder? Yes."

I say I used to laugh until I saw some episodes of true crime documentaries, showing where 'til death they departed---because one of them murdered his or her spouse.

Another key "C" for a happy marriage is communication. So often couples communicate on different levels. After a fight, if the husband buys her flowers, she might think he's trying to buy her love. Talking things out is so helpful. Marriage Encounter weekends teach excellent tools for communicating with each other.

One great question to ask is: "What can I do to prove to you that I love you?" Listen to the answer, and then do it.

The last "C" for a happy marriage I want to highlight is confession---confessing sin and forgiveness of same. "I'm sorry" are some of the most important words in any language.

The Bible says, "don't let the sun go down on your anger." In other words, don't go to bed with a fight unresolved.

So on the anniversary of a third century saint who prized his faith in the Lord and the importance of marriage above his own life, we can renew our commitments to love those whom God has placed in our lives, including our spouse. Happy St. Valentine's Day.

In Remembrance of a True Hero of the Faith---St. Patrick

3/17/14

We live in a time of the anti-hero. Too often, the good guys are the bad guys and vice versa. Celebrities are often held up as heroes, until we learn too much about them.

But to see a true hero, look at the real St. Patrick, who has a day dedicated in his honor. Unfortunately, many people only observe his holiday, March 17, by drinking themselves silly, which is totally contrary to the spirit of the man who Christianized Ireland.

In fact, Patrick shows what God can do through someone who is committed fully to Him.

Thomas Cahill, author of the book, *How the Irish Saved Civilization: The Untold Story of Ireland's Heroic Role from the Fall of Rome to the Rise of Medieval Europe*, notes that Patrick and the Irish came at the moment of a cultural cliff-hanger and played a key role in helping to save civilization.

In the 5th century, barbarians overran the Roman Empire---which was the repository of much of Western civilization---until it finally collapsed. Meanwhile, through the missionary work of Patrick (387-461), the gospel was brought to Ireland; and numerous men became monks as a result, who meticulously copied manuscripts of the Bible and of many of the writings of antiquity.

Cahill writes: "For, as the Roman Empire fell, as all through Europe matted, unwashed barbarians descended on the Roman cities, looting artifacts and burning books, the Irish, who were just learning to read and write, took up the great labor of copying all of Western literature---everything they could lay their hands on."

He notes, "These scribes then served as conduits through which the Greco-Roman and Judeo-Christian cultures were transmitted to the tribes of Europe, newly settled amid the rubble and ruined vineyards of the civilization they had overwhelmed."

Cahill adds, "Without this Service of the Scribes, everything that happened subsequently would have been unthinkable. Without the Mission of the Irish Monks, who single-handedly refounded European civilization throughout the continent in the bays and valleys of their exile, the world that came after then would have been an entirely different one---a world without books. And our own world would never have come to be."

The man at the center of all this was St. Patrick.

Many of the details of his life we learn through a document he wrote late in his life, *Confession*. This was not a book of confessions of his sins, but rather a statement of his beliefs. It is autobiographical in nature.

Patrick (to the surprise of many) was not Irish by birth, but rather grew up in England as a nominal Christian. He said in *Confession*, "I did not know the true God."

At the age of 16, marauding Irish pirates laid waste his city and captured slaves, including Patrick. Later he would write of this: "As a youth, nay, almost as a boy not able to speak, I was taken captive, before I knew what to pursue and what to avoid."

Patrick said, "I was taken into captivity to Ireland with many thousands of people---and deservedly so, because we turned away from God, and did not keep His commandments."

For six years, he worked as a slave for a landowning chief. Cahill notes that during this time, Patrick had two companions---hunger and nakedness.

While he served as a shepherd, he remembered his prayers of his youth and came to know God truly through Christ. After six years of captivity, he was able to providentially escape from Ireland.

The late Dr. D. James Kennedy notes, "[Patrick] vowed revenge---the noble revenge of sharing the gospel with the people who held him captive. He believed that he had been called by God to return to the land of his slavery."

So Patrick, after some theological training, eventually returned to Ireland where he spent the rest of his life (about thirty years) as a missionary. Patrick may well have baptized about 120,000 souls. Some scholars note that he was the most successful missionary since the Apostle Paul.

Patrick wrote this, "Daily, I expect murder, fraud or captivity...but I fear none of these things because of the promises of heaven. I have cast myself into the hands of God almighty who rules everywhere."

There's a famous prayer attributed to Patrick that was inspired by him---although in its present form, it was likely written later. This beautiful statement of faith is called "St. Patrick's Breastplate."

Here is a portion of the prayer: "I arise today through God's strength to pilot me: God's might to uphold me, God's wisdom to guide me...Christ with me, Christ before me, Christ behind me, Christ in me, Christ beneath me, Christ above me..."

So remember the next time you see someone get drunk on St. Paddy's Day, they dishonor the memory a great hero of the faith and of the ages.

What Changed the Vikings?

2/25/14

I saw an advertisement recently for a series on the History Channel on the Vikings. A viewer's guide blurb reads, "Chronicling the medieval adventures of a band of Norsemen."

"Adventures"? I guess that's one way to put it. They went around killing people, raping women, stealing, and destroying things.

For two centuries the Vikings were the scourge of Europe. But what changed them? Who changed them? It's really one of the great stories in human history. However, in our highly politically correct age of multiculturalism, the truth is often obscured.

Norway, my wife's native land—we were married there, in fact-- was once dominated by Vikings. These days, Norway has a reputation as a country committed to peace. The Nobel Peace Prize, is given in Norway.

But it didn't used to be that way...as you can see, I'm sure, in this TV series on the Vikings.

Sometime in the 800s or so, Norwegian Vikings would plant their crops in the spring and then board ships they made to invade all over Europe. They would return with loot, just in time for harvest.

The Christians in the pillaged lands would pray, "God, save us from the Norsemen [Vikings]." Religious institutions (e.g., monasteries) in particular were a favorite target of the Vikings because they often housed treasures and were often poorly defended.

The Vikings pillaged, raped, and killed men, women, and even children. They would systematically put to the torch what was left.

Dr. Kennedy and I noted in the book, *What If Jesus Had Never Been Born?*, "Their fighting men, berserkers, were so fierce in battle that our word berserk comes from them. What changed this horrible scourge of humanity? Jesus Christ did." (They used drug-inducing mushrooms in battle.)

But when one of their leaders, "St." Olaf (995-1030), claimed to become a follower of Jesus, things began to change. I put the "saint" in quotes because by Christian standards, he wasn't always too saintly.

He forced his people to worship Christ instead of their gods, like Odin (from whence we have the word Wednesday, i.e., "Odin's dag" in Norwegian) or Thor (Thursday). As Thomas Jefferson rightly said, "the holy author of our religion" doesn't force Himself on anyone. The gospel should never be imposed by force. But despite this rough start, Christianity began to take root.

Over time, the Vikings were changed. As Dr. Kennedy and I note, "...over time, many of the Scandinavians became true Christians, and so the Vikings stopped their terrible raids. Virtually every Norwegian, Dane, Swede, and even many British [because of the Viking raids] are descendants of these formerly fierce and warlike people."

The gospel had such an effect that by 1020 A.D., Norway passed laws, reflecting these new values. Norwegian historian Sverre Steen writes about that law that "old practices became illegal, such as blood sacrifice, black magic, the 'setting out' of infants, slavery and polygamy."

I recently preached a funeral for a Norwegian/American. The coffin of the deceased had an American flag on one part and a Norwegian flag on the other.

noted to the assembled mourners how the Norwegian flag, and all the flags of the Scandinavian countries, are based on the cross of Jesus. Only the colors are different. The Danish flag (a white cross with a red background) is among the oldest national flags in the world.

Norway has sent out more Christian missionaries per capita than any other country until recent years. Norway is now one of the most humanitarian countries when it comes to helping the world's poor. In short, Norway--a formerly warlike, barbarian nation--now has a good reputation as a peace-loving country.

My wife Kirsti told me, "It was Christianity that changed the Vikings. No doubt about it. Before Christianity came, things like humility, kindness, gentleness were considered a female weakness, instead of as virtues." The Vikings are a trophy of the gospel of Jesus.

A Significant Milestone: the King James Bible at 400
3/11/11

2011 marks the 400th anniversary of the King James Bible. This is a significant milestone, in that the Bible has helped shape much of what is great in Western civilization.

The Bible is the world's bestseller. The King James Version in particular is bestselling Bible; thus, it is the bestseller of the world's bestseller. There are more than one billion copies of the King James Bible in print. And its impact has been profound.

A few years ago (April 2, 2007), *TIME* Magazine had a cover story on why the Bible should be taught (with caution) in the public schools. He noted how influential the Bible has been in Western culture.

Even a leading atheist book, Richard Dawkins' *The God Delusion* (2006) essentially says (and I'm paraphrasing), "Oh by the way, I have nothing against the Bible as *literature*. In fact, it's great as literature. And you're not culturally literate if you are not familiar with the Bible."

This does not mean he in any way respects the Bible as holy writ or anything close. As noted before, he says: "We can give up belief in God while not losing touch with a treasured heritage." That strikes me as a fruitless venture. But I quote it because he refers to the Bible in general, and the 400 year old King James in particular as a "treasured heritage."

The King James Version of the Bible has a fascinating history in and of itself. Essentially, the king was trying to create a copy of the Bible to compete with the Geneva Bible (1560), which was spreading like wildfire among the Puritans and other Christian non-conformists. (It had short notes in the margins of that Bible that so exorcised the king ---for example, stating that on occasion, there is a time to obey God but not the civil authorities.)

King James I disagreed vehemently with Presbyterians and the Puritans. He once said famously: "Presbytery agreeth with monarchy like God with the Devil."

Winston Churchill notes that his slogan was "No Bishop, no King." James, the human head of the Church of England, could control the Church through his bishops.

Thus, the religious nonconformists were troublesome to him. He even said of those Puritan types, "I will make them conform, or I will harry them out of the land or do worse."

The king was galled by the success of the Geneva Bible. His goal in creating the Authorized Version was to usurp it---to dethrone it. He made sure there were no Presbyterians or Puritans working on his committee of fifty-four scholars who created the new Bible, released in 1611.

Eventually, the King James Version did succeed in leaving the Geneva Bible. But that feat didn't occur until a couple decades after his death in 1625.

Whatever his particular motivation, the monarch ended up creating the world's most beloved edition of the world's best-seller.

Reid Buckley, brother of the late William F. Buckley, Jr., trains professional speakers. He said this about the world's most beloved Bible: "Any born English-speaking son or daughter of the Christian West, who has not savored, indeed, soaked him- or herself in the King James Version of the Holy Bible is irreparably ignorant and culturally deprived."

If one has never been "soaked" in such a way, the 400th anniversary is as good as any year to start.

In the Arena

8/1/12

Much of the world is enthralled by watching the Olympics right now. The persistence shown by so many of the athletes is a reminder of the on-going need for tenacity, despite setbacks.

Often during the televised segments, you see portions of the British flag as a backdrop. The British flag is a reminder of persistence, even in the face of outright persecution. The Union Jack, the most common name for the flag of Great Britain, is comprised of a mix between St. George's cross and that of St. Andrew.

The brother of St. Peter, Andrew, was crucified on a cross shaped like an X. St. Andrew's cross is immortalized through Britain's flag---and that of Scotland, of Florida, and of many former colonies of England.

Persistence in the face of opposition is heroic. In our day, there's a great need for persistence in the face of political correctness, which seems to infect virtually every aspect of modern life---even down to our fast food choices.

Consider a few people from the arena of history that refused to quit doing that which was right.

One of my great heroes was Athanasius, the 4th century saint, who was the champion of the Trinity. For his views, he was banished five times from the Roman Empire (outwardly Christian at that time). But he never gave up.

In modern times, in our republic, it's hard to imagine what it would be like to be banished by the Caesar of the world. Yet by the time of Constantine's death in 337, Athanasius was on the outs.

Athanasius' views prevailed and are reflected in the version of the Nicene Creed that is still read week after week by hundreds of millions are the world.

Look at William Wilberforce, perhaps the greatest reformer in history. Because of his strong faith in the Lord, he engaged in a lifelong crusade to rid the British Empire of the evil practice of slavery.

In 1787, this young Member of Parliament wrote in his diary, "Almighty God has set before me two great objectives, the abolition of the slave trade and the reformation of morals." And so with the help of some like-minded colleagues, he formed two societies: The Committee for the Abolition of the Slave Trade, and The Society for the Reformation of Manners (what we would call today morals).

In 1791, after Wilberforce's campaign to end slavery began in earnest, John Wesley, the great preacher and founder of the Methodist Church, wrote to the Member of Parliament, to encourage him. His letter is a classic:

"MY DEAR SIR, Unless the Divine Power has raised you up to be as *Athanasius contra mundum* [Athanasius against the world], I see not how you can go through your glorious enterprise in opposing that execrable villainy which is the scandal of religion, of England, and of human nature." William, writes John, unless God is in this, you will fail.

Wesley continues: "Unless God has raised you up for this very thing, you will be worn out by the opposition of men and devils; but if God be for you, who can be against you? Are all of them stronger than God? Oh, be not weary of well-doing. Go on in the name of God, and in the power of His might, till even American slavery, the vilest that ever saw the sun, shall vanish away before it. That He who has guided you from your youth up may continue to strengthen you in this and all things, is the prayer of, dear sir, Your affectionate servant, JOHN WESLEY"

Wilberforce's anti-slavery campaign came in two parts. First, to get the slave trade abolished. Second, to free all the slaves. Together these efforts took many decades (roughly twenty-five years for each). He finally received word on his death bed in 1833 that the slaves were free.

Even President Obama (many of whose policies I take issue with, on biblical grounds) said this in 2010: "Remember William Wilberforce, whose Christian faith led him to seek slavery's abolition in Britain; he was vilified, derided, attacked; but he called for 'lessening prejudices [and] conciliating good-will, and thereby making way for the less obstructed progress of truth.'"

Take another example. Mother Teresa. Year after year, decade after decade, she helped comfort the dying and the poorest of the poor on the streets of Calcutta (now Kolkata). She once said, "Today God has sent us into the world as he sent Jesus, to show God's love to the world. And we must sacrifice to show that love, just as Jesus made the greatest sacrifice of all."

My mom used to love to tell a story about Mother Teresa. One day a reporter was following the dedicated nun around. As she was helping to clean up a smelly, dying man, the reporter turned away in revulsion and said, "I wouldn't do that for a million dollars." And Mother Teresa shot back, "Neither would I."

Nothing worthwhile seems to come easy. Now is not the time to quit. Now is the time to press on, speaking the *truth* in *love*, even if some falsely smear you.

Winston Churchill famously said, "Never give in. Never give in. Never, never, never, never---in nothing, great or small, large or petty---never give in, except to convictions of honor and good sense. Never yield to force. Never yield to the apparently overwhelming might of the enemy."

On the 100th Anniversary of the *Titanic*

4/10/12

Here's a trivia question for you to ask your friends and family. Who christened the *Titanic*? I'll answer that question later.

April 15, 2012 marks the 100th anniversary of the sinking of the *Titanic*. The steamship was 885 feet long, and it was more than ten stories tall. As of that time, it had been described as "the largest moving man-made object in the world" and a "floating palace."

On its maiden voyage this huge steamship was going from Southampton, England to New York City when it collided with an iceberg about 400 miles from Newfoundland and sank within three hours. There were 2,207 people on board, and 1,500 perished.

Daniel Allen Butler wrote a book I highly recommend, entitled *Unsinkable*. In the Preface, he wrote, "No other disaster in history could have been more easily avoided or was more inevitable...a once-in-a-lifetime combination of weather and sea conditions came together to make the iceberg nearly invisible to the ship's lookouts."

The Greeks had their ancient plays where the flawed hero ended up in tragedy because of his hubris---his arrogance. And when you look at many of the facts surrounding the sinking of the *Titanic*, you find multiple examples of pride, in the worst sense of the word.

The *Titanic* is indeed a reminder of that ancient principle from Solomon the Wise: Pride goes before destruction, and a haughty spirit before a fall. One error compounded on another....but each was predicated on the assumption that the ship was unsinkable.

Before the voyage, one woman, a Mrs. Albert Caldwell, watched "a group of deck hands carrying luggage aboard the *Titanic*. Impulsively, she stopped one of the men and asked him, 'Is this ship really nonsinkable?' 'Yes, lady,' he replied, 'God Himself couldn't sink this ship.'" (Butler, *Unsinkable*, p. 39).

Hindsight is always 20/20. But that wasn't a very smart thing to say.

One author noted about the *Titanic*: "She was the floating embodiment of the new age of scientific optimism, and the international symbol of the century that would finally realize Utopia....Many perceived the ship to be a modern incarnation of the

Tower of Babel. The sinking represented God's unwillingness to allow man to build any edifice of invincibility or to seek salvation through technology."

Meanwhile, it is amazing to think about the hundreds of heroic men who sacrificed their lives because of the chivalrous view ingrained in the culture (because of Judeo-Christian influence) of "Women and children first."

I heard recently about a ferry that capsized in Indonesia, where men pushed women and children overboard to secure their own place in the lifeboats.

Meanwhile, the dust hasn't settled yet from the shipwreck earlier this year of the *Costa Concordia* off the coast of Italy. But from initial reports, the care of women and children first was not necessarily the norm.

The captain of the *Costa Concordia* has been dubbed "the chicken of the sea." (But, in fairness, as of this writing, he has not yet had his day in court). Meanwhile, Captain E. J. Smith of the *Titanic* nobly went down with the ship, after having made sure that the crew saved women and children first as much as possible.

Because of a ten second brush with a 5,000 year old iceberg, April 14-15, 1912 turned the luxury voyage into a night of horror.

I gleaned the following facts from Butler's book. Because the *Titanic* was viewed as unsinkable….

· The crew didn't bother to make sure they had lookout glasses, i.e., binoculars, on-board. (They were actually there, it turns out, but locked up and stashed away, unknown to the present crew because of a last minute change in personnel.)

· They should have gone through a practice drill in case of emergencies, but they didn't.

· They should have had far more lifeboats, one space for each passenger. Instead, as was the custom of the day (which was changed after the sinking of the *Titanic*), they used an elaborate mathematical formula to derive a much smaller number of lifeboats.

· They were going at the fastest speed of the voyage at the time of the brush with the iceberg (22 1/2 knots). The captain was trying to make the trip in record time.

· They would have heeded the six wireless messages from different ships warning them about the ice-fields. The last one, at 11 PM (about a half hour before the accident), came from the

178

Californian ship: "Say, old man, we are surrounded by ice and stopped." To that message, the *Titanic*'s radio operator responded, "Shut up! Shut up! I am busy…"

In retrospect, what made him so busy---compared to 1,500 human lives lost that night?

So who was it that christened the *Titanic*? No one. It was never christened. It didn't need to be. After all, it was unsinkable.

The Bishop of Winchester said, "The *Titanic*, name and thing, will stand for a monument and warning to human presumption." That message is still relevant, a hundred years later.

The Christian and Civil Disobedience

9/9/15

Recent events have called into question the issue of obeying the government in all ways---even in all circumstances.

In the 13th chapter of Romans, Paul says that God has given us the government as a minister of righteousness. It is our duty to obey it. But we also see in Scripture that on occasion, when the government calls for one to disobey God, then civil disobedience is in order.

There's a great lesson to learn from one aspect of World War II related to distortions of Romans 13. I'm not calling anybody a Nazi, but consider this lengthy lesson, wherein the Nazis quoted Scripture in order to demand unquestioning obedience.

On April 9, 1940, without any warning or provocation, the Germans invaded Norway. It was an unexpected battle and an unfair fight with 400,000 German Wehrmacht versus a nation not expecting it. This nightmare lasted until May 1945.

There were, of course, Norwegian collaborators---Norwegians who sold their soul to get ahead during the reign of the Nazis. Foremost amongst them was Vidkun Quisling. His name has been adopted into the dictionary: A quisling is a traitor.

When the Nazis took over Norway, a country full of "pure Aryans," they expected the Norwegians to fully participate in their attempts to glorify the "master race" and purge the "undesirables" from humanity, such as Jews, Gypsies, and Slavs.

The Norwegians would have nothing to do with this. So they resisted, usually in every peaceful way they could. Much of the battle was fought over distributing accurate information.

In Oslo, there is a museum (Norges Hjemmefront Museum) dedicated to the resistance movement in World War II. They have a plaque there in English: "In Norway, Nazi ideology was defeated by the democratic forces rooted in a national, Christian culture."

While the Nazis won militarily (until the end of the war), they never came close to winning the hearts and minds of the people.

Normally, in those days, the churches were full. But during the war, something happened to cause the churches to go empty. The Norwegian bishops and priests, desiring to be faithful to God and the Scriptures, resisted the Nazi efforts to control the churches and the content of sermons. The clergy reasoned that if they all resisted together as one, nothing could happen to them. They were all arrested and sent to concentration camps. Most of them never returned.

Many Norwegian Christians met in private homes secretly for worship and avoided the churches during the war.

The same thing happened with the school teachers. The Nazis took over the curriculum of the schools. The teachers resisted as one group. They too were arrested and sent to concentration camps. Most never returned.

The museum contains a 1941 book, written in Norwegian used in the schools by the Nazis. In it, they quote Scripture: "What are those called in Romans 13:1 who God has set over us? Have you considered that your parents, your school teachers (your principal), policemen, police chief, judges, the priest, the bishop, the county commission, the state government, are the authorities who are installed by God, and that you owe them obedience?"

Then it says: "Overall, we owe the Fuhrer and the government obedience. If you set yourself up against the authorities and against the state, you are standing against God's structure and are subject to punishment."

Talk about the devil quoting Scripture. In reality, the Fuhrer was hostile toward Christianity. Hitler once declared, "The heaviest blow that ever struck humanity was the coming of Christianity. Bolshevism is Christianity's illegitimate child. Both are inventions of the Jew." But he was happy to have his minions twist the Christian Scriptures for his own ends.

God's Word is pure and right. But that doesn't mean it can't be distorted sometimes by evil people intent on achieving goals that are contrary to the message of Scripture. There's a time and a place for everything under the sun, including (on occasion) civil disobedience.

Recently I came across an unpublished letter by D. James Kennedy (11/29/1988), in which he addressed this issue: "The basic Bible principles, I believe, are these: 1) All authority is from God. 2) All human authority is delegated from God. 3) No human authority can countermand the authority of God. 4) If such anti-biblical laws are passed, Christians must in conscience disobey them. 5) They must be prepared to suffer the consequences of their actions."

Then he solidifies the whole point: "The very existence of Christianity depends upon Christians obeying these principles. Had they not done so, Christianity, which was outlawed first in Israel and then in the Roman Empire, would have ceased to exist many centuries ago."

Maria Von Trapp, RIP

8/26/14

Earlier this year, an event happened that did not receive wide notice. The last of the Von Trapp Family Singers, the last of the children—the real ones—died.

Her name was Maria—not to be confused with the lady played by Julie Andrews, Maria Augusta Trapp, who died in 1987. Maria Von Trapp's death in February 2014 marks the end of an era.

The Sound of Music deserves its accolades as the Movie of the Year (1965) and one of the finest films ever made. Even my one-year-old granddaughter is mesmerized by the puppet scene.

As a film it is an icon. One time the great anti-gambling crusader, Rev. Tom Grey was asked on 60 Minutes to respond to those who say gambling is just entertainment. Noting the tragic toll the "entertainment" of gambling often takes on its victims, Grey asked, "Who watches *The Sound of Music* and then shoots himself in the parking lot?"

What's fascinating about the real Von Trapp Family is just how Christian the true story is.

The religious elements come out to some degree in the movie. Yet when the movie was marketed for Brazil, instead of the title we know the movie by, they decided to call it (in Portuguese) "*The Rebellious Nun*." But Maria didn't really rebel per se. She just discovered that God's call on her life was to serve God as a wife and mother, not in a cloister.

In her 1949 book, *The Story of the Trapp Family Singers*, Maria Augusta Trapp said of her marriage to the Captain, Georg Von Trapp, "I greeted it with a heart full of happiness and readiness to serve God where He needed me most—wholeheartedly and cheerfully."

Although her role expanded later, Maria the nun was initially assigned just to tutor Maria, the daughter of Captain Von Trapp. Ironically, Maria the little girl was "of delicate health." She is the one who died earlier this year, after living to be 99, outlasting them all.

Maria didn't mind the assignment to help the children (even though there had been 25 tutors and governesses before her) because she viewed it as temporary: "After all—I don't belong here; I am just loaned." But soon she came to be appreciated by the whole family, including the Captain.

Maria was shocked when she asked Maria Von Trapp, "Don't you have an Advent wreath every year?" The child replied, "No, we never did. What is it?" So the nun on loan to help the children not only brought music to the von Trapp family, but a Christ-centered Christmas as well.

The Captain later confessed, "I always feared Christmas more than any other day. But this year you have made it very beautiful for us. Thank you."

Maria whispered a prayer of gratitude to Jesus, "I thank You so much for sending me there. Please help me to draw them all closer to You."

Her prayer was answered. The Captain said to Maria, "I wish my children would get thoroughly acquainted with Holy Scriptures...Let's start them with the New Testament, and let's read it together every evening until Easter."

Maria said of their Bible-reading: "It proved to be the Book of Books, the only one in the whole world to which a four-year old girl would listen with enraptured interest while all the philosophers are not yet able to get to the bottom of its divine wisdom."

Maria and the Captain got married in 1927; and the Von Trapps began performing musically as a family after a priest friend, Father Wasner, discovered what talent they had. They became a smash hit.

Meanwhile, after the Nazis took over their native land in 1938, the children told their parents: "In school we are not permitted to sing any religious songs with the name of Christ or Christmas."

This was just the tip of the iceberg. So they had a family conference, where Captain Von Trapp said: "Children, we have the choice now." Either keep "the material goods we still have" or "our faith and our honor. We can't have both any more....I'd rather see us poor, but honest. If we choose this, then we have to leave. Do you agree?" They agreed and got away in time.

On a sad note, they later learned that their mansion they had fled back in Salzburg had been seized by the Nazis, who turned their chapel into a beer parlor. Heinrich Himmler himself lived there and Father Wasner's room was turned into a guest bedroom for Hitler.

Maria writes, "One day when Hitler was visiting there, chauffeurs and orderlies were waiting outside on call. One of these soldiers hummed the melody of a Russian folksong." Hitler then had them all shot on the spot.

The family came to America to tour as a music group. But initially it did not go well in this country. Their act was too oriented toward sacred classical music. They were almost reduced to getting menial jobs unrelated to music just to stay in America. Their first manager lost money on them and said, "You will never be a hit in America. Go back to Europe."

Said Maria: "Back to Europe, with the Swastika stretching its black spider legs all over the map."

But they got another chance from a new manager who said, "...we shall start by changing your name. Trapp Family Choir sounds too churchy. I am the manager of the Trapp Family Singers."

Eventually, they settled down in Vermont and created the Von Trapp Family Lodge, which still operates today. So we salute the end of an era, which proved the wisdom of the statement made in the movie: "When the Lord closes a door, somewhere He opens a window." Or as the elder Maria says in her book, "God's will hath no why."

Part 8.

Science

Does Science Disprove God?

11/4/15

A Pew Research Poll released last week reports that fifty-nine percent of Americans see science and religion in conflict. But they also found that, "highly religious Americans are less likely than others to see conflict between faith and science."

I'm not a scientist per se, but it's amazing to me to see how some scientists like to claim that somehow science has disproven God.

Meanwhile, on Bill Maher's television program last month (10/2/15), he and guest Richard Dawkins essentially declared that science has disproved God.

Bill Maher: "You talk about the wonder of science probably better than anybody and, of course, it's a little bit of a difficult mission because the more you explain how wonderful and amazing science is, the more the other side says, 'Well, yeah, because God did it!'"....

Richard Dawkins: "I think that the wonder of science above all is precisely that God didn't do it, the wonder, we do understand how it came about, we do understand how life, in particular, came about with nothing but the laws of physics, nothing but atoms bumping into each other, and then filtered through the curious process that Darwin discovered, it gives rise to us and kangaroos and trees and walruses."

And Dawkins added: "What's truly wonderful is that it came about without being designed. If it had been designed, anybody could do that, it's the fact that it came about just through the laws of physics, naturalism is what's so wonderful about it."

Oh, the glories of science. Now we know better than the ancients, who simply swapped one mystery---the universe---for belief in another mystery---God.

Or do we? G. K. Chesterton (1874-1936) was a great Christian thinker who noted this: "Science must not impose any philosophy, any more than the telephone must tell us what to say."

He also said, "Reason is itself a matter of faith. It is an act of faith to assert that our thoughts have any relation to reality at all. If you are merely a skeptic, you must sooner or later ask yourself the question, 'Why should ANYTHING go right; even observation and deduction? Why should not good logic be as misleading as bad logic? They are both movements in the brain of a bewildered ape?'

The young skeptic says, 'I have a right to think for myself.' But the old skeptic, the complete skeptic, says, 'I have no right to think for myself. I have no right to think at all.'"

By using reason, Dawkins concludes that this world is essentially reason-less. His type did not invent science, nor could it have. It takes belief in reason to understand the laws of science---even to agree that there are laws of science. And reason cannot form in the void of random materialism. That is why it is historically true that science was born in Christian Europe.

Alfred North Whitehead said that Christianity is the mother of science because of "the medieval insistence on the rationality of God." A rational God had made a rational universe, and it was the object of the scientists to---in the words of the great astronomer Johannes Kepler---"think God's thoughts after Him."

In the book, *What If Jesus Had Never Been Born?*, D. James Kennedy and I point out (based on the findings of Henry Morris) that virtually all the major branches of science were invented by Bible-believing scientists, including:

Antiseptic surgery, Joseph Lister
Bacteriology, Louis Pasteur
Calculus, Isaac Newton
Celestial Mechanics, Johannes Kepler
Chemistry, Robert Boyle
Comparative Anatomy, Georges Cuvier
Computer Science, Charles Babbage
Dimensional Analysis, Lord Rayleigh
Dynamics, Isaac Newton
Electronics, John Ambrose Fleming
Electrodynamics, James Clerk Maxwell
Electromagnetics, Michael Faraday
Energetics, Lord Kelvin
Entomology of Living Insects, Henri Fabre
Field Theory, Michael Faraday
Fluid Mechanics, George Stokes
Galactic Astronomy, Sir William Herschel
Gas Dynamics, Robert Boyle
Genetics, Gregor Mendel
Glacial Geology, Louis Agassiz
Gynecology, James Simpson

Hydrography, Matthew Maury
Hydrostatics, Blaise Pascal
Ichthyology, Louis Agassiz
Isotopic Chemistry, William Ramsey
Model Analysis, Lord Rayleigh
Natural History, John Ray
Non-Euclidean Geometry, Bernard Riemann
Oceanography, Matthew Fontaine Maury
Optical Mineralogy, David Brewster

So, are Christians anti-science? Not quite. Science was invented by Christians.

Furthermore, we write: "The prevailing philosophy of the Western world today is existentialism, which is irrational. It would not be possible for science to develop in an irrational world because science is based on the fact that if water boils at 212 degrees today, it will boil at 212 degrees tomorrow, and the same thing the next day, and that there are certain laws and regularities that control the universe." No rational God, no rational universe.

So, does science somehow disprove God? Not at all. On the contrary, the heavens declare the glory of God.

Is Evolution Just a Shell Game?

8/19/15

As the school year begins to gear up again, it's a given that in classrooms across the country, evolution will be taught virtually everywhere and virtually always as a proven fact.

When I was in college, at Tulane in the 1970s, I didn't understand how to reconcile evolution and the Bible. I was taking anthropology classes and learning details on the theory of how we all supposedly came from common ancestry.

Then I spoke with a Christian medical school professor who explained that there is abundant evidence for microevolution---small changes within kind. It's an established fact within biology that nobody disagrees with. But the controversy, he said, surrounds macroevolution, big changes beyond kind. And the evidence for that is not there. The missing links are still missing.

Macroevolution, i.e., common ancestry, is summed up well by its critic Rabbi Daniel Lapin when he told me once: "By an unaided materialistic process, over a long period of time, primitive protoplasm evolved into Bach and Beethoven."

187

Up until his death about a decade ago, the leading evolutionist in America was Dr. Stephen Jay Gould of Harvard University.

Gould admitted: "Everybody knows the fossil record doesn't provide much evidence for gradualism [i.e., tiny, successive changes over time leading to major changes, including speciation]; it is full of gaps and discontinuities. These gaps are all attributed to the notorious imperfection of the record, but this is not an adequate explanation. The fossil record shows one thing which cannot be attributed to its imperfection; most species don't change."

Gould said elsewhere, "New species almost always appeared suddenly in the fossil record with no intermediate link to ancestors in older rocks of the same region."

So then, did Gould abandon belief in macroevolution in light of all this? No, he said, "evolution, like gravitation, is a fact."

In 1972, Gould and Niles Eldredge published a new theory called Punctuated Equilibrium, which attempted to explain the existing geological record in evolutionary terms. A geologist friend of mine says, "Their theory proposed that most species exhibited little net evolutionary change over their geologic history, and that changes came through---restricted to rare and rapid events of branching speciation."

In other words, Gould recognized that the record does not show small, gradual changes from species to species over huge amounts of time. Species appear suddenly in the fossil record, rather than through gradual transition.

It seems to me that evolution (that is, macroevolution) is just a huge shell game. They extrapolate from microevolution to macroevolution.

The late Dr. Colin Patterson of the British Museum was a renowned evolutionist, who spoke at the American Museum of Natural History in New York City (11/5/81): "Gould and the American Museum people are hard to contradict when they say there are no transitional fossils...I will lay it on the line—there is not one such fossil for which one could make a watertight argument."

Creationist Luther Sunderland wrote a letter to Dr. Patterson, and the latter wrote him back. In his book *Darwin's Enigma*, Sunderland reproduces the letter which said: "So, much as I should like to oblige you by jumping to the defense of gradualism, and fleshing out the transitions between the major types of animals and plants, I find myself a bit short of the intellectual justification necessary for the job."

Patterson, author of the textbook, *Evolution*, also said in that letter: "I fully agree with your comments on the lack of direct illustration of evolutionary transitions in my book. If I knew of any, fossil or living, I would certainly have included them."

On December 15, 1987, I called Dr. Patterson in London from our office in Ft. Lauderdale and got to speak with him for several minutes.

He verified the authenticity of his letter to Sunderland. "Great," I said, then I explained how I was working on a film (final name: "The Case for Creation," hosted by the late D. James Kennedy---a type of Scopes Trial in reverse) and asked if we could possibly interview him for this program. He strongly declined to participate because he didn't agree with our premise.

He told me on the phone that despite the lack of evidence for evolution, he nonetheless still believed in evolution.

He said we just haven't discovered *yet* the right mechanism to prove evolution. But I ask: If the evidence isn't there for the premise of macroevolution, then why should we assume the evidence is there for the conclusion?

Indeed, it often appears that macroevolution is a predetermined conclusion in search of proof. If there's no creator God, something like evolution has to be true. One has to wonders if that's why so many tenaciously hold to it despite the lack of evidence.

God and Science---a Comment on the "Hands of God" in Space

1/13/14

Recently, a picture from outer space was posted that some thought looked like the "Hand of God."

Writing about it for space.com (1/9/14), Tanya Lewis said, "The hand might look like an X-ray from the doctor's office, but it is actually a cloud of material ejected from a star that exploded. NASA's NuSTAR spacecraft has imaged the structure in high-energy X-rays for the first time, shown in blue. Lower-energy X-ray light previously detected by NASA's Chandra X-ray Observatory is shown in green and red."

She began her piece, noting, "Religion and astronomy may not overlap often, but a new NASA X-ray image captures a celestial object that resembles the 'Hand of God.'"

This gives me an opportunity to ruminate on God and astronomy or religion and science.

There is often a perceived incompatibility between religion and science. I think that especially true after the rise and acceptance of Darwinism in the late 19th century.

However, it's interesting to note that essentially modern science was born in a Christian milieu about 500 years ago---with early contributions from the ancient Greeks.

All the great leading scientists initially were Bible-believing Christians. They believed that they were---in the words of astronomer Johannes Kepler, as we have seen---"thinking God's thoughts after Him."

They understood that a rational God had made a rational universe, and it was their job as scientists to discover those laws that the Creator had impressed into His creation.

Kepler (1571-1630) wrote, "Since we astronomers are priests of the highest God in regard to the book of nature, it befits us to be thoughtful, not of the glory of our minds, but rather, above all else, of the glory of God." The scientists were thus God's priests.

To the consternation of some unbelievers, Sir Isaac Newton, perhaps the greatest scientist who ever lived, wrote more on Christian theology than he did on science.

Newton saw God's powerful hand in His creation. He once said, "Atheism is so senseless. When I look at the solar system, I see the earth at the right distance from the sun to receive the proper amounts of heat and light. This did not happen by chance."

Sir Francis Bacon, who is credited with having been the inventor of the scientific method---that combination of induction and deduction, of hypothesis and proof (empirical proof). Bacon was a devout Christian.

Bacon noted, "There are two books laid before us to study, to prevent our falling into error; first, the volume of the Scriptures, which reveal the will of God; then the volume of the Creatures, which express His power."

In 1660, the Royal Society of London for Improving Natural Knowledge was founded. This organization is the oldest, perhaps most prestigious such organization.

James Moore of the Open University in England notes it was founded in a Puritan college (Gresham), and virtually all its early members were Puritans---at a time when Puritans were a small minority. He said that Protestantism "encouraged the birth of modern science."

I had the privilege of doing some TV interviews at the Royal Society (for our special on "What If Jesus Had Never Been Born?"---hosted by the late D. James Kennedy).

One of those I interviewed was physicist Sir Alan Cook. He said, "One of the implications of the incarnation that Christ took human form upon Him, including the power of thinking about things and observing things. It seems to me that an implication of the incarnation is that we, those of us who are able to, have a Christian obligation to study the world as God's creation."

I've had the privilege of interviewing on several occasions for my radio show Dr. Steven Meyer, who earned his Ph.D. in the philosophy of science at Cambridge. Dr. Meyer, a fellow at the Discovery Institute, is the author of the *New York Times* bestselling book, *Darwin's Doubt*.

I asked Dr. Meyer for a statement for this particular article. He wrote me: "Far from conflicting, the overwhelming scientific evidence of design in life and in the universe—in the digital code stored in DNA and in the fine tuning of the laws of physics, for example—clearly shows that science can—and does—provide support for a theistic view of reality."

So it comes as no shock to me to see the reported "Hand of God" in the heavens. I believe we see the "Hand of God" even in the study of the heavens.

"Darwin's Doubt"

7/23/13

Every time I log into a computer and have to enter my password, I'm reminded of how impossible evolution is.

One little mistake on the keypad, and I can't log in. There's even a website where I seem to be in permanent "log-in purgatory." I can't login ever. Granted, it's operator error. But still...

How does this tie to evolution? Because if evolution were true, then we are to believe a whole series of complex sequences managed to get everything right---repeatedly.

To use a clichéd example: It would be like a monkey typing at random and coming out with the complete works of Shakespeare without any errors.

There's a new book on evolution that is getting a lot of attention---and deservedly so. It is *Darwin's Doubt* by Stephen Meyer. If you're familiar with the topic, the subtitle is very clever "The Explosive Origin of Animal Life and the Case for Intelligent Design."

This is not some minor book by an "obscurantist backwoods fundamentalist." It is published by HarperCollins and was written by a man who earned his Ph.D. at Cambridge. This 500-page illustrated book made its way to 7th place on the *New York Times* bestseller list.

I had the privilege of interviewing Dr. Meyer of the Discovery Institute on my radio show last week. He said of his book, "The title tells the story. I tell the story of a doubt that Darwin had about his own theory." The doubt centers around what's known as the Cambrian Explosion.

About a decade ago, *TIME* magazine had a cover story on the Cambrian Explosion. They called it "Biology's Big Bang." Geologists place the Cambrian period, which they say was supposedly 550 million years ago, seven geological periods before the Jurassic one, as in *Jurassic Park.*

Meyer explains, "The Cambrian Explosion refers to the geologically sudden or abrupt appearance of the major group of animals early in the fossil record, in a period of time that geologists call the Cambrian." The key word is "abrupt."

In his classic book, *On the Origin of the Species*, Darwin wrote, "If it could be demonstrated that any complex organ existed which could not possibly have been formed by numerous, successive slight modifications, my theory would absolutely break down. But I can find out no such case."

But Meyer says Darwin was aware of the Cambrian period ("at first commonly called the Silurian" (*Darwin's Doubt*, p. 6)). Meyer says, "it was a challenge to his theory because he anticipated that the mechanism of natural selection, acting on random variations, would have to work very slowly and gradually. He thought that the variations would be slow, minute, and incremental. If they were big, the mechanism would create deformities that would not survive, so he thought the mechanism needed to generate small and incremental variations. And that would take a lot of time."

As noted, Darwin was aware of the Cambrian Explosion, but hoped that future discoveries would somehow nullify the significance of the Cambrian. However, they have not.

Meyer told my listeners, "What we see in the fossil record is the abrupt appearance of these animal forms. [Darwin] knew of some of them in his time. But he anticipated or hoped that subsequent generations of fossil-hunters and paleontologists would discover the ancestral precursors to these animal forms in the lower pre-Cambrian layers."

What has happened since *Origins* was first published in 1859? "In fact," says Meyer, "what's happened is that more and more Cambrian animals have been discovered---most of which have still lacked these ancestral forms. And so we have this pattern of very abrupt, discontinuous appearance, in contrast with the picture of the history of life, which Darwin drew of a slow, gradual, unfolding of life."

This problem for Darwinism is not just in the fossils. The so-called missing links are still missing. But Meyer also notes, "It's this deeper problem of coming up with a mechanism that explains complex animal life, especially in the wake of all the things we discovered in the last 50, 60 years in biology about the importance of information---digital code and other forms of information that are stored in DNA and elsewhere in the cell."

Meyer adds, "It's just like in computer science. If you want to have a new function on your computer, you've got to have lots of code, lots of instruction. If you want to build these complex animal forms, we now know, you need information, you need instructions. And that's the crucial question that is really creating an impasse in evolutionary theory. Where does that information come from?"

Oh, I get it---"In the beginning was the Word..."

On Religion and Climate Change

4/19/12

Earth Day is around the corner, and next week a religious group dedicated to the environment will be meeting in Washington, DC.

Their press release on the meeting declares, "Last November, religious leaders, groups and individuals came together to affirm climate change as a moral issue. So began Interfaith Moral Action on Climate (IMAC) a collaborative initiative spanning faiths, spiritual traditions and people of good will."

Their goal for their DC meeting next week will include "urging elected officials to decisively act on the greatest moral crisis of our time."

In their opinion, "climate change is a moral issue" that should be "a priority for the faithful nationwide."

Protecting the environment is surely a worthy goal. But as a layman, I don't understand how the scientists invoked could always be sure of these things. Things like the notion that man's activities (more exactly man's activities in developed countries) are what supposedly cause various catastrophes in nature.

Thirty five years ago, many scientists warned of the catastrophe of the earth cooling. In that short span, it heated up so much so that we're now at risk for global warming?

As I read the Bible, I see disasters in nature as a given in this fallen world. It's a curse because of man's sin. We can do much through science to limit the damage of these catastrophes. But in one sense, we're powerless to prevent them from happening.

Yet the bigger question is this: Are some of our activities, such as burning fossil fuels, actually causing global warming?

It used to be just "global warming" that was condemned. But that didn't sell well during terrible snow storms, such as the one that shut down a prominent presentation Al Gore was going to give against global warming. During such storms, people up north are probably thinking, "We could use a little global warming right now."

So somewhere along the line, "global warming" got morphed into "climate change." But...isn't there always climate change? How convenient.

Like the poor that are always with us, so also is climate change.
If there are specific things we do that harm the environment, like polluting rivers that cause illness for those down river, then such criminal acts should be halted, investigated, and prosecuted to the full extent of the law.

194

I also think that respect for nature improves life for most people. Whenever I visit Central Park, I'm so glad for those with the foresight to not let all of NYC be developed.

Appreciation for nature is one thing. But sometimes the environmentalists worship nature for all practical purposes. Whatever happened to the first commandment---"I am the Lord your God. You shall have no other gods before Me"?

I know Cal Beisner, the spokesperson for Cornwall Alliance, a conservative group opposed to climate change alarmism. The Cornwall slogan is "For the stewardship of creation."

I sent him an email about this upcoming interfaith meeting described above. He wrote me back with this comment: "One thing's for sure: These people don't speak for most American evangelicals, who, backed by solid science, overwhelmingly reject climate alarmism, and, backed by solid economics, reject calls to spend trillions of dollars and trap millions of people in poverty by denying them affordable and reliable energy in a vain attempt to mitigate global warming when even the alarmists' own climate models predict that such efforts would have no discernible effect on future temperature."

Beisner added, "Most American evangelicals stand with The Cornwall Alliance for the Stewardship of Creation, whose *Evangelical Declaration on Global Warming* has been endorsed by over 500 leading evangelical pastors, scientists, and economists."

Robert Nelson is a professor of environmental policy at the University of Maryland and a senior fellow with The Independent Institute of Oakland, California. He wrote, *The New Holy Wars: Economic Religion versus Environmental Religion in Contemporary America.*

Nelson writes, "With Earth Day fast approaching (April 22), Americans might want to consider how environmentalism is becoming a new form of religion. They also might want to ask: Why is it OK to teach environmental religion in public schools, while the teaching of Judaism, Christianity and other traditional religions is not constitutionally permitted?"

Personally, I believe it's best to worship the Creator and appreciate His creation than to worship the creation. After all, we could all wonder if global warming is truly settled science or perhaps just a lot of hot air.

A Baby Reflects the Glory of the Creator

7/8/13

Every day God glorifies Himself in His creation, whether we recognize it or not. That's true at the telescopic level or at the microscopic level and everywhere in between.

When I behold my newly born granddaughter, I can't believe the denial on the part of so many in our culture of the handiwork of the Creator.

Since her birth, I have done a little research on the humanity of the unborn. It's greater than we realize. What He has created and continues to create is mind-boggling. For example, grab a standard pencil and look at the eraser. We'll see the significance of that in just a moment.

It's strange that my daughter, the mom of my new grandchild, gained much weight in pregnancy; yet baby Elizabeth was only 8 pounds, 3 ounces upon birth. What were the extra pounds for? The cord, the placenta, the water, and other auxiliary mechanisms. We see how the mother's body feeds and nourishes the baby, first with colostrum (filled with antibodies, etc.), then with milk. All as God designed.

The Mayo Clinic Staff have put together some great information on fetal development. It seems the miracle begins at the very beginning and keeps on going from there. I didn't even read beyond the first trimester.

The Clinic says that by the time of…

· Fertilization…the baby's gender and "traits such as eye and hair color, and, to some extent, personality and intelligence" are set.

· Three weeks after conception…"your baby is about the size of the tip of a pen"

· Four weeks after conception…"your baby's heart is pumping blood." Also, four weeks after conception: "Basic facial features will begin to appear, including passageways that will make up the inner ear and arches that will contribute to the jaw." Yet at this point your baby's no bigger than the size of a pencil eraser.

· Five weeks after conception…"your baby's brain and face are rapidly developing."

· Seven weeks after conception…the baby's arms, elbows, toes, and eyelids develop. Yet the baby is only ¾ of an inch long at this stage.

· Eight weeks after conception...the eyelids begin to close for protection.

· Ten weeks after conception...fingernails now develop. Yet by this stage the baby only weighs about ½ an ounce.

And on it goes, in the miracle preceding birth. And this is only in the first three months.

Are we supposed to believe all this stuff just happened by chance?

Years ago I had the privilege of interviewing Dr. Michael Behe, a biology professor at LeHigh University in Pennsylvania and author of the book, *Darwin's Black Box*. He said that even the "simplest cell" in our bodies is so complex that it contains a great deal of information.

I asked him if one were to put all the information to be found in one cell of our bodies into books the size of the Encyclopedia Britannica, about how many volumes would this comprise?

He answered about two to three dozen volumes. That is how much information is found in one cell of the body human. And our bodies are comprised of about trillions of cells.

For those with eyes to see, God is glorified in His creation---even at the microscopic level.

Dr. Francis Collins, the director of the Human Genome Project and the author of the book, *The Language of God*, believes in God-ordained evolution. He and I can agree to disagree on that.

But he said, "If you printed out the sequence of the human genome on regular paper with regular font size and you stapled it all together and piled it up, it would be as tall as the Washington Monument. And you have that information inside each cell of your body."

Each of us is a walking miracle. But somehow it is more clearly seen in a baby.

Dr. Behe says the living cell is a masterpiece of design. It could not possibly have originated by chance: "In Darwin's day, scientists were vaguely aware that there were things such as cells, but most of them thought that they were like little pieces of Jell-O, little microscopic pieces of protoplasm. And in the middle of the nineteenth century, some scientists even thought that cells and life could kind of ooze up from the ocean bottom, just spontaneously..."

With advances in microbiology, we know better now. Besides, Milton Berle once quipped, "If evolution really works, how come mothers only have two hands?"

Three thousand years ago, King David said it best...in one of his Psalms of praise (#139).

David exalted God, "For you created my inmost being; you knit me together in my mother's womb. I praise you because I am fearfully and wonderfully made; your works are wonderful, I know that full well. My frame was not hidden from you when I was made in the secret place, when I was woven together in the depths of the earth. Your eyes saw my unformed body; all the days ordained for me were written in your book before one of them came to be."

For this new baby girl in our world, I am most grateful to Jesus Christ, who was not only the co-Creator of everything, including her---but He Himself experienced the miracle of birth.

Part 9.

Islam

A Warning to the West

10/7/10

Geert Wilders is in trouble with the politically correct crowd. Big trouble. Muslims and illiberal liberals of Europe want to make an example of him.

Who is Geert Wilders? He is a flamboyant-looking statesman from the Netherlands. He is a Member of their Parliament. He is the founder of an upstart political party in that country (Freedom Party), which is less than four years old and yet is on its way to becoming the leading party of the Netherlands. He is likely the future Prime Minister of Holland.

He is also a potential prisoner.

Geert Wilders is also a courageous man who is warning the West about the Islamization of the same and the freedoms lost in its wake.

In 2008, Geert Wilders made an Internet movie about radical Islam, called *Fitna* (Arabic for upheaval, chaos), and for that he is on trial in his own country for allegedly violating hate crimes laws. The European Union also wants him tried for hate crimes. The country of Jordan wants to extradite him to have him stand trial there. This is not to mention all the death threats against him.

Mohammed Rabbae of the National Council for Moroccans said of Wilders, "He divides, he creates hate, he creates conflicts between people. Some people can't accept this. Other people can."

His short film simply makes the point that the Jihadists---who attacked on 9/11, at the Madrid train bombing, in London in 2005, etc.---did what they did because they were obeying what the Qur'an tells them to do. That's the essence of his film. Ideas have consequences. Tell the faithful followers of Allah that they should slay the infidel wherever you find them (Surah 9:29 from the Qur'an), and 9/11 happens. That's the point Wilders makes in his movie.

Of course, most Muslims, including Qur'an-readers, do not engage in these Jihadist activities. Wilders admits as much. But those who do get their inspiration from the book, which he calls a "fascist" book, and which he thinks should be banned.

I sat down in early 2009 and had a television interview with Geert Wilders about all the controversy. (He had multiple body guards.) I asked him why he made the movie. He answered: "I've nothing against Muslim, but I fear the Islamization of our societies."

Many demographers have noted the increase in the Islamic population in many nations of Europe. Some are predicting that, if the present trends continue, Europe will be Islamic in about one or two generations.

Geert Wilders is warning about this. He said, "Libyan leader, Muammar Gaddafi, said not so long ago that, we have 50 million Muslims in Europe. We don't need one gun; we don't need one bullet; we will rule this continent in 10, 20, 30 years time, by the *Al-Hijra* [Arabic for the notion of conquest via immigration]. Europe will be ours, in the near future." So says Gaddafi.

Not if I can help it, says Geert Wilders, who has been accused of being xenophobic and even opposed to Muslim immigrants. What he actually says is that they are welcome in the West, provided they don't want to kill us and take away our freedoms. If they accommodate themselves, like other immigrants, fine. But if they have designs to practice their violence so as to impose their religion, that's not fine.

Wilders notes that Muslim men in Europe are overrepresented when it comes to committing crimes. He cites the case of Copenhagen, where about 70% of the crimes are committed by Muslim men (a slight minority compared to the total population).

Wilders has little respect for those European leaders who are constantly caving in to Muslim demands. He notes, "we are, unfortunately, led by appeasers. We have no Churchills anymore in Europe, just a lot of Chamberlains, politicians who are looking in the other direction, singing *Kumbaya*, all year long."

Wilders is paying a high price to make such politically incorrect warnings to the West. Since October 2004 when he started speaking out about the issue, he and his wife have had to have 24-hour armed protection for him everywhere he goes. He is in prison every night or army barracks or some sort of safe house. (Often different places in different nights, so as to avoid assassination). He told me in reference to this lifestyle: "it's something you don't wish your worst enemy, but still, if you have a mission...I always say that if I would moderate my voice, or if I would go out of politics and do something else, then, the people who use non-democratic means, that use violence, that threaten violence, they would win, and I will never let them win....If you don't like what I'm saying, go and do a debate. If you don't like my movie, make your own movie....But never use violence."

Geert Wilders' trial began on Monday (10/4), and he sent a message on Twitter, that he was having a "terrible day." While he can't go to jail any more than he's already in jail (in one sense), there can be a dangerous precedent set, should he lose his case. Speak out against radical Islam, and you will be punished.

The moral of the story? Watch Geert Wilders and what happens to him. He is the proverbial canary in the coal mine. I believe he is fighting the West's battle for freedom. If he loses, freedom loses.

Please, Don't Burn The Qur'an

9/7/10

A pastor in Gainesville, Florida is garnering international headlines because he is threatening to do something bold, but totally misguided, in my opinion. He wants his flock to burn copies of the Qur'an on the 9th anniversary of 9/11.

This minister sees the evil done in the name of Islam, and he wants to make a point. The problem is that the point he wants to make has a price tag. General Petraeus warns that this could cause American troops halfway around the world to be killed. But Pastor Terry Jones of the fifty-member Dove World Outreach Center in Gainesville is undeterred. It's so sad because in one sense the pastor could end up being responsible for the deaths of each every American killed needlessly over this kerfuffle. There were people killed over the false---*false*---report that a Qur'an was flushed down a toilet at Gitmo. There were even people killed by rioting Muslims who were angry over Danish *cartoons*, for heaven's sake.

Remember how Christians were upset in 1988 at Martin Scorsese's blasphemous movie, *The Last Temptation of Christ?* Remember all the violence that occurred when the film was released? There was none, to my knowledge. Remember all the theatres destroyed by protesting Christians? The only theatre destruction I read about took place in France at the hands of a Muslim who was upset because of the mistreatment of Jesus, who is taught in Islam to be a prophet.)

Meanwhile, would Pastor Jones burn a book that says:

· Jesus is the Christ?
· Jesus is the Word of God?
· Jesus is born of a virgin?

· Jesus will return to earth one day?

The answer is that he will burn such a book on 9/11 because the Qur'an says all of these things. It also says, of course, that God has no Son, and it says many other things that directly contradict the Christian message. But that doesn't mean it should be torched. All that does is close the door further (as if it could be) to Muslims potentially interested in the message of Jesus.

Regardless of the message of the Qur'an, the pastor is ill advised to burn it. Since Jesus is the one who originated the Golden Rule, and since the pastor would not want a Muslim to burn the Bible, then I don't think he should burn anyone's holy book either.

That doesn't mean I agree with the Qur'an. The Qur'an commands Muslims to strike terror in the heart of the unbeliever. That is what 9/11 was all about---striking terror in the heart of the Great Satan, America.

Here we are in an extraordinarily tolerant country, America, and yet we get accused of supposedly being "Islamaphobic" because of the vocal (and right-minded) opposition to the Ground Zero Mosque. Why do I say right minded? Good heavens, there are plenty of mosques in New York City. There's even one a few blocks away from Ground Zero. The Ground Zero Mosque is about one thing---a trophy of domination. That mosque, if it's built, will communicate loud and clear: "We won, you lost." They even wanted it to be built and opened up on 9/11/2011---so that on the tenth anniversary of the worst attack on American soil, those in league with the attackers would declare their triumph over their enemies.

If the pastor burns the Qur'an, he will in one sense prove America's critics partially right. He doesn't speak for me, nor you. But tell that to some Afghan villager who hears that his holy book is being desecrated on American soil. The riots have already begun, on just the announcement of the proposed Qur'an-burning.

This ploy to burn the Qur'an is wrong on every front. All it will do is to inflame those who need to be most reached. It will play into the hands of Islamic enemies of the United States, of whom there are many.

I read recently that only 18% of Muslims around the world have a positive view of America. This kind of ploy could make that number even worse.

I suppose the pastor has the right to do so---free "speech" in America even includes burning the flag. But it's so counter-productive for him to do it. It will just make the crazies hate us even more (if that were possible).

Contrary to the prevailing mindset among liberals, America really is not "Islamaphobic." There are approximately 1200 mosques throughout the country, as opposed to even *one* legal church or synagogue in Saudi Arabia. No, not one.

C. S. Lewis, the great Oxford and Cambridge professor and writer, once quipped, The Devil is always trying to trick us to extremes. Sadly, he's doing a good job.

What Part of "Death to America!" Don't We Understand?

8/5/15

No deal at all is better than a bad deal. I think that is especially true with the recent deal with Iran that President Obama and Secretary of State Kerry are touting.

On a weekly basis, Iranian leaders incite crowds with shouts of "Death to America!" and "Death to Israel!" We're the great Satan. Israel is the little Satan. They want our destruction---so why would our government ever pave the way toward Iran possibly getting a nuclear bomb?

I asked Robert Spencer of jihadwatch.org for a statement for this column on Iran and the bomb and Obama's recent deal with them.

Spencer wrote me: "The Iran deal is an unmitigated disaster. Not only does it sanction Iran's nuclear program, but by the removal of sanctions, it finances it. Obama has betrayed (yet again) an ally and endangered the entire free world. That is and will remain his true legacy."

Some of the Iranian leaders have even denied the Holocaust. Yet they seem intent on creating a new one. Liberals, like the president, have said they would like to see the world free from more nuclear bombs. Yet this deal could possibly start a nuclear arms race in the Middle East.

I have even heard some speculate that the mad mullahs in charge in Iran would be willing to use a bomb on Israel, if they got one. They know they would be destroyed by Israel in retaliation, but they would accomplish two things by this:

1) They would take out Israel, "the little Satan," which has been a thorn in the side of radical Islam since it was re-established in 1948; and

2) Even though millions of Iranians would die through retaliation, they would ostensibly die as martyrs for Jihad, therefore they'd go to paradise.

John Wohlstetter is an expert on the Middle East and is a senior fellow with the Discovery Institute. He wrote a book on nuclear weapons, called *Sleepwalking with the Bomb.*

In a recent radio interview about Iran and the bomb, he told me, "America worries about its security. Israel worries about its survival."

He added that if Iran got nuclear weapons, "I think that it is likely they will use them in some way. Now, if they're going to fire a nuclear weapon in the sense of aiming at cities, I think Israel is your most logical target. If they're going to fire at us, maybe they'd try a single shot that is an electro-magnetic pulse attack, which could short out our infrastructure in a worst case---our national grid. That one would be hard to trace."

Thankfully, Israeli Prime Minister Benjamin Netanyahu does understand this very real threat.

In his brilliant speech before Congress on March 3, 2015 (that the president snubbed), he said, "I'm standing here in Washington, D.C. and the difference is so stark. America's founding document promises life, liberty, and the pursuit of happiness. Iran's founding document pledges death, tyranny, and the pursuit of jihad. And as states are collapsing across the Middle East, Iran is charging into the void to do just that."

Netanyahu reminded everyone that Ayatollah Khomeini, the prime mover in Iran's 1979 revolution toward draconian Islam, told his followers to "export the revolution throughout the world."

Although Iran is Shiite (representing roughly 15% of all Islam), the vast majority of Islam, the Sunni population, includes many radical Muslims as well. ISIS and Al-Qaeda are Sunni groups. Hezbollah is Shiite. One is tempted to say, pick your poison.

A Christian couple best known for their music ministry, Jimmy and Carol Owens, wrote an open letter recently to the president and secretary of state, wherein they quoted some of the Haddith, the sayings of Mohammed, showing that deception to advance Islam was okay.

Their open letter stated, "Here are some quotes from their founder himself, the prophet Mohammed:

"....Bukhari 4,52,267 Mohammed cried out, 'Jihad is deceit.'

"Bukhari 5,59,369 Bin Maslama volunteered to kill an enemy for Mohammed, then said, 'Give me permission to deceive him with lies so that my plot will succeed.' Mohammed replied, 'You may speak falsely to him.'"

And they summarize all this in a sentence: "If deception to an enemy is advantageous to Islam, it is not a sin."

The Bible is very clear. We should be as wise as serpents and as innocent as doves. This deal is so bad it should be opposed by all Americans, especially the legislative body which Obama deliberately sought to avoid by not calling it a treaty. But a rose by any other name... What part of "Death to America!" doesn't he understand?

To paraphrase satirist Tom Lehrer, "We'll try to stay serene and calm...when the Ayatollah gets the bomb!"

"Enough, Enough, Enough"

2/10/11

The Egyptian uprising has been dominating the news lately. But there's a story beneath the surface that needs to be told as well.

And that is all the Christians that are at risk, not only in Egypt but throughout the Middle East.

The Muslims have persecuted the Christians for centuries now. But sometimes there has been a fragile peace. In recent times that peace seems to have been shattered.

For example, Christians came to worship at a Catholic cathedral in Baghdad on Sunday morning on November 1, 2010. Suddenly, militant Islamists burst into the building armed to the hilt, and they began to systematically kill worshipers, including the priest at the altar.

An American nun wrote about one of the most remarkable aspects of this slaughter, which claimed at least 58 people:

> Among the victims of this senseless tragedy was a little boy named Adam. Three-year-old Adam witnessed the horror of dozens of deaths, including that of his own parents. He wandered among the corpses and the blood, following the terrorists around and admonishing them, "enough, enough,

206

enough." According to witnesses, this continued for two hours until Adam was himself murdered.

When you look at the photo of Adam (reproduced below) and you look how happy he seemed to be, and then you consider how tragically his life ended, it puts a human face on all the suffering going on in the Christian communities of the Middle East.

At the very beginning of this year, on New Year's Day, 2000 Christian worshipers were leaving a church in Alexandria, Egypt. A suicide bomber detonated a bomb, killing himself and at least 21 Christians and wounding about 100 more, some seriously.

The scene was out of a horror movie. As body parts were scattered all over, some Muslim extremists came out of the shadows and jumped on these remains, screaming, "Allahu Akbar!"

What's interesting to note about this bombing is that an hour before the suicide bombing went off and killed all those Christians and wounded so many others, several of the security forces left the church they were supposed to guard, leaving only a skeletal crew behind. Many suspected that somebody received a tip off as to what was about to happen.

Tragically, incidents like these in Baghdad and in Alexandria are starting to become more common, at least on a smaller scale. I spoke recently with Rev. Julian Dobbs, who heads the Church and Islam Project of the North American Convocation of Anglicans. He said, "too often in places where there was a relative peace, Christians, our brothers and sisters, are now living with the regular threat and challenge of persecution and suffering for their faith."

One of the problems, of course, involves changing religion. You can come and go within Christianity. But you apparently only leave Islam in a pine box. Says Dobbs, "As painful and difficult as it is for us to understand this in this modern generation, Islam is the only religion I know of in the world which calls for the execution of those who leave the faith."

Not all Muslims are terrorists, of course, but these days it seems that virtually all terrorists are Muslims. You would think that the non-violent Muslims would have a vested interest in speaking out against their violent brethren, lest they all be condemned with the same brush.

I know a man who fled his native Lebanon two decades ago because of anti-Christian persecution. In his native land, he was a lawyer and an advocate on behalf of Christians in Lebanon. Today, he's a spokesman on Middle Eastern issues in Washington, DC. His name is Dr. Walid Phares, and you often see him on major media outlets, CNN, Fox News, ABC, NBC, CBS, etc.

Dr. Phares has often written on the issue of Jihad, and his latest book---which was written before the upheaval in Tunisia and now in Egypt---is entitled, *The Coming Revolution: Struggle for Freedom in the Middle East.*

He told me recently, how for the "Al Qaida and its cohorts in the region are openly saying that they are at war, at jihad with the Christians, and they want to, ethnically cleanse them from the region."

Dr. Phares added, "If there is any emergency worldwide for the international community to support a community, endangered community, would be the Christian in the Middle East."

If extremist groups in Egypt, such as the Muslim Brotherhood, gain much power, this does not bode well for those who want to live in peace---including the millions of Christians there.

Just like little Adam of Baghdad, we must say in reference to the Muslim slaughter of the innocent Christians in the Middle East, "Enough. Enough. Enough!"

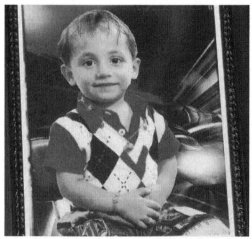

Photo of Adam of Baghdad, posted on the Christians of Iraq.com website: He cried out to the Islamic attackers (before they killed him), "Enough, enough, enough!"

Faithful, Even Unto Death

2/18/15

The AP reports that 21 Coptic Christians were beheaded in Libya. They were faithful unto death. Their murderers were Islamic State (IS) members, in affiliation with the main body of IS, which is in Syria and in Iraq.

The video shows 21 captives in orange jumpsuits with each captive being led by an IS member at the Libyan shores of the Mediterranean Sea. The Christians are forced to get down on their knees, and are then beheaded. All of the captors had their faces covered, to hide their identities.

I suppose you could say this was IS's version of the St. Valentine's Day Massacre---although we don't know when the executions actually took place.

In the video, the leader of the Islamic militants says to the camera: "All crusaders: safety for you will be only wishes, especially if you are fighting us all together. Therefore we will fight you all together."

He also says, "The sea you have hidden Sheikh Osama bin Laden's body in, we swear to Allah we will mix it with your blood."

And he adds, looking across toward Italy, only 500 miles away or so: "We will conquer Rome, by Allah's permission."

Amazingly, the Obama White House will only claim that the victims were Egyptians (not naming them as Christians), nor will it identify the murderers as Muslims, but rather it says that the Islamic State "is unconstrained by faith, sect, or ethnicity."

Coptic Christians are from Egypt, and they trace their movement back to when St. Mark, writer of the second Gospel, came there and proclaimed the gospel and was martyred there.

The word Coptic is derived from the word Egypt, and it was the dominant religion until the forces of Islam conquered Egypt in the 7th century.

It's fascinating to me that in Revelation, the final book of the Bible, there is a depiction of the saints of God who are waiting to be avenged since they have been unjustly killed.

"How long, O Lord?" is their cry. When will He vindicate them? The fascinating aspect of all this is that many of them are beheaded, which is not necessarily the most common historical form of martyrdom. But it is certainly used by the radical Muslims on many occasions.

Of course, there was anti-Christian persecution and martyrdom centuries before the followers of Mohammed (died 632) unleashed more persecution on the Church.

Jesus told His disciples that they were to be His witnesses for Him unto all the world. The Greek word we translate as "witness" is the word from which the word "martyr" is derived. So many of those early Christians, including almost all of the apostles, were witnesses for Christ unto death that the word came to mean, "one who testifies unto death."

After having seen and even touched Jesus following His resurrection from the dead, the disciples were willing to be put to death for their message rather than deny what they had witnessed.

My long-time pastor, the late Dr. D. James Kennedy spoke about how one of the heroes of the faith that really touched him was Polycarp, who lived in the first and second centuries. He was a direct disciple of John, who wrote the fourth Gospel.

Said Dr. Kennedy of this man: "Polycarp was brought to trial when he was eighty-six years old. He said that as a child and through all of his life he had followed Christ, and Christ had never failed him. He had ever been faithful. How could he deny Him now? And Polycarp was martyred for his faith and received that crown of life."

Martyrdom has been a common occurrence for many Christians through the centuries. In his classic book, *The Cost of Discipleship*, Dietrich Bonhoeffer, Christian martyr of the Nazis, said, "When Christ calls a man, he bids him come and die." That is, to die unto himself. Martyrdom would be the ultimate example of that.

I pray in reference to the persecutors of the Christians, e.g., the radical Muslims, that God would redeem them---or remove them.

Meanwhile, Christ calls His followers to be faithful, even unto death, as were those 21 brave Coptic Christians last weekend.

The Hundredth Anniversary of a Tragedy--- Eerily Familiar

7/16/15

A hundred years ago around this time a terrible massacre was taking place against Christians. It was the Armenian massacre, where literally hundreds of thousands of Christians were slaughtered just for being Christian by Muslims in what is now Turkey.

It is eerily similar to the crisis of today, where ISIS and Boko Haram and other radical Islamic groups are killing Christians just for being Christian. Masterminds of ISIS are scheming of new sadistic ways to kill their enemies, to videotape it, and post it on the Internet.

The 20th century was the most anti-Christian century on record. It was also the bloodiest century on record. In fact, the term genocide was coined in the 20th century.

The first of the genocides of the bloodiest century on record was that of the Armenians, who were all professing Christians, in Turkey. The world did nothing about it at the time, despite being informed.

Henry Morgenthau, the American Ambassador to (what was then) Constantinople, sent a telegram back home, dated July 16, 1915, describing the ongoing attacks against "peaceful Armenians."

He wrote: "…from harrowing reports of eye witnesses it appears that a campaign of race extermination is in progress under a pretext of reprisal against rebellion."

Years ago, I had the privilege of interviewing the late church statistician, Dr. David Barrett, who has been recognized as a pioneer researcher of Christian missions. He spoke with me at length about martyrdom, including the slaughter of the Armenians.

He told me that the genocide of the Christians in Turkey began earlier than 1915, "There was an official attempt to wipe out the Christian population of Turkey from about 1880 onwards, which finally succeeded by the year 1915….Most of the Christians were Armenians or Assyrians, and so those two races were decimated in clear cases of genocide."

Later, hundreds of thousands of Armenian Christians were massacred "in the final stages of getting these people out of the country," he noted.

Barrett said that in addition to the ones directly killed, there were also hundreds of thousands of Armenians who were displaced: "Nobody knows what happened to them. They just disappeared into the deserts; they were literally taken to the end of the bus or train journeys, dumped and told to move in that direction. So this is one of the worst cases in the history of martyrdom."

Meanwhile, how did the Muslims directly kill the Christians?

Dr. Barrett says, "They would arrive in the village fully armed, of course. They lined up everybody and would go from one person to another saying, 'Mohammed or Christ?'"

The Armenians have a liturgical phrase "Christ, only Christ." This is similar to phrases we are familiar with in English, such as, "Lord, have mercy. Christ, have mercy…"

Barrett continues: "Christian after Christian, even the small toddlers, would say 'Christ, only Christ,' and then they were bayonetted to death. Then on to the next person, and on to the next person, and on to the next person."

He says that was not the only way they killed the Christians, but he noted "to this day the Turkish government will not admit that this was genocide."

All told, somewhere between 600,000 to 1.5 million Armenian Christians were slaughtered.

Two decades later, Hitler justified some of his own actions and the way they'd be viewed by history, noting, "Who, after all, speaks today of the annihilation of the Armenians?"

Martyrdom is as old as the Christian church. I've been watching a good Christian movie recently on the life of Polycarp, the 2nd century saint who died in Smyrna, which is today also in Turkey.

The lead character says of a young martyr for Christ: "Germanicus did not have his life taken from him. He gave it willingly….He did not fear death, only denying the Lord."

Then he adds, "One cannot truly live…until he knows what he's willing to die for. Germanicus had the love in him that overcomes fear. Our sorrow is real….He is alive in the Lord. Great is his reward."

As we think about what happened to the Armenian Christians a hundred years ago, it is hard not to think about what radical Muslims are doing to Christians in many parts of the world today, especially the Middle East.

As noted, in the book of Revelation, we read about martyrs for Christ: "They cried out with a loud voice, 'How long, O Sovereign Lord, holy and true, until You judge and avenge our blood on those who dwell on the earth?'" The day is coming when God will set everything right. Meanwhile, as we have opportunity, we should speak out on behalf of today's victims of anti-Christian vitriol and violence.

Political Correctness on Islam
Can Lead to More Killings

7/21/15

Last week a young man shot and killed five of our military men in a recruitment center in Chattanooga. Initially, everyone was asking why. Some of those interviewed on TV seemed to have no clue as to the motive.

My colleague at D. James Kennedy Ministries, John Rabe, wrote a whole book along these lines. It's called *None Dare Call It Islam*

In reference to this tragic bloodbath in Tennessee, Rabe says: "Once again, the Obama Administration—along with much of the U.S. media—is playing its 'My, my, my, *whatever* could've been his motive?' game with Mohammod Youssef Abdulazeez, the young man who killed five U.S. servicemen at a recruiting station in Chattanooga before he was himself killed by police. His family blames "pot and alcohol" and says he suffered from depression."

Many months ago *TIME* Magazine (9/29/14) had a quote from British Prime Minister David Cameron on ISIS: "They are not Muslims. They are murderers." With all due respect to the Prime Minister---they *are* Muslims, and they *are* murderers.

Our president said something similar after the beheading of American James Foley in August. "ISIL speaks for no religion. No just God would stand for what they did yesterday, or what they do every day. No faith teaches people to murder innocents" (presstv.com, 8/20/14).

It's news to ISIL that they have nothing to do with Islam. Whatever you call them, ISIL (the Islamic State of Iraq and the Levant) or ISIS (Islamic State of Iraq and Syria) or IS (Islamic State) certainly has to do with Islam. They are informed by Islam which says to slay the infidel wherever you may find them (Surah 9:5) and to kill the Muslim who leaves his religion. This doesn't mean every Muslim is a terrorist. But very often these days every terrorist is a Muslim.

Many in the West deal with Islam through the prism of political correctness. Yes, the thinking goes, there are a few bad apples among the Muslims today, but the Christians had their crusades.

The crusades lasted roughly from 1100-1300 AD, where "Christian" armies sought to make Jerusalem safe once again for

Christian pilgrims. They came in response to the aftermath of the Muslim conquest of Jerusalem in 637. No conquest of Jerusalem, no crusades, perhaps.

I don't often agree with Bill Maher, and I was even a guest on his program four times when it was on ABC-TV. It was usually four against one, and I was the one.

But Maher eloquently showed how ludicrous it is to draw this moral equivalence between Islam and Christianity. He was a guest on Charlie Rose's PBS program recently, and he wouldn't let Rose equate Islam to Christianity, as the mainstream media so often does. Here is some of their dialogue:

"MAHER: Vast numbers of Christians do not believe that if you leave the Christian religion you should be killed for it. Vast numbers of Christians do not treat women as second class citizens. Vast numbers of Christians --

"ROSE: I agree with that --

"MAHER: -- do not believe if you draw a picture of Jesus Christ you should get killed for it.... There was a Pew poll in Egypt done a few years ago -- 82% said, I think, stoning is the appropriate punishment for adultery. Over 80% thought death was the appropriate punishment for leaving the Muslim religion. I'm sure you know these things.

"ROSE: Well I do. But I don't believe --

"MAHER: So to claim that this religion is like other religions is just naive and plain wrong. It is not like other religious. The *New York Times* pointed out in an op-ed a couple weeks ago that in Saudi Arabia just since August 4th, they think it was, they have beheaded 19 people. Most for non-violent crimes including homosexuality....[I]n Mecca where infidels, non-Muslims, are not even allowed in the holy parts of the city....They do behead people. Now if they were beheading people in Vatican City, which is the equivalent of Mecca, don't you think there would be a bigger outcry about it?"

I never thought I'd say it, but, good for Bill Maher. If we can't speak the truth about what motivates the radical Muslims, then we'll enable them to go on killing innocent people. Yet our politicians and news media so often cover up for Islam.

We are ill-served by our officials and the mainstream media these days in their treatment on Islam. We are told that Islam is a religion of peace and that most Muslims just want peace. But where are they? Why are they not marching in the streets against these violent Jihadists?

When the religious motivation (to serve Allah by killing the infidel) is censored out by politicians and the media, then we misread and miscategorize what's going on---thus, opening the door for more such killings. It was wrong to call the Fort Hood shooting an example of "workplace violence." The shooter gave ample instances that he was motivated by his interpretation of Islam. He shouted, "Allahu Akbar," in his attack. He had given out copies of the Qur'an in advance. His calling card even used the acronym "SOA"---Soldier of Allah.

Political correctness disarms us in advance from protecting the innocent in this ongoing conflict.

What Was Left Out of the 9/11 Memorials?

9/13/11

Now that the dust has settled from the memorials commemorating the 10th anniversary of 9/11, we can see what was included and what was excluded.

I was pleased that the president read Scripture (from Psalm 46).

I was displeased that the mayor of New York City chose not to invite any Christian clergyman to participate, as this would supposedly violate the separation of church and state.

Never mind that the founders of this country ---by their words and by their actions---showed over and over again that they intended religion (by which they meant Christianity in its various stripes) to flourish, even in the public arena, on a voluntary basis.

Technically, if the mayor's interpretation of the first amendment is right, what in the world is the president doing reading from the Holy Bible---at an official function, no less?

It is good that the dead of 9/11 were honored. It is good that also honored were the many heroes of that time---such as the firemen, who rushed into the World Trade Center to save as many lives as they could.

But there was something else generally missing from the 9/11 commemorations. Conspicuous by its absence.

If you had no idea about the history of 9/11, and you observed Sunday's commemorations, you might well think that all these poor people were killed by a natural disaster, not a deliberate attack.

The threat of radical Islam was not mentioned (or if it was, I missed it). This is a threat that is alive today, just as it was alive on that Tuesday ten years ago.

Thereligionofpeace.com maintains a counter, keeping track of how many separate attacks there have been, worldwide, by Jihadists since 9/11. The Madrid train bombing counts as just one. The 7/7/05 double-decker bus bombings, etc. in London count as another one. How many have there been? 17,729. [Editor's note: As of 3/23/16, the number is 238025. These figures are available at www.thereligionofpeace.com.]

Although Christians and Jews (and atheists and others) are often the targets of these attacks, usually, radical Islamists kill Muslims, who don't share their radical views---more than any other group.

Why are they doing this? The radical Muslims are obeying their understanding of the Qur'an that they are to slay the infidel wherever you find them (Surah 9:5). (Heretics can be viewed as infidels.)

It's estimated that of the 1.5 billion or so Muslims around the world, less than 15% are committed to a radical version of Islam. The problem is that 15% of 1.5 billion people are still tens of millions of people.

As we've seen, political Correctness keeps us from naming the enemy---radical Islam. Why do they hate us? Because we won't convert.

Again, not every Muslim believes the way of the terrorist. On my radio show last night, I interviewed a living Muslim hero, Dr. Zuhdi Jasser, the president of the American Islamic Forum for Democracy, who is the host of the documentary, *The Third Jihad*.

I asked Dr. Jasser about the Fort Hood shooting. Eyewitnesses said the alleged shooter cried out, "Allahu Akbar" ("Allah is the greatest," which is what radical Muslims cry out before they kill someone), as he shot and killed thirteen and wounded others; his card had "SOA" printed on it (standing for Soldier of Allah).

Yet the Pentagon came out in 2010 with an 86-page report on the Fort Hood shooting, and it didn't mention: Islam, Muslim, Qur'an, "Allahu Akbar," etc. It didn't even mention the shooter's name (Nidal Hasan), presumably because it is a Muslim name.

How can we win in this war that we didn't ask for, if we can't even name the enemy that wants to kill us?

Dr. Jasser noted, "I think [the Pentagon report] is demonstrating that we are completely wasting our time, and that we're not addressing the root causes which are the separatism of political Islam from American-type societies." He added that as a medical doctor, he has to diagnose illnesses all the time, or he'll never be able to properly treat the patient. Because of political correctness, we're not treating the threat of radical Islam properly.

Vengeance is *Ours*, Says the Islamist

1/13/15

In the Bible is a remarkable statement: "'Vengeance is Mine,' says the Lord, 'I will repay.'" This means that God's honor is not up to us to defend in the ultimate sense---not that we should not lovingly, graciously speak out when we can, if He is dishonored.

But this is a huge difference between the Christian and the Islamist. The Islamist is the radical Muslim committed to Islamic superiority and willing to kill for it. In effect, the Islamist says, "Vengeance is *ours*. We will repay."

It was Islamists that engaged in the infamous slaughter in Paris at the cartoon magazine offices.

In reaction to the violent attack in Paris last week, Howard Dean said on MSNBC, "I stopped calling these people Muslim terrorists. They're about as Muslim as I am."

He continued, "I mean they have no respect for anybody else's life, that's not what the Qur'an says. And, you know, Europe has an enormous radical problem....I think ISIS is a cult. Not an Islamic cult. I think it's a cult."

It fascinates me that liberals, who are quick to blame Christians for anything---justly or unjustly---engage in semantic gymnastics to try and separate Islam from the frequent and widespread killing by Islamists. But that is a futile exercise and just leads to impotency in dealing with this very real threat to all of us.

John Wohlstetter, a senior fellow with the Discovery Institute, is a national security and foreign policy expert. I interviewed him for my radio show in the wake of the Paris killings. I told him that as a follower of Jesus, I would not want to publish those anti-Muslim cartoons because I want to reach Muslims for Christ, not offend them.

He responded, "That makes sense as manners. But....what is at stake here is, Do we define the ambit [the range] of our freedom of speech or do our adversaries?"

After the Paris massacre, Wohlstetter noted in his blog at letterfromthecapitol.com, "Ditch multiculturalism, or kiss freedom goodbye...We cannot prevail unless we identify the enemy." I would add that we don't to read Sun-Tzu's *Art of War* to know how critical that last point is.

In Christianity, God will right all wrongs in the end. He will judge and He will hold all accountable. In Islam, it is up to the individual to uphold the honor of Islam, Mohammad, and the family honor. Any slights against these should be avenged by Muslims.

That explains much of the bloodshed from radical Muslims. In contrast, forgiveness is a Christian concept. In Christianity, God's divine Son even submits Himself to crucifixion for the forgiveness of His enemies. We Christians, rather than killing to defend His honor, are to share the message of reconciliation with God through Christ to everyone, personally forgiving our own enemies as we go. Not that Christians always live up to that, but it is the ideal taught by our faith.

Jesus is the source of our freedom and forgiveness. For example, in 1777, when he was an active member of an orthodox church, Thomas Jefferson wrote the Virginia Statute for Religious Freedom. It was passed in 1786. It was a key forerunner to our First Amendment.

Jefferson said, "Almighty God hath created the mind free...all attempts to influence it by temporal punishments...are a departure from the plan of the holy author of our religion [i.e., Jesus], who being lord both of body and mind, yet choose not to propagate it by coercions on either, as was in his Almighty power to do, but to exalt it by its influence on reason alone..."

Since Jesus gives humans freedom to accept or reject Him, it is wrong for us to compel belief.

All religious force does is to "beget habits of hypocrisy," according to Jefferson.

I know some Coptic Christians from Egypt, whose people are routinely persecuted by Muslims. They told me that the Copts have a saying to this effect: "God will protect the Bible. But the Muslims need to protect the Qur'an."

This is why after the slayings in the satirical magazine in Paris, one of the shooters was heard to say, "Now we have avenged the Prophet."

Meanwhile, Christians peacefully protest anti-Christian bigotry, which never seems to end; but we don't kill anybody over it, nor should we. After all, "Vengeance is *Mine*," says the Lord. "I will repay."

Praising Allah at the National Cathedral

11/19/14

Recently, I had the privilege to visit the National Cathedral in Washington, DC. Someone asked me, "What were you doing there?" My response: "Worshiping Jesus Christ."

Before and after the beautiful service, it was a delight to walk around and see what's there---such as the stone sarcophagus of Woodrow Wilson, with just his name and the years of his birth and death. He died in 1924. The cathedral was built in 1907. This was the only presidential grave I saw there in my abridged, unofficial tour.

The National Cathedral is part of the Episcopal Church. It is not officially part of the U. S. government, in that we have "no establishment of religion" in America. By design. A good design. The founders wanted to make sure there would be no religion "by law established" in America at the federal level.

That does not mean the founders did not welcome the acknowledgement of God in public life. After all, the same men who gave us the First Amendment set up the chaplain system and paid clergymen to serve in the legislatures and military. By design. A good design.

There were many things to see at the cathedral that fascinated me---reminders of our nation's rich Christian heritage. There is a huge statue of George Washington, the lifelong Anglican, who said in his Farewell Address that "religion and morality" are "indispensable supports to our political prosperity." He also said that morality cannot be maintained without religion. (He said it at a time when about 99% of the country was professing Christians.)

How sad, then, it was to learn that the National Cathedral recently invited a Muslim imam to praise Allah in an official worship service there.

One report noted, "The planners say this is the first time the cathedral has invited Muslims to lead their own prayers there, which they call a 'powerful symbolic gesture.'"

Columnist Robert Knight, in his article "A Brave New World of Intolerance" (*Washington Times*, 11/17/14), notes: "The cathedral, indeed, sent a powerful message---of weakness. Many Muslims will see it as akin to raising their flag over a conquered enemy."

The imam came and said his prayers there last Friday (11/14/14). Meanwhile, the officials kicked out a brave, unruly Christian lady who was objecting out loud to this event.

It is ironic to me that on the day I write this (11/17/14), I received an email from Christian Concern out of England on their plan to "launch an initiative to help protect those in the UK who want to leave Islam but fear the consequences of doing so."

They write: "Entitled 'Safe Haven', the project has been launched in response to the brutal treatment in the UK of some who have left Islam and become Christians." Some of those who will participate in their campaign on 11/18/14 include former Muslims who have converted to Christianity. According to strict Muslim law, the penalty for leaving Islam should be death.

One of those ex-Muslims who plans to testify for "Safe Haven" said, "My own family would rather see me dead." In short, tolerance toward someone else's religion seems to come only from the Christian side of the fence, but never the other side, where "tolerance" is crushed under the bulldozer of a totalitarian ideology.

America is a free country, and if the Episcopal Church wants to invite an imam to say prayers at the National Cathedral, who can stop them?

But are these professing Christians pleasing the Lord? Jesus Christ said, "I am the way, the truth, and the life. No one comes to the Father but by Me." I'm sure their answer would be something like: "Tolerance. That's why we invited the imam. We all worship the same God anyway."

G. K. Chesterton once said, "Tolerance is the virtue of the man without convictions."

The aforementioned Woodrow Wilson, whose body is entombed at the National Cathedral, said in a 1911 rally in Denver: "A nation which does not remember what it was yesterday, does not know what it is today, nor what it is trying to do. We are trying to do a futile thing if we do not know where we came from or what we have been about..."

In the same speech, he said, "America was born a Christian nation. America was born to exemplify that devotion to the elements of righteousness which are derived from the revelations of Holy Scripture."

Too bad the powers that be at the National Cathedral seem to be oblivious to what Washington or Wilson or, more importantly, Jesus has had to say. I'm reminded again of a quote from Chesterton: "These are the days when the Christian is expected to praise every creed except his own."

Shariah Law—Incompatible with Basic Rights
2/15/11

In the wake of a largely peaceful revolution in Egypt—a people's revolt, if you will—we keep hearing more and more about Shariah law.

In fact, some surveys of the Egyptian people have found widespread support for Shariah.

What exactly is Shariah, and what would it mean for Egyptians?

Very simply, it is strict Islamic law.

I spoke recently with an Egyptian woman who grew up in a Muslim household and has since converted to Christianity.

She lives safely in the United States. But if she lived back in Egypt, she could easily be murdered because of Shariah law.

The Egyptian woman I spoke with is Nonie (pronounced NON-ee) Darwish, author of the books, *Now They Call Me Infidel* and *Cruel and Usual Pun*ishment.

She said, "The word Shariah is an Arabic word meaning literally 'the way.' It's the way to live. And Shariah is a set of very detailed laws."

These laws are found both in the Qur'an and also the Hadith, which are the collection of the sayings of Mohammed.

Nonie notes, "Whatever Mohammed did in the 7th century became the law for the Muslims to live by forever."

Shariah law is often presented to the West as religious law, simply governing how Muslims live out Islam in their private lives. Shariah law governs everything from how to wash your hands to how to run a country.

If you want to get a picture of what strict Shariah looks like, look at Saudi Arabia. Because of strict Shariah law, virtually every Friday in that country, convicted thieves have a hand and a foot chopped off. And converts to Christianity from Muslim backgrounds get beheaded.

Shariah even teaches Muslims that, in some circumstances, it is OK to take the law into your own hands.

Nonie told me, "There's a law in Shariah that tells Muslims…anybody on the street can murder an apostate and he will not be punished for it."

That's why she would take her life into her own hands just by returning to her native land—even though her own father died by an Israeli letter bomb to retaliate for his anti-Israeli terrorist work.

Muslim terrorists would be inclined to embrace her, if for no other reason than that her father died as a Muslim "martyr," fighting the Jewish infidels.

But she has committed the ultimate sin---converting to another religion.

Another aspect of Shariah law is honor killing. Nonie says those who engage in honor killing in the Muslim world are often tolerated, and the police look the other way.

An honor killing, for example, is when a father kills his own daughter for violating the family's honor by allegedly doing something immoral, such as engaging in pre-marital sex.

Tragically, some of these honor killings are now even taking place in the Western world—and for much lesser offenses—like the Muslim man in Germany, now jailed for life, who killed his German-born wife because she was "too independent."

An Egyptian man in Texas reportedly shot in cold blood his two teenage daughters because they had boyfriends. Then, before his crime was discovered, he flew back to his native Egypt to escape American justice. Such honor killings may seem rare, but they're not uncommon.

It's interesting that so many American liberals who always clamor about women's rights can't seem to see how repressive strict Islamic law is toward women.

Wherever Shariah law is in effect, women (not to mention minority religious groups) are second class citizens.

For example, because of Shariah law, women can't drive in Saudi Arabia.

Under strict Shariah law, a woman's testimony in court is worth half of a man's testimony.

If a woman claims to be raped, it can only be established to be truthful by the testimony of four male eyewitnesses.

A woman cannot be caught with a man in public who is not her husband or relative. Nonie notes, "The police go into coffeehouses to check if the male sitting with the female is a blood relative or not." If a woman is caught with a non-relative, she will face public flogging—under Shariah.

A woman under strict Islamic law must be covered from head to toe.

And on and on it goes with strict Shariah law.

I wonder if the Egyptians realize what they are clamoring for when they claim to want strict Shariah law.

If they get it, they'll learn the hard way that the cure is worse than the disease.

Plans to Take Over the World--- Temporarily Put on Hold

5/6/11

He's dead, but unfortunately it's not over.

Osama Bin Laden has finally been killed, and he was only 30 miles or so from Pakistan's capitol.

About a decade ago, I was in Islamabad myself, staying at the Islamabad Holiday Inn. I remember being awakened about 4:30 in the morning with the Muslim call to prayer. I said to myself, "No wonder this country's so poor. They don't let anybody sleep!"

In our short travels there, we were even in Rawalpindi, the neighboring outpost where KSM was later captured.

Rawalpindi is the same place where former Pakistani prime minister Benazir Bhutto was murdered a few years ago. At Osama's direction.

Someone I met in Rawalpindi sent me a joke recently in a Facebook entry. "What does Taliban 1 say to Taliban 2? Happy Birthday, and have a blast."

The death of Osama Bin Laden gives us a good time to reflect on the overall goal of radical Muslims.

When I was a child sometime in the mid-1960s, I discovered a book in our local library (Winnetka Public Library) which stated that the Communists actually had a plan to take over the whole world.

That was astounding to me because it was a credible threat.

Thankfully, forty years later, the Western world has made great strides in vanquishing Communism, although there are vestiges left here and there. Like in many university classrooms in America.

There's another ideology that plans to take over the whole world.

Radical Islam.

Remember how, after 9/11, some people said Osama Bin Laden had "hijacked Islam"?

I question how accurate that is, in light of the 1400-year track record of Islam.

Mohammed himself said, "I have been ordered to fight against the people until they testify that none has the right to be worshiped but Allah, that Mohammed is Allah's prophet, that they offer prayers and give obligatory charity. If they perform all of that, they save their lives and their property" (Sahih Bukhari, Volume 1, Book 2, Number 24).

After Mohammed's death in 632, Muslims spread Islam by the sword, conquering from the Arabian peninsula throughout the Mediterranean world.

They even conquered much of Spain and tried to conquer France, until Charles Martel, the grandfather of Charlemagne, defeated them at the Battle of Tours in 732.

Meanwhile, by A.D. 950, 50% of what had been Christendom had been conquered by the Islamic sword. Most of that territory has never returned.

As noted, the crusades, which we hear about ad nauseam, were a violent reaction to almost five centuries of all these Muslim conquests.

Robert Spencer, director of jihadwatch.com and the author of *The Politically Incorrect Guide to Islam and the Crusades*, told me that the crusades "are very likely to have saved Europe from conquest and Islamization and saved France and Germany and Britain and Italy from the same fate that overcame Christian Egypt, Christian Syria and the other lands that earlier had been subjected to jihad conquest. It is very likely then that we owe Western Christian civilization, the civilization that is at the foundation of our own society and culture, to the crusades and that we owe the crusaders a great debt of gratitude for what they did."

Spencer quickly added that that appreciation for the crusaders does not excuse some of the excesses the warriors "of the cross" committed.

I would add that I agree with those who say that Christianity should never use force to enforce doctrine. It's bad for everybody---including the Christian cause. Meanwhile, there certainly is justification (at the last resort) for fighting in a just war.

Jump ahead to the early 20th century, when the Ottoman Empire collapsed at the end of World War I. Within a decade, the new dictator of Turkey had abolished the caliphate---the successor of Mohammed.

The Muslim Brotherhood was born in the 1920s to try and recreate a worldwide caliphate.

Then in the late 1970s, Ayatollah Khomeini helped bring a resurgence of Islam. Even though he was a Shiite (about 15% of Muslims, compared to the 85% who are Sunnis), he was able to unite many millions of Muslims with a dream of triumphant Islam.

The more he imposed fundamentalist Islam, the more he woke up millions of moderate Muslims against strict Islam.

Osama Bin Laden entered the picture in the 1990s. He stated, "I am confident that Muslims will be able to end the legend of the so-called superpower that is America." As the *New York Times* put it in his obituary: "In his vision, he would be the 'emir,' or prince, in a restoration of the khalifa, a political empire extending from Afghanistan across the globe. 'These countries belong to Islam…not the rulers.'"

It's a good thing Obama got Osama. But he would have been more classy---and more accurate---if he had given President Bush a little credit.

If it hadn't been for Bush's policies, Obama wouldn't have gotten Osama.

It would be nice to think that the threat of radical Islam is over with the death of Osama Bin Laden. But in light of the ideology inherent to Islam "Slay the idolater [infidel] wherever you find him…" Qur'an 9:5), that's wishful thinking. Don't be surprised if someone arises soon to take Osama's place.

Why Did The Marathon Bombers Do It?

4/24/13

Last week, when it became clear that some radical Muslims were behind the bombing, the question came up as to why? What was the motive? It's the same motive that has caused so much of the violence of radical Muslims all over the world; it's basically men seeking eternity in Paradise.

I'm thankful that as a Christian, I can *know* that I am going to heaven. Not because I'm good; not by works---that is *my* works; but certainly by the work of *Christ* at the cross.

John the Apostle writes, "God has given us eternal life, and this life is in his Son. He who has the Son has life; he who does not have the Son of God does not have life. I write these things to you who believe in the name of the Son of God so that you may know that you have eternal life."

But within Islam there is no guarantee of going to Paradise when you die. They have instead, a false hope of entering by dying in the process of committing Jihad. This will supposedly guarantee them eternity into Paradise where they will be wed to 70 virgins. The suitcase of 9/11 hijacker Mohammed Atta was misdirected to another airport and contained his wedding garb.

Stephen Massood of Pakistan is a former Muslim and head of *Jesus to the Muslims*. About Jihadists, he said, "They believe that, 'Well, if we are killed, we will go straight into Paradise.'"

The website, www.thereligionofpeace.com, maintains an ongoing register of how many Islamic attacks have been foisted on the world since 9/11. The Boston Marathon bombing would count as just one. As of 4/23/13, the number is 20,742.

Here is a recount of five prominent examples of those 20,742:

* Bali, Indonesia, October 12, 2002: Jihadi bombs in a nightclub kill 202 people and injure an additional 300.

* Madrid, Spain, March 11, 2004: At the train station, a series of bombs placed by Jihadists kill 201 people, and injure an additional 1,841.

* Beslan, Russia, September 3, 2004: Jihadists kill at least 350 people at a school---mostly children---and injure 600.

* London, England, July 7, 2005: A series of blasts in the subway (that is, "the tube") and in buses---killing 52 and injuring 750. The bombers turn out to be British-born Jihadists, so-called "home grown terrorists."

* Mumbai, India, November 26, 2008: Jihadists attack civilians and tourists, killing 178 and injuring 370. In addition, 5 Jews were singled out and tortured to death.

I spoke once with a Member of Parliament, David Liddington, about this. He said, "Most Muslims are people who absolutely loathe violence and terrorism. But, of course, only a relatively small number of very hardline radicals can cause an awful lot of trouble."

Robert Spencer of www.jihadwatch.org once told me, "In the Qur'an and in the teachings of Mohammed and in Islamic tradition of theology and law, there are mandates commanding Muslims to wage war against unbelievers." For example, he notes, see Surahs 2:191, 4:89, 8:39, 9:5, 9:14, 9:29, 9:73, 47:4, etc.

I once asked him, "Why would they kill an innocent child?" (Something we saw just last week in the case of the eight-year-old boy killed at the Boston Marathon.) He said, "This is something that is actually mandated by Islam; the Qur'an says in Chapter IX Verse 123 to 'fight the unbelievers and let them find a harshness within you.'"

I don't mean to imply that every Muslim is a terrorist. But these days a preponderance of terrorists are Muslims. Presumably, seeking an entrance to Paradise---in all the wrong ways. Spencer estimates only about 10% of Muslims are radicalized, but out of 1.3 billion or so people, that's a lot of radicalized individuals who could cause us harm.

Between the time of the bombing and the revelation of who was behind it, we heard all sorts of speculation about who might be responsible. We heard "right wing" terrorists, bandied about it, as if there was some sort of moral equivalence. Really?

As noted before, in his book, *The God Delusion*, the atheist Richard Dawkins talks about "the American Taliban." He doesn't come out and directly define them, but it became clear from the context that he was talking about those supposed Christians who do violence to abortionists. How many human beings does that represent?

Every time an abortionist has been murdered, and it's happened about four or five times I can think of, Christian leaders can't get to a microphone fast enough to denounce this despicable act. Rev. Paul Hill was a Presbyterian minister who murdered an abortionist, and he was put to death for it. At least he got due process, unlike the abortionist he killed. The AP (April 23, 2013, 4:43AM) says that the bombers were "motivated by religion." Again, moral equivalence.

As we've seen, Zuhdi Jasser, M.D. is a Muslim and an American, who is terribly opposed to violence, including that done in the name of Islam. He is outspoken against Jihadist violence.

Dr. Jasser said of such Jihadist attacks, "The root cause, I believe, as a Muslim, is the ideology of Islamism. The ideology of wanting to create Islamic states that are supremacist; that believe there should be an Islamic law and government. That no other legal system takes precedence. That government should be ruled by clerics or those that believe in Islamism."

He adds, "...until we start to build relationships with Muslims that are working against political Islam and the establishment of the Islamic state, I think we are going to continue chasing our tails domestically and globally for the next many generations to come."

Adam Savit of the National Security Policy said of our war on radical Islam: "we consider it a traditional war with men on the battlefield. Unfortunately, it is an ideological war and everyone, including Americans in America are combatants on that battlefield." Innocent victims learned that last week in Boston. Let us continue to pray for them and pray for opportunity to share with our Muslim neighbors the true Gospel, which grants them access to eternity in Paradise.

The Scapegoating of the Christians in Egypt
8/21/13

In the Bible, on the Day of Atonement, the High Priest was instructed to sacrifice one goat for the forgiveness of sins (for a year). He laid his hands on another goat and confessed the sins of the people, and then banished it to the wilderness.

This second goat we have called the "scapegoat" in English, ever since the phrase was coined by the first major translator of the Bible into English (from the original Hebrew and Greek), William Tyndale (c. 1494-1536). (Wycliffe translated it from Latin.) Much of Tyndale's work was used in the King James Bible (1611) and thus popularized all over the world.

Christians view Jesus' death as fulfilling all the ceremonial sacrifices, including that sacrificial goat and the scapegoat---and the Passover lamb and everything else.

Scapegoating means taking punishment, out on an innocent party, the sins of someone else. Right now Christians are unfairly being made the scapegoat by the Muslim Brotherhood in Egypt, since Morsi was ousted from power last month.

The crazy thing is that the pushback against the government of Mohammad Morsi, the elected president of Egypt until early July, came not just from Christians---but also middle class youth, political liberals, and secular Muslims---all of whom opposed the leader's ties to the Muslim Brotherhood and his imposing a strict Islamist regime.

Millions of Egyptians---again, most of them Muslims---protested against Morsi, until the army stepped in on July 3 in a coup. So why are Christians alone being singled out by Morsi's supporters, who cry, "Victory or Martyrdom"?

With somewhere between 10-15 million (in a country of 85 million), Egypt has the largest Christian population of any Middle Eastern country. For now.

Samuel Tadros, a Research Fellow at the Hudson Institute's Center for Religious Freedom, is quoted as saying that last Wednesday (8/14/13) appears to have been the worst single day of violence against Egypt's Coptic Church since the 14th century.

He says the Muslim Brotherhood blames Christians for ousting Morsi, so it can paint the military-backed government as anti-Islamic.

Tadros says the Coptic pope has gone into hiding, and many surviving churches have canceled Sunday services as Christians huddle in their homes, fearing for their lives.

In *National Review Online* (8/20/13), Rich Lowry writes, "Egypt is in the midst of an anti-Christian pogrom. Supporters of ousted Muslim Brotherhood president Mohamed Morsi are lashing out at the country's Copts for the offense of being Christian in Egypt."

Bishop Julian Dobbs from the Convocation of Anglicans in North America, who has on occasion visited the Christian communities in Egypt, sent me an email on the situation.

He notes, "Supporters of ousted president Mohammad Morsi have gone on the rampage against Christians in Egypt. A ten-year-old girl was gunned down as she was walking home from her Bible study class, and churches and other Christian property have been torched by rioters. Egyptian Christians have come under frequent attack since the uprising that led to Morsi's removal; they are being scapegoated for his fall."

Estimates vary as to how many Christian churches, orphanages, and schools have been destroyed. Some have put the number as high as 80, just since last Wednesday.

Rev. Dr. Mouneer Hanna Anis, Bishop of the Anglican Diocese of Egypt recently wrote, "Please pray that the situation will calm down, for wisdom and tact for the police and the army, for the safety of all churches and congregations, and that all in Egypt would be safe."

The Muslim Brotherhood is an international Islamic organization that was founded in Egypt in 1928, and it's dedicated to restoring the caliphate; the caliph was the successor of Mohammed as the political, military and spiritual leader of the Muslims

Perhaps the Muslim Brotherhood is best understood by their creed: "Allah is our objective. The Qur'an is our law. The Prophet is our leader. Jihad is our way, and death for the sake of Allah is the highest of our aspirations." No wonder the Egyptian Christians are feeling their wrath.

In their book, *Shariah: The Threat to America*, the Center for Security Policy notes that the Muslim Brotherhood is "the root of the majority of Islamic terrorist groups in the world today."

Pray for the Christians in Egypt as they have been scapegoated by the Muslim Brotherhood.

Forgotten Heroes of 9/11

9/11/13

Greater love has no man than he lay down his life for his friends. So said Jesus Christ.

There are many heroes we can honor on 9/11. Such as those who fought back on the plane that went down in a field in Pennsylvania. (Said Todd Beamer: "It's time. Let's roll.") Such as all those firemen who went up the Twin Towers as they were burning from the terrorist attacks.

Thousands commemorated some of those heroic firefighters in runs across the US, including one called "Tunnels to Towers," to remember fallen fireman, Stephen Siller, who died on 9/11, trying to rescue as many as he could. At my pokey pace, I even got to run such a race in Ft. Lauderdale.

But there are at least three forgotten heroes from 9/11 that I want to highlight here. Three heroes from 9/11---2012. From the attack in Benghazi. Perhaps, there are others. But because so much about the Benghazi attack that killed our Ambassador, Chris Stevens, and three others, is still surrounded in controversy, we still don't know all the details, definitively. Perhaps because the attack didn't fit the narrative that Al-Qaeda was on the ropes and bin Laden was dead.

On November 2, 2012, CBS news provided a clear timeline of the fateful events that night, the 11th anniversary of 9/11.

All sides might not agree on some of the specific details, but this seems to be agreed to by all: Four Americans died on the attack on the consulate outpost in Benghazi, and they were the ambassador, information officer Sean Smith, and two Navy Seals, Ty Woods and Glen Doherty, who died in a gunfight to protect Americans.

From what I can tell, both Ty Woods and Glen Doherty fit well with what Jesus said about "greater love." As I understand it, because of their sacrifice, the lives of others were saved.

Another hero of that night was agent Scott Strickland, who apparently returned into harm's way, into a burning building, to try and save the ambassador; but it was too late.

These should be household names---and perhaps there are others that didn't make the reports. Who knows? Maybe they'll all be honored properly some day in the made-for-TV movie.

There have been many hearings about Benghazi, the most famous being the one on January 23, where Hilary Clinton erupted in anger at one of the senators, asking: "What difference, at this point, does it make…?" As to the cause of the attack---i.e., a terrorist attack vs. a spontaneous mob protest brought on by a video. Why hold a hearing if the motive made no difference?

Geoffrey Dickens of the Media Research Center wrote an article (9/9/13) called "Benghazi Blackout" on the mainstream media's collective yawn on details of last year's attack.

For example, Dickens writes: "On July 18 Republican Congressman Frank Wolf went to the House floor to claim survivors of the Benghazi attack, State Department and CIA employees were forced to sign non-disclosure agreements. Total Big Three Network stories? 0."

No wonder these three heroes (and probably there were others) are largely forgotten. They've been ignored by the dominant media.

Ty Woods' father, Chuck Woods, did everything he could *not* to politicize his son's death or to make it a campaign issue (during the heated 2012 campaign). But he wondered if the administration has been forthright in how they have handled the Benghazi killings.

Chuck Woods delivered this statement: "I want to honor my son, Ty Woods, who responded to the cries for help and voluntarily sacrificed his life to protect the lives of other Americans. In the last few days it has become public knowledge that within minutes of the first bullet being fired the White House knew these heroes would be slaughtered if immediate air support was denied. Apparently, C-130s were ready to respond immediately."

Woods states the White House knew what was going on, but for whatever reason chose not to respond: "In less than an hour, the perimeters could have been secured and American lives could have been saved. After seven hours fighting numerically superior forces, my son's life was sacrificed because of the White House's decision."

He added, "This has nothing to do with politics, this has to do with integrity and honor. My son was a true American hero. We need more heroes today. My son showed moral courage. This is an opportunity for the person or persons who made the decision to sacrifice my son's life to stand up."

Apparently, Woods and Doherty even defied orders to "stand down," to save lives.

Although the White House seems to acknowledge now that it was a terrorist attack (trying to claim that they did from the beginning), initially they tried to shift the blame on an anti-Mohammed Internet video. That video was so poorly made, as a video, that Saturday Night Live couldn't do a better job in a parody against it.

For about two weeks, the President, Secretary of State Clinton, Jay Carney, and other White House officials tried to make the video the cause of the attack on Benghazi. The whole world now knows differently. (Yet as of this writing, the film-maker is still in jail for reportedly violating something else.)

In our remembrances of heroes of 9/11, Ty Woods, Glen Doherty, and Scott Strickland should also be included. Too bad political correctness has obscured the memory of their sacrifice, so far.

Killing Christians With Impunity?

10/2/13

Next month will mark the International Day of Prayer for the Persecuted Church. The official date is November 10, 2013. However, their website states: "...you are free to choose another date if you wish." Voice of the Martyrs and Open Doors have chosen November 3.

When I was a child, I somehow picked up the notion that persecution against the Christian church basically ended with the collapse of the Roman Empire.

But it turns out that the last century was the worst century ever for the persecution of Christians and martyrdom. Dr. David Barrett, a leading church statistician, says there were more Christians martyred in the 20th century than had been murdered in all previous centuries combined.

Persecution today continues to rear its ugly head in various places around the globe, such as in remnant Communist countries, like Vietnam or North Korea. But anti-Christian persecution is especially found in the Middle East and those places where the philosophy of Islamism---a supremacist form of Islam---prevails.

It's a cliché by now, but it's true: The Arab Spring has turned into the Christian Winter.

Dr. Peter Hammond of Frontline Fellowship says that just in the last few years the Christian population in the Middle East has shrunk from about 15 million to 13. Most of these have fled the homes their families have occupied for multiple generations---or perhaps even millennia.

Hundreds of years before Mohammed was born or Islam conquered that region, these families lived basically in peace and safety. Even after the Islamic sword swept over their lands and forced them into dhimmi status (a second class status, not unlike the old Jim Crow laws blacks lived under in the deep South), these families still remained in Iraq and Syria and Egypt.

But in recent years, due to events like the "Arab Spring" and the war in Iraq, the region has dramatically destabilized for Christians. We need to pray for these hurting fellow Christians. Paul says, "And if one member [of the Body of Christ] suffers, all the members suffer with it..."

More than 100 or so Christian cathedrals, churches, schools have been destroyed in Egypt just in the last couple of months. One Cairo-based church cancelled the Sunday-morning service in August for the first time in 1300 years.

In a recent weekend, Islamists killed dozens of Christians at a Pakistani church service and shoppers at a Kenya mall. (To the Islamists, virtually all non-Muslims are infidels.)

Recently, American attention has been focused on Syria, though it has somewhat subsided as of late, since a US strike has seemingly been averted for the moment.

Clearly, Syria is undergoing terrible developments. Some call it a civil war. Others would say that foreign invaders are taking advantage of the chaos that came in the aftermath of the Arab Spring, especially after the fall of Mubarak in Egypt.

In any event, Islamists are creating more and more havoc throughout the whole region.

Syria played a key role in the start of Christianity. It was in a city of Syria that the famous moniker for believers in Jesus was first created. Luke tells us in the Book of Acts: "the disciples were fist called Christians in Antioch."

Saul of Tarsus was on the road to Damascus, when Jesus appeared to him and changed him into the greatest missionary ever---Paul the Apostle. He went on to write half the New Testament.

It was out of Antioch, that the early Church sent Barnabas and Paul out on the first missionary enterprise. They were the first we know of to bring the gospel to Europe.

My good friend, Bill Federer, bestselling author and speaker, told my radio audience recently that after Greek (the Koine version of which was the language of the New Testament) and after Latin (the main language for Church writings for more than a millennium), Syriac (a language based in Syria) contained the most amount of Christian writings.

Even now, thousands of Christians still live in Syria, but their lives and future are in jeopardy, as are the lives of many Muslims who do not buy into the Islamist philosophy of the Syrian rebels.

Reports show that our government is funding many of these rebels in Syria or providing them with guns. Most agree that Syrian president Bashar al-Assad is a bad guy. Yet the rebels opposing him include Muslim terrorists committed to the same deadly philosophy of Al-Qaeda, whether directly affiliated or not. Christians in Syria, meanwhile, plead with foreign powers to stay out of the battle and to not support the Muslim rebels.

Saddam Hussein was a bad guy by anybody's reckoning. But, reflecting the "law of unintended consequences," the change in government in Iraq has been devastating to Christians---the majority of whom have been killed or driven out by Islamic militants.

For *TheDailyBeast*, Kirsten Powers, wrote, "A Global Slaughter of Christians, but America's Churches Stay Silent" (9/27/13). She notes, "Christians in the Middle East and Africa are being slaughtered, tortured, raped, kidnapped, beheaded, and forced to flee the birthplace of Christianity. One would think this horror might be consuming the pulpits and pews of American churches. Not so. The silence has been nearly deafening."

It's time to shatter the silence and mobilize the prayer warriors. The least we can do is pray.

Author's note: In March 2016, the US Congress and the State Department have now officially acknowledged that genocide is being committed against Christians in the Middle East at the hands of some Muslims.

Celebrating Christmas Can Be Dangerous---in Egypt
1/1/14

Our Christmas has come and gone. But for the Coptic Christians in Egypt, Christmas is commemorated on January 6, the day tradition holds the wise men (the Maji) came from the East, bearing gifts for the Christ child.

Western Christians have celebrated Christmas on December 25, the date held early on as the day of Christ's birth. Eastern Christians celebrate His birth on January 6. As noted before, an early Church council tried to reconcile the two dates. The best they could come up with is a compromise between the two dates---hence, the origin of the Twelve Days of Christmas, December 26-January 6.

But as Coptic Christians in Egypt prepare to celebrate Christ's birth, there is danger in the air.

As January 6, 2014 approaches, so also does January 8, the date when deposed Egyptian president Mohammed Morsi is scheduled to go on trial. The Muslim Brotherhood, of whom Morsi is a prominent member, are out for blood. Christians make an easy target.

We should recall that in July, tens of millions of Egyptians took to the streets to protest Morsi and his attempts to impose strict Islamic law, Shariah, on the whole country. The millions protesting surely included many Christians. But also there were far more Muslims protesting than any other group because of the largely Muslim makeup of the population.

Then for three days in August (14-16), many angry Muslim extremists went on a destructive rampage, targeting Christians as a means to vent their rage for Morsi's downfall.

Norwegian writer Dr. Arne Fjeldstad (1957 -2014) was the director of the Media Project, an international consortium of Christian journalists from all over the world. The Media Project's headquarters is in Washington, DC. Arne was also my brother-in-law. He had lived in Egypt for about five years, beginning in the early 2000s.

Arne writes, "Over the last few months, Christians in Egypt experienced an intense wave of attacks against churches, orphanages, schools and other Christian institutions---in the name of God (Allah). A few weeks ago, I visited Egypt once more and experienced many encounters with Christians. This time considerably more tainted with uncertainty and fear than I could remember from several previous visits (and my own time living in the country)."

Arne quotes a Hudson Institute fellow, Samuel Tadros, a Coptic scholar: "Egypt has not experienced anything similar to the attacks and destruction of churches since 1321."

Dr. Fjeldstad also notes that more than 100 Christian buildings were destroyed during the August rampage and afterwards.

He adds, "Violence against Christians is not just happening in Egypt. The last few months have shown horrific images from Pakistan, Nigeria and Syria, to name a few. A year ago, the German chancellor Angela Merkel said: 'Christianity is the most persecuted religion in the world.'"

Jesus warned that the day would come when men would kill you (His disciples) and think that in so doing they were offering a service unto God. Surely this is one of those times. Many of the Muslim extremists think Allah is pleased as they shed the blood of the infidel.

Often when they do this, they scream "Allahu Akbar!" (Allah is the greatest).

Sen. John McCain said recently that that is the Muslim equivalent of Christians saying, "Thank You, Lord." In reality, it means Allah is the greatest---greater than all gods.

In a normal year, Christians in Egypt will celebrate the evening of January 6 in church services. They likely will alter some of their plans this Christmas time so as not to become easy prey for militant Muslims, scapegoating the Christians for their own political troubles.

Any objective observer of the American media would have to agree that the dominant mainstream media is biased to the left. Usually, this bias is annoying. But their bias seems to lead generally to silence when it comes to the plight of Christians in the Middle East. The media's sin of omission is part of the reason we don't know about these things.

The Pope spoke on the plight of Christians on 9/25/13: "When I think or hear it said that many Christians are persecuted and give their lives for their faith, does this touch my heart or not?"

Even Prince Charles, often silent on such matters, spoke out about the plight of Christians at this present time.

We should contact our representatives to request Egypt to protect the minority Christians. But most of all, we should remember them in prayer.

The great 4th century Christian leader Ambrose said, "Not only for every idle word must man give an account, but for every idle silence." It seems like an appropriate thought as we consider the danger that our Christian brothers and sisters face in Egypt---as they are about to celebrate their Christmas.

Multiculturalism Is Disproven by Europe's Immigration Crisis

9/16/15

Masses of people are leaving countries in the Middle East and North Africa and streaming into Europe for the chance of a better life. It's an enormous tragedy. More than four million refugees have come out of Syria since 2011 because of its civil war.

How did such a disaster happen? No one takes a perilous journey to leave home unless home has become unsafe or impossible to stay in. No parents put their children on a dangerous, rickety old boat unless it is better than the alternative. They are desperate. Our hearts go out to them.

Writing for the *Wall Street Journal* (9/12-13/15), Walter Russell Mead penned "A Crisis of Two Civilizations." He described this migration as "one of the worst humanitarian disasters since the 1940s." He noted that even "the sick and the old are on the road."

The main reason behind the mass migration appears to be the suppression of freedom and the violence wrought under various Islamic governments, and the relative freedom afforded by formerly-Christian Europe.

Mead writes, "Today we are watching the failure of Islamism. From the Muslim Brotherhood to Islamic State, Islamist movements have had no more success in curing the ills of Arab civilization than any of the secular movements of the past."

This crisis shows how cultural relativism---the idea that one culture is just as good as another----and that all cultures are basically equal---is just not true. People are voting with their feet, whether they realize it or not, and going to countries with a Christian base.

I am not saying that European nations, or America for that matter, officially acknowledge the contributions of the Christian faith to their civilization. But it is Christianity that has helped shape the positive aspects of the West.

Daniel Lapin, an Orthodox Jewish rabbi, who appreciates the contributions of Jesus, made an interesting point when I interviewed him years ago for our television special, *What If Jesus Had Never Been Born?*, which was based on the book that I co-wrote with Dr. D. James Kennedy.

Said Rabbi Lapin, "The easiest way to answer the question of whether life on planet earth is better because Jesus walked Jerusalem or not is very simple, and that is: Just watch the way people vote with their feet. Watch where the net flow of immigration is in the world today. Is it from Christian countries to non-Christian countries or the other way around? It is so obvious."

This current crisis in Europe reminds me of the plight of Cubans who have desperately been trying to get to America, as they flee the bankruptcy of atheistic communism.

One time I came across one of these Cuban refugee rafts on the beach, about 350 miles away from Cuba. This homemade craft was composed of three wooden doors, with flotsam at the bottom to keep it afloat.

One of the doors served as the hull and the other two made up the raft's sides, with window shutters nailed across to serve as crossbeams. It was literally as if someone had torn apart his own home to put this thing together. Items of clothing in the raft indicate that it had held as many as ten people. I don't know what became of them.

Since it is illegal to leave the island, those fleeing would have had to make this raft secretly. Then they would have to get safely out of Cuban waters. If they were discovered by the Cuban coastal authorities, they could have been shot on sight to prevent them from leaving. Yet they embarked upon the trip nevertheless.

And all cultures are equal?

Having escaped to international waters, the occupants of this doors-turned-into-a-raft had to row it or float a few hundred miles over several days. They would have had to deal with the grueling sun and the potential threat of sharks along the way in order to try and get to America.

Why? So that maybe---just maybe---they could get a chance to enjoy what you and I enjoy every day. Freedom. The chance for a better life.

Meanwhile, millions of Americans born here think little of the freedom we have. The tragedy is that because we are jettisoning our Christian roots, our freedom is now at risk.

Freedom is a great blessing and flows directly from the Judeo-Christian tradition. It may sound like heresy to modern ears, but all cultures are not the same. Some ideas are better than others. Millions of people would not risk everything, even the lives of their own children, if it were not so. There is certainly no mass migration of people into radical Islamic or communist countries. The supposed glories of multi-culturalism are sinking into the Mediterranean.

Europe's Only Hope is Christian Revival

11/11/15

Europe is on the eve of changing forever. Hundreds of thousands of refugees have been leaving the tumult of the Middle East and Northern Africa to stream into Europe. One report estimates that three million more refugees are yet to come. This could mean the Islamization of Europe.

Many demographers have noted the increase in the Islamic population in a number of European nations, and mass-Muslim immigration comes with the importation of rigid Islamic customs and, often, Sharia law. Some are predicting that, if the present trends continue, Europe will be Islamic in about one or two generations. Now, it seems to be coming at an accelerating pace.

What the forces of Islam could not accomplish at Tours, France in 732 or Granada, Spain in 1492 or in Vienna in 1683, they may be able to accomplish without firing a shot.

As noted before, Geert Wilders, a controversial statesman from Holland, once told me in 2009: "Libyan leader, Muammar Gaddafi, said...we have 50 million Muslims in Europe. We don't need one gun; we don't need one bullet; we will rule this continent in 10, 20, 30 years' time, by the *Al-Hijra* [Arabic for the notion of conquest via immigration]. Europe will be ours, in the near future."

Wilders has been sounding the alarm for years about the Islamization of Europe and the loss of freedom that will result. For his efforts, he has been charged with hate crimes.

Wilders is frustrated with many fellow European leaders because they are not taking the Islamic threat seriously.

Already some Germans are frustrated about the rapid changes they see happening. Breitbart.com (10/27/15) transcribed many German comments about the new immigrants: "None of us want this. We're all scared." "What is this? How will it be in 100 years?" "Look at the women. They're all veiled!" "This is our future."

But is Europe reaping what it has sown? Europe is post-Christian for the most part, and nature abhors a vacuum. For years now, it would seem that there have been more worshipers in the mosque on Friday than in the cathedral on Sunday.

My friend Bill Federer, a best-selling author and speaker, said that the Islamic takeover in Europe has been in the works for a while.

In a 2011 interview, Bill told our viewers, "Europe has gone from Judeo-Christian to the secular. The theme song for secular Europe is John Lennon's 'Imagine:' 'Imagine there's no heaven, it's easy if we try...nothing to kill and die for and no religion too.' So, once you get rid of religion, nobody's going to kill and die to defend Europe. I mean, who is going to die for diversity? 'Here's a gun, give your life for pluralism.'"

The result of this jettisoning of Judeo-Christian beliefs then "emasculates them," he says. Bill continues: "And so, into Europe comes Sharia Law Islam, and it's taking over entire cities and communities. And they're blocking the streets and the Europeans are thinking, 'How did we get here?' Easy, you go from drive into neutral before you go into reverse. You had to go from Judeo-Christian to secular before you became Islamic."

Is it possible that modern Europe has essentially rejected the love of Jesus and could suffer the sword of Mohammad as punishment?
This may seem far-fetched. But in Isaiah 10, the Hebrew prophet, writing more than 700 years before Christ, proclaimed that the Assyrians were the rod of God's anger because Israel would not repent. My wife pointed this out to her Bible group recently.

"It is possible," she adds, "that God is using the same basic people group to again punish His unrepentant people?"

But is there any hope? Yes, true Christian revival in Europe. Let's be frank. The Muslim asylum-seekers are not fleeing the glories of Christendom; they are fleeing the brutalities of Islam.

Bishop Michael Nazi-Ali in the Church of England says of the asylum-seeking crisis: "The first and immediate thing is to say is that we must not fail in compassion.... Having said that, we must also ask about the causes of the crisis and what can be done to address them."

Hope for Europe is the same as hope for the rest of the world. True repentance and turning to Jesus.

As one convert to Christianity from Islam, Faisal Malik, once put it: "The only answer to Islam and what's happening around the world is the Gospel of Jesus Christ. There's no other solution, absolutely no other solution."

And he added, "The more Muslims come to Christ, there's less Muslims left for the terrorists to recruit in the midst of dissolution in our world to create more problems around the world."

Who Are the Real Terrorists?

1/27/16

Imagine sacrificing to send your children off to college---forking over thousands of dollars, so they can have a future. Then they end up in an introduction to psychology class...where they are taught that Christians are more dangerous than radical Islam.

At a recent "Introduction to Psychology" class at the University of California, Merced, Dr. Ross Avila raised quite a few eyebrows. Thecollegefix.com (1/11/16) reported on this class, which happened this past fall.

In a recording made of the class, Avila can be heard to claim that terrorism on American soil by foreigners, e.g., Muslims from other countries, is a myth (beyond 9/11) and that white Christian men commit the most terrorism in America.

He says that since 9/11, about 90 percent of those who perpetrate terrorist attacks in America are "white, Caucasian men….usually, the people who are religiously motivated and politically conservative. And these are the type of people we always think of being like really against terrorism."

To bolster his case, the professor cites an example of a supposedly Christian man who attacked the Texas state house with an AK-47 and "literally fired around 60 rounds at the state house…. that's an act of terrorism….Did you hear about that?"

I had not heard about it, and only one person in his large class had. Avila said if the would-be attacker had been Muslim, we all would have heard about that case.

As it turns out, the Austin shooter, though he was killed by the police, did not injure anyone else---though not for a lack of trying. He did indeed have right-wing political motivations and identified with a tiny, fringe "Christian identity" heretical sect, the likes of which have been roundly denounced by Christians of all stripes.

But can we seriously believe that attacks like this constitute the majority of attacks---and that such wacko militia types have amassed a higher body count since 9/11?

Professor Avila's erroneous assertions were apparently drawn from a 2015 New America Foundation study, which claims that in the last 14 years, 48 Americans were killed because of "right wing attacks" versus 45 killed by "violent jihadist attacks."

Robert Spencer, the best-selling author on all things Islamic, is the author of the new book, *The Complete Infidel's Guide to ISIS*. He maintains the website, jihadwatch.org. I have interviewed him numerous times to get a Jihad update.

In a 1/19/16 post, Spencer says, "Contrary to media myth, you're actually 62 times more likely to be killed by an Islamic jihadist than by a 'right-wing extremist.' Professor Andrew Holt shows that…the New America Foundation wildly exaggerate[d] the threat of 'right-wing extremists,' and fudge[d] the data to do so…"

I reached out to Robert and asked him for a statement on the professor's remarks for this column. He emailed me: "Academics such as this professor are convinced that Muslims, as (in their view) non-Christian, non-Western, and non-white, are and can only be victims of the aggressive, imperialist and colonialist West."

Spencer adds, "Accordingly, they will go to any lengths, no matter how absurd, to exonerate Islam of the crimes committed daily in its name and in accord with its teachings, and to denigrate Christianity, which they find much more noxious and threatening than Islam."

Spencer notes, "Their views, however, are so tremendously contrary to fact that they are clearly impervious to all actual evidence and sound reasoning." Facts are stubborn things, to paraphrase John Adams.

The bias of many college professors today toward traditional Christianity is deep-seated. Several years ago, *World* magazine reported (8/18/2007) on a study conducted by Gary A. Tobin, president of the Institute for Jewish and Community Research. He wanted to find out how prominent anti-Semitism was among faculty members. Thankfully, it turned out to be very low.

In this study of 1,269 college professors from 712 separate colleges and universities, they found only 3 percent of professors were biased against Jews. But what about evangelicals? *World* reports: "53% [of professors] admitted to harboring unfavorable feelings toward evangelicals." Tobin said, "The prejudice is so deep that faculty do not have any problem justifying it. They tried to dismiss it and said they had a good reason for it."

Thus, I suppose it should come as no surprise that a college professor would promote the idea that we need to worry more about alleged "Christian terrorism" than Muslim terrorism.

I would add that Jesus taught us to love even our enemies. Christians, of course, have not always lived up to that. But that is in contrast to the plain teaching of "Fight against those who believe not in Allah." Politically correct attempts to divert our attention from the real threat can only endanger us all.

What Good Is the Right of Free Speech If You Can't Exercise It?

5/12/15

By now, gallons of ink have been spilled on the recent meeting (over the May 2-3 weekend) in the Dallas area where the contest was held on who could draw the best picture of Mohammed.

Anti-jihadist blogger Pamela Geller of New York organized the contest. Two American jihadists drove hundreds of miles to kill the "infidels" and were killed in the process.

Franklin Graham remarked that the recent Garland conclave was misguided. As a Christian, he says we shouldn't insult anybody's religion. Like me, he believes the ultimate answer to the radical Islam issue is the gospel of Jesus Christ, who is more than just a prophet.

But Graham also pointed out that that radical Islamists "have no right to go around shooting people because someone mocks them."

Free speech rights are found in those countries rooted in Judeo-Christian tradition. They are not found in those places built on other worldviews.

One of the most amazing aspects of the story was the largely unreported fact that Geert Wilders came all the way from Holland to attend the Garland meeting.

Who is Geert Wilders? As noted before, he is a controversial Member of Parliament in the Netherlands and the founder of an upstart political party (Freedom Party), which has already begun to make its mark on that country's politics.

Geert Wilders is taking a courageous stand by warning the West about the Islamization of the same and the freedoms lost in its wake.

He never sleeps in the same place more than two nights in a row because of the multiple death-threats he faces from "the religion of peace."

As we've seen, in 2008, Geert Wilders made an Internet movie about radical Islam, called *Fitna* (Arabic for upheaval, chaos), and for that he is on trial in his own country for allegedly violating hate crimes laws. The European Union tried him for hate crimes, but after a grueling trial, he was exonerated.

His short film simply makes the point that the jihadists---who attacked on 9/11, at the Madrid train bombing, in London in 2005, etc.---did what they did because they were obeying what the Qur'an tells them to do. That's the essence of his film. Ideas have consequences. Tell the faithful followers of Allah that they should "slay the infidel wherever you find them" (Surah 9:5 from the

Qur'an), and 9/11 happens. That's the point Wilders makes in his movie.

Of course, most Muslims, including Qur'an-readers, do not engage in these Jihadist activities. Wilders admits as much. But those who do get their inspiration from the book.

I sat down in early 2009 and had a television interview with Geert Wilders about all the controversy. He had multiple bodyguards.

I asked him why he made the movie. He answered, "I fear the Islamization of our societies." He also said, "Sure, there are moderate Muslims. We should try to invest in moderate people."

This is a long-term fight over free speech. Pamela Geller, the event's organizer, once told me in an interview: "One big problem that America really has to watch out for [is] where they're imposing Sharia drip by drip, by shutting up people like myself and my colleagues, like Robert Spencer [publisher of jihadwatch.org], by defaming us because we speak...you know they call it 'Islam-a-phobia.'"

She adds, "What it is, is jihad-phobia, and you should be afraid of the jihad frankly...But it's part of this Islamic supremacist narrative...you cannot criticize Islam." She said these things in 2011, some three years before the Garland incident.

Liberals used to at least pay lip service to the notion of free speech. Remember the ACLU? Lately, they seem to have found a religion they can finally get behind---radical Islam. My guess is that since both hate conservative Christianity so much, they have found common cause.

The ACLU used to argue that attacks on free speech rights are a slippery slope. If someone loses their right to free speech, we all lose it.

So in the late 1970s, they offended virtually everybody by going to court on behalf of the free speech rights of a group of neo-Nazis to march in Skokie, Illinois, which at the time had some 7000 survivors of the Holocaust residing therein.

In this current battle, Pamela Geller, Geert Wilders, and Robert Spencer are the proverbial canaries in the coal mine. They are fighting the West's battle for freedom. If they lose, so does freedom. As one pundit recently noted, if free speech protections do not protect unpopular speech---at the height of its unpopularity---then they aren't really free speech protections.

Part 10.

Miscellaneous Musings

"Truth" in a Post-Christian West

2/4/15

A great quote attributed to George Orwell, author of *1984*, is, "During times of universal deceit, telling the truth becomes a revolutionary act."

In poring over the news of late, it's amazing how much untruth there is, mixed with partial truth. Spin and euphemisms often replace truth.

I read recently that an abortion doctor was honored for his work. But not once was there a mention of the word "abortion" or even a hint of the grisly work he is involved in.

Just last month, noted Matt Rocheleau for the Boston Globe (1/8/15), "Up to 64 Dartmouth College students — including some athletes — could face suspension or other disciplinary action for cheating in an ethics class this past fall." Cheating in ethics class? This speaks for itself.

Meanwhile, a Christian publisher pulled a book detailing the alleged foray into heaven of a boy who died and came back. The boy admits now he made it all up to get attention.

When people preface what they say with the phrase "Well, to tell you the truth," do they mean to imply that they normally don't tell you the truth? Note to self: Try to drop that phrase from my speech.

One of the most amazing exchanges in the history of the world was when Pontius Pilate, governor of Judea, was trying Jesus of Nazareth and the prisoner referred to "the truth." Pilate then asked Him, "What is truth?" and he pivoted and walked away.

Just a few hours before, Jesus had said to His disciples during the Last Supper, "I am the way, the truth, and the life. No one comes to the Father but by Me." Here was Truth incarnate standing before Pilate, and the blind governor had no clue.

As the famous line in the movie puts it, "You can't handle the truth!" Or as the great American short story writer Flannery O'Connor once said, "The truth does not change according to our ability to stomach it."

In our day of relativistic ethics, where there is supposedly no real right or wrong, how can we condemn lying---truly? Unless, I suppose you get caught.

But that wasn't the way George Washington saw things. Before he retired, he imparted a masterful written speech in 1796, his Farewell Address.

In that Address, he famously noted: "Of all the dispositions and habits which lead to political prosperity, religion and morality are indispensable supports."

He went on to say that we can't expect morality to continue if we undermine religion. Keep in mind, this was at a time when the vast majority of Americans were professing Christians.

He also said, "Let it simply be asked: Where is the security for property, for reputation, for life, if the sense of religious obligation desert the oaths which are the instruments of investigation in courts of justice?"

In other words, how can we expect someone to obey a sworn oath to tell the truth if they have no "the sense of religious obligation," undergirding that oath?

The founders understood that belief in a God who sees all things and who will one day hold us accountable made a huge difference. That's why in our days truth is breaking down---even among some professing Christians. But let God be true and every man a liar.

This isn't just an American problem. It is a problem in the post-Christian West.

George Weigel, an insightful Catholic writer, said in the *LA Times* in 2006: "If the West's high culture keeps playing in the sandbox of postmodern irrationalism---in which there is 'your truth' and 'my truth' but nothing such as 'the truth'---the West will be unable to defend itself. Why? Because the West won't be able to give reasons why its commitments to civility, tolerance, human rights and the rule of law are worth defending."

He added, "A Western world stripped of convictions about the truths that make Western civilization possible cannot make a useful contribution to a genuine dialogue of civilizations, for any such dialogue must be based on a shared understanding that human beings can, however imperfectly, come to know the truth of things."

The battle for truth has major stakes.

On Avoiding Scandalous Sin

6/3/15

It is so sad to read the news about the latest sex scandals involving prominent Christian leaders. I pray for them, and I pray for their victims. I also pray that more Christians would not be led into temptation, but delivered from evil.

Too often we fall for Satan's mousetrap. We focus on the cheese, while ignoring the big trap ready to break the neck.

These news stories give us an opportunity to reflect on ways to avoid such scandals going forward. Moses once said that you may be sure that your sins will find you out.

Motivator Zig Ziglar said something once I have never forgotten. He said the only real failure in life is moral failure. We may have temporary setbacks in trying to achieve success, but moral failure can bring devastation.

There are lessons to learn from this for all of us, since we all have feet of clay. The Bible has much to say on this front.

Consider the case of Joseph, a son of Jacob. He was sold into slavery by his own brothers, who hated him because they envied him.

He ended up in Egypt in the household of man named Potiphar. Genesis 39 notes, "Now Joseph was well-built and handsome, and after a while his master's wife took notice of Joseph and said, 'Come to bed with me!'"

He asked her how he could "do such a wicked thing and sin against God?" Constantly, "day after day," drip, drip, drip, she attempted to seduce him. But he "refused to go to bed with her or even be with her."

Then one day she dismissed everyone out of the house. So it was only she and Joseph. She grabbed his cloak to get him into bed, but he fled. She screamed and lied about him.

Joseph was thrown in prison. But he stayed true to his integrity. Eventually, he was completely exonerated and even became second only to Pharaoh in all of Egypt. He had passed the test.

I find it interesting that when the wife was trying to tempt him, he didn't sit down with a tablet and chisel out a pro and con list. He simply fled. He put on his running shoes. What a great model for us.

Unfortunately, King David, many centuries later, shows us what not to do on this front. During the season when kings go off to war, David was at home relaxing. As he looked down from his roof, he happened to see a beautiful woman, bathing. One thing led to another and, before long he had committed adultery and was responsible for killing the woman's husband to cover it up.

Then God brought judgment on David and his household. What David had done in private, God judged in public.

All of this could have been avoided by that second look. You can't always help that first glance of something tempting---unless you purposefully expose yourself to temptation, in which case you've already lost the battle. But you can be careful with that second---and third and fourth glance.

Job said, "I made a covenant with my eyes not to look lustfully at a girl." Pastor Kent Hughes makes the point that "Job's covenant forbids a second look." Jesus warned us to not look at a woman lustfully and so sin in our heart. It always begins in the heart.

It is important, though, that we distinguish between temptation and giving in to temptation. Martin Luther said you can't stop a bird from flying overhead (temptation), but you can keep it from building a nest in your hair (sinning).

One time a Christian writer decided to study the problem of pastors committing adultery. What he found was that through lust, they had committed adultery in their hearts repeatedly. Then when the opportunity finally made itself available in a real life situation, they simply acted out what they had envisioned so often before.

If this is a problem for you, find a trusted brother or sister in Christ to whom you can confide. Not the church gossip, but someone who can hold you accountable. Often by sharing the truth with someone else, the stronghold of evil is broken.

One of the big traps to avoid is a smug attitude---"this could never happen to me." Paul warned, Let him who thinks he's strong, watch out lest he fall.

Ultimately, the key to purity is renewing the mind. The key to that is the Bible. When Jesus was tempted by the devil, each time He responded, "It is written..." and then He quoted the Bible.

As we see one scandal after another rocking the church, I remember the adage: The Bible will keep you from sin or sin will keep you from the Bible.

A Hymn for Our Time

8/25/15

"Mere anarchy is loosed upon the world," wrote Yeats in "The Second Coming." He penned those words in 1919, but as David Lehman observes, those words provide a "summary of the present age" (WSJ, 7/25-26/15).

Yet through it all, God is at work even when things look bleak---perhaps especially when things look bleak. There's a great hymn from the 1800s that reminds us of this. It's is James Russell Lowell's classic, "Once to Every Man and Nation."

It is a hymn for our time---with all the setbacks and ebbs and flows in the advance and seeming regress of the gospel and Judeo-Christian morality.

This hymn, sung to the tune of "O the Deep, Deep Love of Jesus," is such an American classic that Dr. Martin Luther King, Jr. read the words to his followers as an encouragement at a critical juncture in his movement.

Everyone knows that fifty years ago, the civil rights marchers had their famous struggle across the bridge in Selma, Alabama on the way to Montgomery. What is not as well known is that when they finally made it over, the Baptist minister read the words of this obscure hymn.

Here are the words of that hymn, which I slightly updated for clarity:

"Once to every man and nation comes the moment to decide.
In the strife of truth with falsehood, for the good or evil side.
Some great cause, some great decision, offering each the bloom
or blight. / And the choice goes by forever, between that
darkness and that light.

"Then to side with truth is noble, when we share her wretched crust.
Before her cause brings fame and profit, and 'tis prosperous to be
just. / Then it is the brave man chooses, while the coward stands
aside, / Until the multitude make virtue of the faith it had denied.

"Though the cause of evil prosper, yet the truth alone is strong.
Though her portion be the scaffold, and upon the throne be wrong.
Yet that scaffold sways the future, and behind the dim unknown
Standeth God within the shadow, keeping watch above His own."

This last verse in particular is the one that gets me. Sometimes it does seem like evil is triumphing. But then in a moment God changes things. Even when nobody expects it.

My long time pastor, Dr. D. James Kennedy, once said this:

"Who would have thought:

* In that hour when Lazarus lay stinking in his tomb, that soon he should be rejoicing around the table with his Redeemer;

* That when Jonah was in the depths of the sea that soon he would be preaching at Nineveh;

* That when Nebuchadnezzar, the mighty monarch of Babylon, was out munching on the grass in the forest, that one day soon he would again be sitting upon the throne in Babylon;

* That when Joseph was deep in the prison in Egypt, that soon he would be prime minister of the greatest nation in the world at that time;

* That when Job was sitting there on a dunghill scraping off his sores in the midst of his sorrow, that soon he would be rise up and be richer and more blessed in everything in this world?"

God turning things around unexpectedly happened many times in the life of Athanasius, the 4th century saint, who was the champion of the Trinity. For his views, he was banished five times from the Roman Empire (outwardly Christian at that time). But he never gave up.

Athanasius' views prevailed and are reflected in the version of the Nicene Creed that is still read week after week by hundreds of millions around the world.

Athanasius was on the scaffold many times, but that scaffold swayed the future. More than a millennium later, the Christian Member of Parliament, William Wilberforce (1759-1833), was fighting slavery in the British Empire. As evangelist John Wesley was dying, he wrote Wilberforce a letter (see Part 7. Christian History. "In the Arena"), saying in effect, "William, unless God is in this, you will fail."

Often in history it seems the bad guys are winning. But we should take heart because the Lord knows what is going on and in His time will make things right.

Those who have written off the Christian cause in our world---and certainly it has seen its share of defeats lately---may yet be surprised when God arises. As another hymn puts it, "So from the beginning the fight we were winning; Thou, Lord, were at our side, all glory be Thine!"

"The Music of the World"

3/22/12

Once upon a time, an old man was walking down the street, so says Aesop in one of his fables. As he shuffled along clutching his cloak, the wind and the sun got into an argument as to which of them was able to make the man part from his blanket.

The wind went first. He blew and blew and blew, but to no avail. The harder he blew, the harder the man clung to the cloak.

Then it was the sun's turn. He simply slid out from behind the clouds and caused the man to wipe his brow so that within minutes, he quickly took off his cloak. In the end, gentle persuasion is better than blustery explosions.

As Ben Franklin once put it, "Tart words make no friends: a spoonful of honey will catch more flies than a gallon of vinegar." If we want others to treat us well, there's no better way than for us to treat them well.

Who says nice guys always finish last? Who says good deeds never go unpunished? There's a powerful, short book on the subject of encouragement, called, *Being Nice—a Winner's Secret Weapon: How it Pays to be Nice.* The author is Mike LeFan of Temple, Texas, who notes, "Kind words are the music of the world."

LeFan writes: "'It's odd,' says a Texas businessman, 'but big businesses and corporations spend thousands and even millions of dollars on creating products and services and on advertising them, but they neglect the one thing that both customers and employees really respond to—appreciation.' What could be simpler or more effective than offering appreciation? It costs nothing. Yet it's practically ignored at work, at home, and in the community. Most of us dole out more criticism than approval."

LeFan points out the importance of encouragement. He writes, "Where there's praise, there will be second effort."

He quotes Mark Twain who said, "I can live for two months on a good compliment."

A 2008 study at Harvard involving gamesmanship found that it actually pays to be nice, rather than to be a jerk. LeFan asserts, "When faced with an offensive opponent, turning the other cheek and continuing to cooperate—or at least not inflicting punishment—paid off better in the long run. In other words, 'playing nice' was more profitable than playing in a cutthroat fashion."

LeFan has culled through the wisdom of Western civilization for many fine thoughts on being a nice guy, such as Sophocles from the

5th century BC: "Kindness will always attract kindness." Or Frederick William Faber of the 19th century, "Kindness has converted more sinners than zeal, eloquence, or learning."

This little book stands on its own merits. But I happen to know something about the author that makes it absolutely remarkable to me.

In my work at Coral Ridge Ministries (now D. James Kennedy Ministries), I've interviewed some interesting people. Michael LeFan is one of them. He contracted polio when he was eight years old in 1954. Yet he doesn't complain about it and is sustained by his faith in the Lord.

LeFan writes, "My polio left me totally paralyzed—almost. I needed someone else's help to eat, bathe, dress, and take care of all personal necessities. And I still need that. But as months and years passed, I found that my left leg and foot had movement, even dexterity. It began as a way to entertain myself, but over time I learned to pick up a pencil in my toes and eventually even to scribble with it."

Every word I just quoted was tapped out, stroke by stroke, by his left foot---with a pencil in between his big and next toe, using the eraser side to hit a computer keyboard. Stroke by stroke. He has written books this way, including his new book on being nice and including the book from which the above quote comes, called, *Patience, My Foot!*

Despite his polio, despite sleeping in an iron lung each night, Michael has gone to college earning an undergraduate degree. He took notes using his left foot.

In fact, he discovered he had dexterity enough with his left foot to do all sorts of things. He has painted pictures with a brush between his toes; he's even served as president of the local ham radio club, operating the radio with just his foot.

Setbacks and disappointments come to us all. Sometimes it's easy in life to feel sorry for yourself, holding back any kindness to those whom we perceive have mistreated us. But I believe we can learn much about encouragement (not to mention perseverance) from a polio victim, who persists in his writings---stroke by stroke, tap by tap, using just his left foot.

In his new book comes this gem from Ian Maclaren: "Be kind; everyone you meet is fighting a hard battle." Surely, Michael LeFan is fighting a harder battle than most of us.

So show a little kindness today, and be a part of the music of the world.

A Pope Named Francis? Well, it's About Time

3/20/13

One thing amazed me about the new pope being appointed last week. For the first time in Church history---after about 800 years---a pope chose the name Francis, in honor of St. Francis of Assisi. I hadn't realized this was the first time ever. Well, it's about time.

Francis of Assisi, for whom one of our great cities is named (San Francisco) was a delightful Christian example for Catholics, Protestants, and Orthodox Christians alike.

If more of us who profess to follow Christ were more like him, we would have a much stronger witness before the watching world.

Francis Bernardone (1182-1226) grew up the son of a wealthy merchant, but upon receiving a divine calling, he forsook a life of comfort and ease, choosing instead a life of poverty and simplicity to serve the Lord. Centuries later we still remember him.

According to author Marc Galli (now the editor of *Christianity Today*), "'Lord, Make Me an Instrument of Thy Peace,' sometimes called 'The Prayer of Saint Francis,' was not written by Francis though it does embody his spirit. It was probably composed at a Catholic congress in Chicago, in 1925" (*Christian History Magazine*, Issue 42, 1994.)

I find the Prayer of St. Francis prayer quite liberating. After some recent personal conflicts, I make it a conscious goal to pray it, along with the Lord's Prayer, every day.

Part of that prayer includes: "O Divine Master, grant that I may not so much seek to be consoled, as to console; to be understood, as to understand; to be loved, as to love. For it is in giving that we receive. It is in pardoning that we are pardoned, and it is in dying that we are born to Eternal Life."

I'm reminded of the opening concept of Rick Warren's mega-bestseller, *The Purpose-Driven Life*. The key to understanding life is this: it's not about you, but the Lord.

This is such a winning approach to life, come what may. I especially find helpful the line, "It is in pardoning, that we are pardoned." As was said by Christ, whom Francis patterned his life after, we should pray, "Forgive us our debts as we forgive our debtors." Forgive others instead of clinging to simmering resentments, which ultimately ruin *us*.

Human nature, being what it is, is bound to produce conflicts. Francis recognized that. One of the geniuses of the founding fathers of America was recognizing man's moral limitations, and putting in place safeguards to protect us---from each other.

James Madison, direct student of the Scottish Presbyterian head of Princeton, Dr. John Witherspoon, said, "All men having power ought not to be trusted." That's not a cynical view of human nature. It's a realistic one.

Ben Franklin said that if you had a 100 kings, only one would not tend to be like Pharaoh (the evil one described in the early chapters of Exodus), if given the chance.

Because of the founders' realistic, and biblical, belief in man's corrupt nature, Americans have experienced a great deal of freedom. Countries built on a foundation of man's supposed innate goodness---like the failed Soviet Union---end up with endless bloodshed.

The Bible also says, inasmuch as it is up to you, be at peace with all men. It's not always up to us. Francis strikes me as one who tried to live up to that ideal.

Francis was a great peace-maker. He attempted, unsuccessfully, to stop the Crusades. But at least he was able to peacefully present Jesus to the Islamic leader---and live to tell it.

Samuel Escobar notes, "What we learn from history is that the inhumanity of the Crusades was not the only way in which Christians related to Islam in those days. Francis of Assisi pioneered a different approach. In 1219 he managed to cross the lines of battle and gain entrance to the sultan of Egypt. There Francis presented to the sultan the message of Christ in its simplicity and beauty" (*Christianity Today*, 1994).

G. K. Chesterton added this tribute to Francis: "He...saw the image of God multiplied but never monotonous. To him a man was always a man and did not disappear in a dense crowd any more than in a desert...."

Chesterton added, "What gave him his extraordinary personal power was this; that from the pope to the beggar, from the sultan of Syria in his pavilion to the ragged robbers crawling out of the wood, there was never a man who looked into those brown burning eyes without being certain that Francis Bernardone was really interested in him…."

Francis is the one who created manger scenes---live nativity sets. Galli writes how on Christmas Eve, 1223, he "set before our bodily eyes how he [Jesus] lay in a manger."

I watched a movie recently on this great leader. The man who directed the classic movie, *Casablanca*, made a film called *St. Francis of Assisi* in 1961. It's well done---if you can get past the dreadful music during the opening credits (just one man's opinion).

Francis, the new leader of the Roman Catholic Church---some 1.2 billion people today---has some pretty big shoes to fill---those of St. Francis of Assisi.

The End of the World? Been There. Done That.

12/18/12

Is it the end of the world?

Is December 21, 2012 the end of the world? The Mayan calendar says as much.

Many around the world fear the end has come, and they are preparing for it. Writing for the Associated Press (12/11/12), Jack Chang notes: "[T]housands are getting ready for what they think is going to be a fateful day."

He adds, "The Maya didn't say much about what would happen next, after a 5,125-year cycle known as the Long Count comes to an end. So into that void have rushed occult writers, bloggers and New Age visionaries foreseeing all manner of monumental change, from doomsday to a new age of enlightenment."

Chang notes, "Even the U.S. space agency NASA intervened earlier this month, posting a nearly hour-long YouTube video debunking apocalyptic points, one by one."

Chang quotes one descendant of the Maya who views December 21 not with hype or dread, but rather as opportunity for renewal. Jose Manrique Esquivel says, "For us, this Dec. 21 is the end of a great era and also the beginning of a new era. We renew our beliefs. We renew a host of things that surround us."

Some of the plans of preparation for the December 21 day include preparing for all the tourists. "Mass tribal drumming, circles of energy and ritual dancing are also planned."

Meanwhile, the Vatican is reassuring their followers that the world will not end on that day. The Associated Press (again, 12/11/12) notes: "The Vatican's top astronomer has some assurances to offer: The world won't be ending in about two weeks, despite predictions to the contrary." The astronomer said of the Mayan prophecy: "[I]t's not even worth discussing."

It's tempting to be snug over the prophecy not being fulfilled. But we as Christians shouldn't gloat. We have had more than our share of major false prophecies that ended up not being fulfilled.

Christianity teaches that history is linear, not circular. Christ divided time in half. B.C. (Before Christ) and A.D. (Anno Domini, "in the year of our Lord," so, for instance, the US Constitution is signed "in the year of our Lord" 1787).

The politically correct folk now refer to these distinctions as BCE and CE. No, that doesn't mean Before the Christian Era or Christian Era---although it could because the Christian era still defines the date in question. (The C stands for the word "Common.") But how is time reckoned in the so-called "Common Era"? The birth of Jesus (which was most likely during the winter of 5-4 B.C.).

The idea of the world coming to an end gets back to teaching from Jesus Himself and the apostles. He talked about His return as a day of reckoning, as a day of accountability.

Tragically, at various times during Church history (and even in our own time), many professing Christians have speculated about the day or time of His return and have given the Church a collective black-eye for it. The end of the world on such-and-such a date? Been there, done that.

Consider, for example, what happened when the year 999 was drawing to a close, before the ushering in of A.D. 1000. Thousands crammed into St. Peter's in Rome, awaiting the momentary end of the world had come—since 1000 years were over from the time Jesus had come to earth.

Richard Erdoes, author of *A.D. 1000*, describes it this way: "On the last day of the year 999, according to an ancient chronicle, the old basilica of St. Peter's at Rome was thronged with a mass of weeping and trembling worshippers awaiting the end of the world. This was the dreaded eve of the millennium, the Day of Wrath when the earth would dissolve into ashes. Many of those present had given away all of their possessions to the poor—lands, homes, and household goods—in order to assure for themselves forgiveness for their trespasses at the Last Judgment and a good place in heaven near the footstool of the Almighty" (p. 194).

But the year ended, and the next year came (and went).

Since Jesus Himself said, "No man knows the hour or day, not even the Son of Man" (referring to Himself), then who are we to speculate? In fact, if anybody claims they have an actual date of Christ's return, to me that's a tell-tale sign that they are wrong---by definition. His return will be a big surprise.

There are sects within Christendom that even began because of a prediction (false, of course) of Christ's return. One thing all the would-be prophets seem to forget is the element of surprise.

Jesus said that it will happen when people least expect it. Paul said that day of the Lord will come "like a thief in the night."

So the key is to be ready for His return at all times. Meanwhile, until He comes, we should "occupy"---i.e., go about doing His will on earth, as it is in heaven. One slogan mocked, "Jesus is coming. Look busy." That's not what He has in mind. We should work "heartily as unto Him."

So is December 21, 2012 the end of the world? Well, let's talk it over---on December 22.

Ten Trends to Watch in 2012

1/3/12

I'm not a prophet, nor the son of a prophet. But it doesn't take a prognosticator to predict a few trends that I believe we'll see in the next year. Here are a few trends to watch in 2012, in my humble opinion.

1. The world will not end in 2012, contrary to Mayan predictions.

2. There will be major turnover at the ballot box, as many Americans are tired of business as usual.

3. Americans will continue to become more pro-life. Science will do the talking. Sonograms are revealing that babies in utero are clearly human beings, not "clumps of tissue."

4. The ABC (Anything But Christ) principle seen in the public arena (schools, governments, etc.) will continue. But we will also see a push back against it by everyday people.

5. There will continue to be a deep hunger for information on America's true history. Things like Kirk Cameron's upcoming movie will help feed this hunger. I believe that in 2012, more

Americans will rediscover how belief in God had a lot to do with why so many of the settlers came here in the first place.

6. In America, the rich will get richer and the poor will get poorer---until the government chains that choke economic growth are thrown off. That would most likely begin to happen in 2013, after much turnover at the ballot box. When there are good economic policies at work, everyone---rich or poor---gets richer. In contrast, the politics of envy and class warfare hurt everyone---especially the poor.

7. There will be more and more attempts in the U.S. to throw Israel under the bus. Even some Jews, who are more committed to liberal politics than they are to that nation state, will participate in this. Jews and American evangelicals will continue to be the main true friends to the only committed democracy in the Middle East.

8. Europe will become less important in world affairs, as it continues to turn its back on the Gospel.

And two final trends, with some elaboration:

9. Europe will continue to become more Islamic. There will be more worshipers in the mosque on Friday than in the cathedral on Sunday---that is already the case.

Just weeks ago, the *New Statesman* magazine published an interview between the world's leading atheist, Richard Dawkins, of Oxford University, and Christopher Hitchens, another notorious atheist who has since died and gone to his reward.

Dawkins wondered aloud if all his and Hitchens' anti-Christian crusades in the West were just helping pave the way for a Muslim takeover in those parts of the world. By merely asking the question, Dawkins essentially admitted what he and his co-anti-religionists are actually accomplishing.

My short answer to Dawkins' insightful question is "yes." Nature abhors a vacuum.

10. China will continue to rise in influence around the world--as the Gospel continues to silently rise in the world's largest country. If we in America listen to the siren song of the atheists and continue to turn our backs on God, China will easily become the world's next super power–especially if influential Chinese officials increasingly realize they need God's help.

Let me elaborate further on this point as well. Writing in the Iona Institute for Religion and Society (March 3, 2011), Tom O'Gorman opined, "In the West we are doing our best to destroy our Christian heritage; but in China, Chinese intellectuals are coming around to the view that it is precisely this heritage that has made the West so successful."

A member of the Chinese Academy of Social Sciences noted that Chinese thinkers were trying to understand the success of the West, and ultimately it came back to religion. He said (as quoted in Harvard University's Niall Ferguson's new book, *Civilization: The West and the Rest*): "The Christian moral foundation of social and cultural life was what made possible the emergence of capitalism and then the successful transition to democratic politics. We don't have any doubt about this."

Well, those are ten trends I think we should watch in 2012. As you can see, I think a lot of reward or punishment ultimately revolves around our response to Jesus Christ. But if you think I exaggerate on that point, consider even just one example. Why is this year *2012* in the first place? Because it's reputed to be 2012 years after His birth.

As Psalm 2 notes, We should kiss the Son (show reverence to Christ), lest we perish on the way. Let's make it a great year by living for Him.

Has the Milk of Human Kindness Curdled?

5/22/12

Recently, the boxer Manny Pacquiao from the Philippines was thrown some punches below the belt because of his favoring of traditional marriage.

He opposes the legalization of same sex marriage, as he said in an interview. However, in the *Examiner* article highlighting the interview, the writer quoted a passage in Leviticus (that Pacquiao wasn't even familiar with), which says that homosexuals should be put to death. This was a law in ancient Israel that the vast majority of Christians (and Jews for that matter) would agree was part of the now-defunct theocracy of Israel. (See Additional Note at the end of this essay.)

In short, words were put into Pacquiao's mouth. He never said he hated gays or that they should be killed. He just said, "God only expects man and woman to be together and to be legally married." But a group with the name "Courage Campaign" successfully petitioned Nike to drop sponsorship of the boxer.

Meanwhile, a savage boxing match took place on a recent Saturday (April 28, 2012) in Atlantic City. The only reason it made news is because the knockout punch was so nasty.

Daily Mail of the U.K. (5/1/12) reported on this, showing graphic photos of the punch and the distorted image (caused by the punch) of the hapless face of the knockout victim. The headline reads: "That's going to hurt in the morning: Brutal knockout blow turns boxer's face to jelly." The article also said his face was turned into "mush."

The 23-year winner of the bout was quoted as saying, "I was so excited that I did a little dance for the fans, but that was before I saw how badly he was hurt." He also noted, "I felt that punch all the way up my shoulder and back, so I knew he wasn't getting up."

Is it just me? It seems there's something savage about the whole sport.

I find it ironic that Muhammad Ali is the most successful boxer of my lifetime. But hasn't he spent the last 30-40 years in terrible health---possibly because of so many punches received? If that's success in boxing, what is failure? I suppose it would be getting your face turned into "jelly" or "mush."

Sorry for being a party pooper, but do people find this entertaining?

I consider Matt Barber a friend. He's a former part-time professional boxer turned culture warrior (on the right side too). He won most of his matches, but his wife convinced him to quit when he endured a blow that impacted his windpipe. Now he fights in the court of ideas for religious liberty and through his columns. A book of his columns even played off of the boxer theme---*The Right Hook*. Like the Philippine boxer, Matt is a committed Christian.

Don't get me wrong. I think it's terrific when people discipline their bodies and get them into top athletic shape. What I don't like is when they use their bodies as weapons to decimate others for the entertainment of others; it just becomes an appeal to old-fashioned bloodlust.

One of the saddest stories I remember reading was about a man who had no money but wanted so badly to go see his mother. Not being able to afford the airfare, he agreed to go into a boxing ring--- although he was out of shape---to somehow earn a few bucks. But he was killed in that bout. He never got to see his mother.

Speaking of bloodlust, as of this writing, a major blockbuster movie is *Hunger Games*. This film depicts a bleak future, where human life is even cheaper than it is now. The film shows how a group of twenty-four teens have to battle it out with each other until only one is left alive---all for the entertainment of society, which sees it on TV.

One announcer at the start of this contest declares, "We have a bloodbath about to take place." At least you can say for violent movies today, presumably no animals were even hurt in the making of the movie, much less any actors or actresses (or stunt-people).

But it wasn't always this way. That is to say, prior to the humanizing influence of the church, it used to be that human beings killed one another for sport. In the gladiatorial contests of ancient Rome, slaves would fight until death. They were forced to do it. Half the population of Rome was slaves. As a trailer for Hunger Games declares, "Kill or be killed." That's what these gladiators had to do---kill or be killed.

Perhaps, the climax of this orgy of blood was when Emperor Trajan held a spectacle wherein 10,000 gladiators were killed in a span of only four months.

When Emperor Constantine professed Christianity in the early part of the 4th century, he decreed that these games should cease. For a while it was so.

But slowly the contests crept back, until one day in 404, when a humble monk, Telemachus, stumbled across one of these cruel contests in the arena. He yelled out, "In the name of Christ, forbear!" In other words, "In the name of Christ, stop this thing!"

The late Chuck Colson writes, "The fighting began, of course. No one paid the slightest heed to the puny voice. So Telemachus pattered down the stone steps and leapt onto the sandy floor of the arena. He made a comic figure---a scrawny man in a monk's habit dashing back and forth between muscular, armed athletes. One gladiator sent him sprawling with a blow from his shield, directing him back to his seat. It was a rough gesture, though almost a kind one. The crowd roared."

Telemachus ended up getting murdered that day, trying to interpose his body to get the gladiators to stop. When the emperor heard about this, he abolished the games once and for all.

Colson sums up, "There were other forces at work, of course, but that innocent figure lying in the pool of blood crystallized the opposition, and that was the last gladiatorial contest in the Roman Coliseum. Never again did men kill each other for the crowds' entertainment in the Roman arena."

Competition is healthy. The Apostle Paul even likens the spiritual life to a foot race. Sports can be beneficial and exhilarating. But we should never take pleasure in human beings, created in the image of God, destroying one another for mere entertainment.

Additional Note: There were three types of law in the Old Testament---civil, moral, and ceremonial. Our view is that the first type (civil) includes laws that applied in the theocracy, such as the above-cited command in Leviticus, that no longer apply today. (The principle behind the law may apply, but not the specifics. Jesus says we are to love our enemies. The civil law commanded ancient Israel to slay the Canaanites. This is another example of a civil law that no longer applies.) The moral law of God, best encapsulated in the Ten Commandments, still applies today. The third type of law is ceremonial. All of the sacrifices and feasts of ancient Israel were fulfilled when Jesus, the Passover Lamb, was sacrificed on Good Friday, which is our Day of Atonement.

Part 11.

The Seven Deadly Sins

Pride—the Sin Behind Many Headlines

8/1/13

In scanning the headlines today, I noticed how there's an untold story that lay at the root of so many of the developments in the news---human pride. I'm not talking about pride in the sense of self-dignity or self-respect, but in the sense of arrogance, hubris, and haughtiness.

This month marks the 50th anniversary of Dr. Martin Luther King, Jr.'s classic speech, "I have a dream." In that speech, the Baptist preacher quoted Isaiah from the Bible, including the point that in due time, the humble ("every valley") shall be exalted and the proud ("every hill and mountain") laid low: "I have a dream that one day every valley shall be exalted, every hill and mountain shall be made low, the rough places will be made plain, and the crooked places will be made straight, and the glory of the Lord shall be revealed, and all flesh shall see it together."

This is a common theme of the Bible: God opposes the proud, but gives grace to the humble.

Said Solomon famously, "Pride goes before destruction, and a haughty spirit before a fall."

Charles Haddon Spurgeon once said, "Be not proud of race, face, place, or Grace." There's a classic story told about Spurgeon, the terrific Reformed Baptist preacher of 19th century London. One day after church, a proper Victorian woman was commending him for his sermon, when a drunk happened to stumble by.

The woman made a face, expressing her disgust at the drunk, and said, "Well, I never!" And Spurgeon, looking over at the same drunk, said, "But for the grace of God go you or I, Madam."

Pride often robs us of our ability to see things properly. We compare ourselves with our neighbors and come off better (in our minds) than we really are before an all-holy seeing God.

To the Christian, the sin of pride is among the greatest evils. C. S. Lewis likened it to spiritual cancer. In fact, listen to what the great British scholar (a professor at Oxford, then later Cambridge) had to say on the subject: "...the essential vice, the utmost evil, is Pride. Unchastity, anger, greed, drunkenness, and all that, are mere fleabites in comparison....it is Pride which has been the chief cause of misery in every nation and every family since the world began."

One of the greatest rulers from antiquity was King Nebuchadnezzar II (605-562 B. C.). He has a lot to teach us about pride and its destructive nature. Thankfully, the important lessons surrounding him were recorded in the Bible and thus preserved for all time.

Nebuchadnezzar II was Babylon's greatest king. As a conqueror, he was feared by all. A great builder, he had enlarged the city of Babylon to an area of six square miles, beautified it with magnificent buildings, and surrounded it with impenetrable walls. He had hanging gardens around his palace, so spectacular, that they were one of the seven wonders of the ancient world.

Nebuchadnezzar had indeed accomplished many things, but he wouldn't have been able to do any of these things were it not that God had given him his life, his health, his talents, his genetic make-up, his family background, etc. This is true of anybody great or small that accomplishes anything. As Paul notes, What do you have that you did not receive? The answer is nothing.

But full of pride, Nebuchadnezzar bragged, "Is this not great Babylon, that I have built for my royal dwelling by my mighty power and for my majesty?"

God was not pleased with Nebuchadnezzar's overinflated opinion of himself. Listen to what happened next, as found in the book of Daniel: "While the word was still in the king's mouth, a voice fell from heaven: 'King Nebuchadnezzar, to you it is spoken. The kingdom has departed from you! And they shall drive you from men, and your dwelling shall be with the beasts of the field. They shall make you eat grass like oxen; and seven times shall pass over you, until you know the Most High rules in the kingdom of men, and gives it to whomever He chooses.'"

Then what happened? Daniel continues, "That very hour the word was fulfilled concerning Nebuchadnezzar; he was driven from men and ate grass like oxen; his body was wet with the dew of heaven till his hair had grown like eagles' feathers and his nails like birds' claws."

After seven years he acknowledged God, and his mental health and kingdom were restored. I remember in an "abnormal psychology" class at Tulane, this story was in our textbooks. Of course, as I recall, it discounted the divine element which is critical to the story.

In all the universe, the most devastating example of pride run amok is Lucifer. He was once a highly exalted angelic being. How did Lucifer fall? Through the sin of pride. As C. S. Lewis puts it, "it was through Pride that the devil became the devil."

To me, the key to overcoming pride is in reversing the phrase "alter ego" (and alter the spelling of alter to altar): We leave our ego on the altar.

Greed---The Bible Proven Right Yet Again

6/19/13

I enjoy collecting information about studies that relate to some aspect of the Bible. Over and over, social science data tends to confirm the Scriptures.

A new study verifies the truth revealed in Paul's statement in the Bible that the love of money is a root of all kinds of evil.

Paul didn't say that money is the root of evil---although I've heard people misrepresent the Bible as supposedly saying that. Nor did he say it's the lack of money that is the root of evil, although I've heard some people say that's what it should say.

Yet I've known some poor people who were very greedy, and some rich who were not.

Well, a new study validates what the Bible said 2,000 years ago--- not that it needs validation---that the love of money is indeed a corrupting influence.

Writing for CNBC (6/13/13), Mark Koba penned a report, "Just the Scent of Money is Corrupting: Study."

Koba writes, "The report by University of Utah and Harvard researchers found that individuals who could gain monetarily through unethical behavior were more likely to demonstrate that behavior than those who weren't offered a financial gain."

Kristin Smith-Crowe, professor of management at the University of Utah, co-authored the recently-released study. She said, "We certainly found that the love of money is corrupting and just the mere exposure to it makes people do bad things"

In our highly materialistic age, it's easy to forget that ancient Christians classified greed as one of the "Seven Deadly Sins."

The sin of greed is as old as time and as current as today's news. Do you realize that a significant minority of Americans today would be willing to kill you if the price were right?

These are among the many disturbing findings reported in a book about twenty years old, entitled, *The Day America Told the Truth*.

This ground-breaking work revealed just how immoral we have become as a nation. Anecdotally, of course, we read about that every day in the news. But this book was based on extensive surveying where the respondents were guaranteed anonymity.

One of the findings is related to greed. Pastor R. Kent Hughes writes about the disturbing results to an intriguing question the respondents were asked: "The survey…posed the question, 'What are you willing to do for $10 million?'"

Hughes reports, "Twenty-five percent would abandon their families, 23 percent would become a prostitute for a week, and 7 percent would kill a stranger. Think of it. In a gathering of 100 Americans, there are seven who would consider killing you if the price was right. In 1,000 there are seventy."

Gulp.

For his short 2012 movie, *Genius*, evangelist and film-producer Ray Comfort took to the streets of California and interviewed a lot of people about values and morals.

Here is my paraphrase of one of his questions on the topic of greed: "Would you be willing to poison a total stranger if you would be paid a few million dollars for it?"

Guest after guest basically said, "Yes." With some of them, they said it as if were a joke. But they still said it.

The film has been described this way: "It is shocking to hear how many are willing to kill another human being for simply a few million dollars. Such is the moral state of North America."

Again, greed is nothing new. A neighbor of Abraham Lincoln's in Springfield saw Lincoln passing by with his two sons. Both were crying loudly. "What is the matter with the boys?" asked the neighbor. "The same thing that is the matter with the whole world," answered Lincoln. "I have three walnuts and each boy wants two."

In writing against greed, of course, the Bible in no way condemns striving for more money, to earn a better living. More power to you.

In fact, in the same letter (1 Timothy) where Paul says that the love of money is a root of all kinds of evil, he also says, "Anyone who does not provide for their relatives, and especially for their own household, has denied the faith and is worse than an unbeliever."

But greed is not a matter of meeting basic needs. Greed involves breaking the Tenth Commandment: "You shall not covet your neighbor's house. You shall not covet your neighbor's wife, or his manservant or his maidservant, his ox or donkey, or anything that belongs to your neighbor."

Greed is "the desire for more"---and more and more and more, and there is no end to it. Both the Bible and the social science research documents that the love of money corrupts

Envy, the Green Monster

7/27/12

Envy has been called the Green Monster. It's a sin we don't talk about very much. Yet it envy was the motive for the very first murder, where Cain killed Abel

Envy has continued to be responsible for countless other murders since the dawn of time.

Envy can be summed up in two short sentences that were uttered by a thief when he held up a pharmacy in Gulfport, MS about two decades ago. He held a gun to the pharmacist's head, demanding money and drugs. He shouted: "You've got it! I want it!" That's a great definition of envy. It cuts to the chase; it cuts through any religious games or sanctimonious ways to hide our jealousy: You've got it. I want it.

The irony of envy is that a person may be fabulously wealthy compared to the vast majority of the rest of the world. Yet he may envy that small population that has more than he...and that gnaws at him so he ends up not enjoying the abundance he has because of these feelings of envy. Happiness and envy can't co-exist. As different authors have pointed out, one can be lustful and happy. One can be gluttonous and happy. One may even enjoy indulging his temper by flying off in a rage. But one can't be envious and happy simultaneously. They are mutually exclusive.

Here's a quick test to see if the deadly sin of envy rests in your heart: Do you envy Bill Gates? Do you envy the latest movie star? Do you envy the latest pop star? If you're a minister, do you envy Billy Graham? Do you envy the wealthy? I think if we were honest, we would see that some degree of envy resides in all of our hearts. "Not me," you say? But suppose a co-worker were promoted this very week, would that *immediately* elicit thanksgiving in your heart or resentment?

Envy is likened to a sickness, and we're all vulnerable to its icy grip in our hearts if we're not careful. From the smallest resentment of another's possession or advantage to the blinding desire to destroy that person, too often envy raises its ugly head and wreaks havoc.

What was the greatest single crime ever committed in the history of the world? What was the greatest single injustice ever perpetrated on any one person? The answer, of course, is the crucifixion of Jesus Christ. He was not only innocent; He was the only perfectly innocent person who ever lived. Yet He was executed like a common criminal. What was the *motive* of those who sought His death? Envy. "For [Pilate] knew it was out of envy that they had handed Jesus over to him" (Matthew 27:18).

Emperors, kings, and dictators through the centuries have likewise committed murder because of their envy. Much of the history of England, for instance, contains episodes where the brothers, sisters, or other relatives of the monarch ended up in the Tower of London because of envy, lest they rival his or her power. Many of these siblings were murdered simply for having been born. Consider other examples in history of leaders killing others because of their envy:

· Herod was envious of a little baby, Jesus, who, it was said, was born a king. Herod couldn't bear to have this potential rival to his political power, even though the "rival" was a little infant. So Herod massacred all sorts of baby boys to try and remove this threat to his power. Having been warned in a dream, Joseph and Mary had fled before. They were safely in Egypt by the time this slaughter of the innocents took place.

· The French Revolution spilled the blood of one perceived enemy of the people after another. Eventually, the revolutionaries rivaled each other for political power, and virtually each one ended up getting killed during the reign of terror.

· Josef Stalin massacred 40-60 million of his own people in order to force Communism on Russia, a portion of whom were killed because of his paranoid envy. His envy of the Capitalist West was so great that when soldiers returned from the European theater, he had them eventually killed in what is known as "the hero's purge" because they saw what life was like outside of Communist Russia. Consider also his murder of all his former colleagues who helped bring about the Russian Revolution with him, such as Leon Trotsky, one of the key architects of the Soviet Union. Stalin was so envious and paranoid of his former comrade that he had his henchmen chase Trotsky more than halfway around the globe until they caught up with him in Mexico and stuck an icepick in his head.

As it was with Cain and Abel, so it has been with many other children. What they are envious of is love, affection, and acceptance. Whether this is perceived or real, it can cause rage which can lead to violence. What sometimes happens is that a parent can withhold his or her love from one child, and yet lavish it on another one. For example, Joseph was clearly Jacob's favorite son; this brought untold trouble on the family.

The Smothers Brothers sometimes captured this sibling rivalry in a humorous way. One brother complained, "Mom always liked you best. She gave you a dog as a pet and only gave me a chicken." Then the other brother piped in, "Yeah. But your chicken ate my dog."

All humor aside, some families are ruled by such rivalry. Look at what happened when Jacob loved his son, Joseph, more than all his brothers. All of which is detailed in the last several chapters of Genesis.

Envy is something that thrives in the dark. But when the light is shown on it, it sometimes withers away. Psychologist Betsy Cohen, author of a book about envy called *The Snow White Syndrome*, says: "We must bring envy 'into the light.' It is a dark and hidden emotion but easily disarmed. When unacknowledged, envy is dangerous. Bring it into the light, use the word, and it becomes less potent. We must call it by name—envy."

Covetousness, which we find forbidden at the end of the Ten Commandments, is really the only commandment dealing with thoughts about and towards other people. (The first commandment forbids wrong thoughts and attitudes about God.) But covetousness forbids us to want and desire anything belonging to our neighbor. We seldom recognize envy or covetousness for what it is, and we seldom confess it as a sin. As a matter of fact, an elderly Catholic priest once said that in all his years of hearing confessions, he had never once heard a person confessing to the sin of covetousness.

May God give us grace, by uprooting the envy in our hearts.

The Antidote to our Culture's Sexual Anarchy
10/21/14

This culture is obsessed with sex. Even burger ads sometimes use sex to sell their product. Pornography is rampant. Gender confusion rules the day. Some even want laws to let men use the ladies' room. And if you are a pastor and don't agree, they may subpoena your sermons.

Tragically, the church is not immune from sexual problems. Every so often another prominent minister falls publically because of private sexual sin. Dr. Mark Laaser of faithfulandtrue.com says pastors can be vulnerable because of loneliness: "The ministry in whatever denomination or form is sometimes a very lonely profession."

He notes, "Fantasy is the cornerstone of sexual addiction. All sex addicts and all people who get into trouble with adultery, to a certain extent, have problems with fantasy. Fantasy is an attempt by addicts to heal any woundedness of their spirit. So if they're lonely, they're going to find a fantasy that helps them feel a lot less lonely."

Dr. Mark Laaser knows firsthand about sexual addiction and healing. By the grace of God, he overcame a 25-year addiction himself and now counsels people in this realm regularly. At his ministry in Minnesota, they even hold treatment workshops that usually last three intense days.

Sexual sin often loses its grip once the light is shone on it. As has been said, sunlight is the greatest disinfectant. Accountability to a trusted source is a key help. I have interviewed Dr. Laaser a few times for Christian radio and television. Here are some of his insights.

He says: "The physical consequences [of sexual addiction] are profound. Most of us have known people who have lost jobs, careers. We work in our ministry with a number of pastors who have fallen, and that's a terrible thing to happen---when you lose in a way, God's calling on your life."

And there are other losses too: "We've had people who spent hundreds of thousands of dollars on sexual activity....We've had men who have actually started robbing banks in order to pay for their prostitution habit. We're seeing a lot of crazy things. People being arrested....People being sued, those kinds of things. And then there's the divorce rate, the broken marriages, broken homes, abandoned children, as a result of sexual addiction. That's all very profound."

He says, "Most sex addicts can trace their addiction back into childhood and adolescence. So it generally starts early and just develops over the course of the life until they are found out."

While leading a secret double life, Dr. Laaser was both a minister and a Christian counselor. When he was "found out" in the mid-1980s, he was fired by the church's trustees. But one of them was a recovering alcoholic who had undergone treatment to deal with his problem, and he noted the similarities between his problem (in recovery) and Dr. Laaser's. So he recommended Laaser to be sent to a treatment facility. It turned out to be just what the doctor ordered.

Laaser tells how it all had begun: "I started looking at pornography at age 11. I got really hooked into that for 25 years following that. That, of course, got progressively worse over time. I mean I needed more and more forms and the volume of that needed to increase in terms of frequency and other kinds of things." He thanks God that he found help before the Internet hit.

He said, "The sex addict will always want more and more of the same thing or more and more of other things to achieve the same effect on their brain. That's the kind of an effect that we call tolerance. Sex addicts build up a tolerance to sex---where they're going to need more excitement, more activity or so forth to have the experience."

He says three myths kept him from seeking help: "The first one was if you professed Christ, God would remove all lust from your heart. The second one was if you go into the ministry, God will prevent you from all sexual temptation. And the third one was that if you get married, and have a regular sexual partner, you'll never have a problem with sexual temptation."

The distortion of sex today is a twisting of God's design. Says Laaser: "God's intention for sexuality is that a man and a woman in marriage should be together in a totally spiritually and emotionally intimate relationship first, and then sexuality is an expression of that....it should be self-sacrificing, and it should be our hearts' intention in marriage to give to our partners."

Keeping connected to Jesus is the key. A former homosexual once told me, "I went to sleep one night and was just praying, 'Lord, I can't do this anymore.' And I closed my eyes and I saw a vision of the cross...and I heard that still small voice again say to me, 'Whenever you get tempted to fall, think about the cross, and everything I've done for you.' And in that moment, there was a healing that took place inside of me." That began his new freedom in Christ.

Dr. Laaser concludes, "My heart is to reach out to those who are as lonely as I was---who are as isolated as I was, who are as hopeless as I was. Our ministry's main mission is to reach out to the sexually broken, so they can find a source of strength and hope." As Jesus said of Himself, "If the Son sets you free, you shall be free indeed."

A Sad State of Affairs

11/14/12

The Drudge Report calls it a "Four-Star Circus." It's certainly like a national soap opera.

Perhaps, the worst part is its obscuring of what really happened in Libya on 9/11 of this year.

Of course, the "it" is the unfolding scandal involving the four-star General David Petraeus (which he apparently has admitted to) and his biographer, Paula Broadwell, and now allegations of flirtatious emails from General John Allen, former commander of our troops in Afghanistan, and a Tampa socialite. Allegations he denies.

Being embroiled in adultery clearly is a betrayal to one's family, and for a military leader to guard national secrets is clearly compromising, potentially to the country.

In reading some of the stories on the scandal on various news sites on the Internet, I have been struck by how many times they have enticing photos on the side. Here's a story, blasting the former head of the CIA for committing adultery, with lustful photos in the margins. (They often have these enticing photos, regardless of the news item featured.)

Since this story is front and center and virtually inescapable, this gives us an opportunity to ruminate on the issue of adultery from a spiritual perspective.

When did the word "affair," which sugar coats reality, replace the word adultery? Whenever it happened, it was before the 1980s.

I remember many years ago, when I interviewed Dr. J. Allan Peterson on an open-line radio show in the Chicago area to discuss his book on adultery, *The Myth of the Greener Grass*.

I asked for phone callers to ring up to discuss "adultery;" no one called. Dr. Peterson suggested during the commercial break that I ask for callers to discuss their "affairs;" suddenly the board lit up like a proverbial Christmas tree. This was on Christian radio no less.

We might envy our neighbors for their greener grass, but you should see their water bill!

Apparently, people today can't "relate" to the old-fashioned, outmoded concept of "adultery" (sin), but they readily know what you're talking about if it's an affair (an indiscretion, a choice, nobody else's business). But a rose is a rose by any other name; or perhaps I should say, a thorn is a thorn by any other name.

In Puritan times, one preacher charged another with having committed adultery. He accused him of "nefarious breachments of the 7th commandment," a phrase not easily forgotten.

A lot of people thought that Jimmy Carter invented the phrase "lust in the heart." But that concept comes from Jesus. The Lord said it's bad enough to commit adultery, but also to commit adultery in the heart. And the Bible not only says, "Thou shalt not commit adultery," but also, "Thou shalt not covet thy neighbor's wife," which is adultery in the heart.

It is said, We don't break the Ten Commandments---we break ourselves by violating them.

Look at how a man or woman could work for decades, building up a positive reputation and a great record of service---all to be destroyed for a few minutes of pleasure?

In the classic art film, *Koyaanisqatsi* (meaning "life out of balance"), it's amazing to see one building after another blown up---with the driving music of Philip Glass. It took years to build those buildings, and with a few explosives in just the right places, they collapse in seconds.

Zig Ziglar is right. As noted, he once said the only real failure in life is moral failure.

From a biblical perspective, lust battles with our very souls. I can think of people who claim they fell away from faith because there was some alleged deficiency with Christianity. But the reality is that it was lust that got the better of them.

For example, one famous anti-Christian humanist of today claims he left the church because God didn't answer his prayers, yet at the same time he "had a girl in every port," to quote *TIME* magazine. Church lady might say about his arguments against the faith, "How conveeeenient."

Psychologists describe a condition known as "cognitive dissonance" which is a fancy way of describing the idea that you can't hold two mutually exclusive beliefs at the same time for too long. Eventually, one will win out over the other.

While God forgives those who repent, there are still the consequences we pay for our sin.

But if you think you're strong, watch out lest you fall. Ellen Williams once wrote, "If you are thinking to yourself, 'An affair could never happen to me,' you are in trouble. To believe that we are immune leaves us wide open and unprotected."

Of course, this is not a new problem. David---the greatest king of ancient Israel (and also one of its leading generals)---fell prey to his own lusts. While he was forgiven, he paid a terrible price for it all, including a civil war against him from one of his own sons, Absalom.

I give Ben Franklin the last word: "Samson, for all his strong body, had a weak head, or he would not have laid it in a harlot's lap."

The Deadly Sin of Anger on the Rise

5/28/14

If you can control your anger, you're greater than being able to control a city. That's a paraphrase from Solomon the Wise, about a thousand years before Christ.

I like to write sometimes on the Seven Deadly Sins, of which Anger is one---even though a person can be angry without sinning. In one form or another, anger is in the headlines.

A report came out this month on the subject of nagging, which is often a muted, frustrated form of anger.

CBS New York reported (5/9/14) that "...a new study suggests husbands of nagging wives can actually be nagged to death. Danish researchers from the University of Copenhagen said having a nagging partner can significantly shorten one's life, and could result in three extra deaths per 100 people per year. The study also said people nagged by their spouses are more likely to get heart disease and cancer." Anger on the part of the one who nags can hasten the death of others.

Anger can also kill in more dramatic ways, including the one who is angry. How horrible it is when someone snaps and even commits violence because they can't control their rage.

A new report just came out on angry outbursts by motorists, i.e., road rage. Paul A. Eiesentein summarizes it in an article called, "Get Out of My Lane!" (cnbc.com, 5/23/14): "According to a new study by travel site Expedia, some of the most rage-inducing behaviors are slowpokes who won't move out of the left lane, tailgaters and people who text while driving."

Then we see people going crazy on killing sprees fueled by anger, like the recent stabbing and shooting of victims in Santa Barbara, California. Anger seems to be on the rise in our time.

Our nation's founding fathers designed our government on the premise of self-control. The more people could control themselves, including their anger, the less need for government control. To paraphrase Speaker of the House Robert Winthrop in an 1849 speech: We'll either be ruled by the Bible or by the bayonet. Take your pick. Control from inside or control from outside.

In *The Dance of Anger*, Harriet Goldhor Lerner says, "Anger is a signal, and one worth listening to. Our anger may be a message that we are being hurt, that our rights are being violated, that our needs or wants are not being adequately met, or simply that something is not right."

She adds, "Our anger may tell us that we are not addressing important emotional issues in our lives, or that too much of our self—our beliefs, values, desires or ambitions—is being compromised in a relationship...."

The Bible has much advice about handling anger, but nowhere does it forbid us to get angry per se. Indeed, God made us in His image. In addition to being a God of love, He is a God of wrath.

God's anger is not petty, nor whimsically vindictive, but always in keeping with His eternal plan.

Over and over again in the Old Testament, God became angry with His people, especially when they turned to other gods, or when they forgot His mercy and His help in the past. The purpose of God's anger was to bring His children back into a right relationship with Him.

When Jesus came to earth, He also became angry. For example, in the Gospels, He cleansed the temple because they had changed a place of worship into just a marketplace. *Killing Jesus* by Bill O'Reilly and Martin Dugard provides some excellent background on the temple cleansing.

In Mark, Jesus overthrew the tables and drove the moneychangers out, declaring, "It is written, 'My house will be called a house of prayer', but you have made it a 'den of robbers.'"

In His anger, He did not sin---and that's the point. However, the rest of us have, according to the Bible, a sin nature---which severely limits our ability to be righteously angry. We are more likely to import our own selfishness and own sense of entitlement in our anger.

The Bible (especially the Psalms) is honest about our feelings towards God, but it also warns us against being angry with God: "Woe to him who quarrels with his maker," says Isaiah. When Job was angry with God, the Lord answered: "Would you condemn Me to justify yourself?"

When it comes to our relationships with other people, the Bible has much to say regarding anger:

• "Refrain from anger and turn from wrath; do not fret—it leads only to evil."

• "A gentle answer turns away wrath, but a harsh word stirs up anger."

• "Do not make friends with a hot-tempered man, do not associate with one easily angered, or you may learn his ways and get yourself ensnared."

• "A man who controls his temper is better than one who takes a city."

The key advice on anger is found in the Old Testament and New: "Be angry, and do not sin." The New Testament warns not to give in to sinful anger, lest we give the devil a foothold.

Because Christ died on the cross and justifies us, we don't have to worry about justifying ourselves. Therefore, when we are wronged, we can forgive (as we have been forgiven) and leave vengeance to God, who will settle things in His timing. This will disarm anger.

On a lighter side, I always remember Art Carney, as Ed Norton on "The Honeymooners," saying, "Sheesh, what a grouch!" whenever Jackie Gleason, as Ralph Cramden, blew his stack. Humor can be like releasing a pressure valve to relieve the stress of anger.

How much better our world would be if we could learn to keep the deadly sin of anger in check.

If My Body is the Temple of the Holy Spirit, Then Why Do I Look Like the Buddha?

12/31/12

Every year most of us go through the ritual of setting New Year's resolutions, around January 1.

For many people, there is a perpetual goal to lose weight---a goal I've often struggled with. If you're overweight, please don't take offense at any of this. Who knows? Perhaps, I may inspire someone to work toward taking off unwanted weight. You might be able to add years to your life---and quality and better health to those years. I recognize that for some rare bodies, nothing they do can change their weight. But, thankfully, they're the exception. For most of us, it's simple mathematics: input versus output.

Suppose you took a backpack and put in it a five-pound sack of sugar. Then put that on your back and walk around with that extra five pounds. Now, put in two. That's ten pounds extra. Put in three. That's 15-pounds. Put in five such sacks. That's 25 pounds extra weight.

Walk around with that extra 25 pounds weight. It might hurt your knees for a while and your back. Yet if we're 25 pounds overweight, isn't that already happening? We're carrying around that extra weight.

Unfortunately, many Americans are now grossly overweight. That includes many Christians. One statement in an anti-Christian book really bothered me. Sam Harris in his *Letter to a Christian Nation*, says that Christians are fat. Ouch. That hurts because it seems to be so often the case. Perhaps, because so many church functions center around eating.

I have noticed that it is easy to use food as a means of therapy---as a pick me up, when dealing with life's difficulties. But when you eat to feel better, then you get fatter. And you feel worse because of your girth. This becomes a vicious cycle.

About ten years ago, I did two things that helped me in this area. First, at the gym I go to, I hired a trainer, as part of a group rate. (It's nowhere near as expensive as I thought it would be---or as it could be, I suppose, in other contexts).

Secondly, I began to participate in runs, .e.g., 5k's, 10k's, 5 milers, etc. A friend who got me into the serious running used to always say of running: "It sure beats the doctor's bills." I'm very slow. But I've learned that I compete against myself, i.e., by trying to improve my times, and the other runners around help me to go faster.

Obviously, excessive running can have its issues too. I know some people who have run multiple marathons and now have knee problems.

My dad used to always say, "Everything in moderation." I remember the cynical bumper sticker that says, "Eat right, exercise, die anyway."

Chuck Swindoll once said this about progress in life in general: Three steps forward, two steps backwards. If it's true that virtually any habit can be made by doing it 21 days in a row, then why not get going now---to start a new lifestyle?

Through a lot of directed training, I was able to really get a handle on my weight and to lose about 30-40 pounds, most of which I have been able to keep off. (All except those last five pounds or so). And I think it has improved the quality of my life. Obviously, get your doctor's advice before starting any serious regimen.

Thankfully, I have been able to lose many pounds and keep them off. However, it is an on-going struggle. It is not easy.

A great key to weight loss is counter-intuitive: eat often. Eat small meals about every two hours, including protein. Don't be like a camel where you eat a large meal and store it.

Fat is our friend. Fat was designed by God to help us through lean times. But now in modern times, where we have such abundance, we generally don't go through such lean times, so we don't need the extra fat that keeps getting stored.

In the ancient Church, gluttony was viewed as one of the seven deadly sins. In its own way, it is still deadly, and not only to the body. In modern Christendom, it seems that many don't care about the issue. We just let ourselves go---and go and go and go. We need to remember that self-control is one of the fruits of the Spirit.

I believe we will never have victory in this area until we see gluttony as a sin. Food is one of God's greatest gifts, but like all of His gifts, it can be abused.

I know that God is sovereign and He determines our days. But I also know that He who ordains the ends ordains the means. The research on the deleterious effects of being overweight abounds. In short, we need more discipline.

My brother and his family got into a friendly argument about which was the best exercise? Swimming? Running? Walking? Weight-lifting? Their conclusion was simple: The one you actually do.

As a Christian, I view my body as the temple of the Holy Spirit. I remember once thinking: If my body is the temple of the Holy Spirit, then why do I sometimes look like the Buddha? Well, in 2013, I hope to see you at the finish line, hopefully looking more like Jesus than Buddha.

Food for Thought on America's Obesity Problem

5/10/12

Food is one of God's greatest gifts, but like all of His gifts, it can be abused.

A recent report from the Atlanta-based Centers for Disease Control and Prevention just released a new study showing a 130% increase in the number of "severely obese" Americans. The *LA Times* (May 8, 2012) reports this is defined as having a Body Mass Index (BMI) of 40 or above.

Meanwhile, the Centers also report that if the present trends continue to 2030, we will see an increase from 34% to 42% of Americans who are obese (as defined by a BMI of 30 or more).

America seems to be losing the battle of the bulge.

I know that God is sovereign and He determines our days. But I also know that He who ordains the ends ordains the means. The research that is out there about the deleterious effects of being overweight is so abundant. We don't need more studies, more research. We just need more discipline.

Some people have medical issues or glandular problems that result in obesity. I have sympathy for them. But this is relatively rare. Most people who are overweight are overweight because of their behavior. It's pure mathematics for most of us---input vs. output.

As noted before, in my personal struggle with keeping the fat off, I have appreciated what Chuck Swindoll says about accomplishments in general: three steps forward, two steps backwards.

If you're overweight, please don't take offense at any of this. It wasn't until a close friend began calling me to account for tipping the scales that I began to take action. He has probably added years to my life, and certainly more quality to my life.

My friend encouraged me to start running and competing in races (primarily against myself, by striving to do faster next time) as a means of losing weight. He said, "It sure beats the doctor's bills." When I started, I used to joke all the time, "I'm in shape---round is a shape." But I have been able to lose many pounds and keep them off. After a while, the joke rang hollow. However, it is an on-going struggle. It is not easy.

I know many Christians who are disciplined in many ways, but they have let themselves go as far as being overweight. I discussed this once with a friend---about all the fat we find in the body of Christ. He said, "What other sin is left?" We can't smoke or do other things. But we can eat. And do we ever. We often build many functions around food.

The results do not go unnoticed. One time, when my son was little, we went to a Christmas singing-presentation at a church. He turned to me and asked, "Dad, why are all those ladies so fat?" Out of the mouths of babes.

Of all people, Christians should be excellent examples in this area. The Holy Spirit resides in us and can give us self-control.

In the ancient church, gluttony was viewed as one of the seven deadly sins. In its own way, it is still deadly, and not only to the body. In modern church circles, it seems that many don't care about the issue. We just let ourselves go---and go and go and go. We need to remember that self-control is one of the fruits of the Spirit.

Those of us who take our hope and comfort from the Lord should take a hard look at how we use food. One thing I had to stop doing is using food as a means of therapy---as a pick me up, when dealing with life's difficulties. In short, avoid "comfort foods."

I like the way overweight comedian Allan Sherman once put it: "Fare thee well, Metrecal, / And the others of that ilk. / Let the diet start tomorrow, / 'Cause today I'll drown my sorrow / In a double malted milk." (Metrecal was a brand of diet foods in the 1960s.)

When you eat to feel better, you get fatter. And you feel worse because of your girth. So you eat more to soothe your bad feelings, and the vicious cycle repeats. Some people feel discouraged because they have worked hard at losing weight, and their lack of results has discouraged them to the point of giving up.

Ironically, the people who gain the least weight usually eat often, literally throughout the day. They just eat smart and in smaller portions. And they exercise regularly.

If we Americans are ever going to control our obesity problem, we need to get our eating habits in check and increase our exercise. The great thing about more discipline in this area is that it tends to spill over into other aspects of your life---giving you more energy. Thomas Jefferson said (August 19, 1785): "Give about two [hours] every day to exercise; for health must not be sacrificed to learning. A strong body makes the mind strong." That's often true for the spirit as well.

So which is the best exercise for you? The one you actually do.

Overcoming the Sin of Sloth

1/8/14

At the start of the New Year, it's often good to review our life's direction and goals. One thing to consider is how much any of "the Seven Deadly Sins" (Pride, Greed, Envy, Anger, Lust, Gluttony, and Sloth) have a hold on our lives.

The Seven Deadly Sins are not listed as such in the Bible. Yet each one is independently condemned in various passages of the Scriptures. In fact, most of the Seven Deadly Sins have several Bible verses against them. The one I want to focus on here is Sloth.

We don't think of Sloth or Laziness as a sin per se. But surely it is. Leonardo da Vinci once said, "God sells us all things at the price of labor." Sadly, today, millions are choosing to live off of the labor of others without even thinking about it. (Of course, if someone is disabled and unable to work, that is a different matter.)

Did you ever hear about the patient who went for a very thorough examination by a doctor? The patient said that he wanted the doctor to be frank about what was wrong with him. The doctor asked him if he was quite sure about this. The patient replied in the affirmative.

Said the doctor, "There isn't a thing in the world wrong with you, except that you are just lazy." The patient answered, "Okay, doc. Now give me the medical term for it, so I can tell my wife."

God created work before the fall. Work is good. Since the fall, the earth is under a curse, and we experience that curse in one way or another each day.

God declared to Adam in judgment: "Cursed is the ground because of you; through painful toil you will eat of it all the days of your life. It will produce thorns and thistles for you, and you will eat the plants of the field. By the sweat of your brow you will eat your food" (Gen. 3:17-19).

Nevertheless, we are still commanded to do our own work, even if it is difficult. In the Ten Commandments (and elsewhere in the Bible). God tells us, "Six days shall work be done." The Apostle Paul commends work (Col. 3:23), and even connects it with having food (2 Thess. 3:10).

The Greeks and the Romans used their slaves to do their hard work. In ancient Greece, about 75 percent of the population was slaves. In Rome, it was about half. Larry Burkett points out: "The Greeks degraded into a nation of idle talkers who were easily overrun by the Romans."

We get a taste of that in Acts 17, when Paul spoke before the Areopagus in Athens: "For all the Athenians and the foreigners who were there spent their time in nothing else but either to tell or to hear something new" (Acts 17:21).

Thus, the condemnation of sloth as a sin fits with the Judeo-Christian view but not necessarily other traditions. As the late Dr. D. James Kennedy once pointed out: When Jesus worked as a carpenter, He dignified labor.

Jump to today. Many employers are often complaining that one of the greatest difficulties they face is workplace theft. Not so much stealing pencils or paper clips, but rather time. One study written up years ago found that time theft by employees "cost companies more than all other crimes, including pilfering, insurance fraud, kickbacks, and embezzlement."

In one study, they found 33 percent of American workers have confessed to researchers that they have phoned in sick—when they really weren't. All of these are symptoms of the sin of sloth.

I think it's interesting to note that the Bible gave an apt description—more than 3,000 years ago—of the slothful employee and the impact he has on his boss. Solomon wrote: "As vinegar to the teeth and smoke to the eyes, so is a sluggard to those who send him" (Proverbs 10:26).

The Book of Proverbs has much to say about sloth and diligence:

• "Lazy hands make a man poor, but diligent hands bring wealth. He who gathers crops in summer is a wise son, but he who sleeps during harvest is a disgraceful son."

• "Diligent hands will rule, but laziness ends in slave labor."

• "The sluggard craves and gets nothing, but the desires of the diligent are fully satisfied."

• "The plans of the diligent leads to profit as surely as haste leads to poverty."

There is a great deal of spiritual sloth today. How many of us intend to spend time in the Bible and in prayer and in service to others, but never really get around to it?

Howard E. Butt, Jr. once told a church audience that too many churchgoers tend to regard sermon-listening as an end in itself. Church attendance is a great first step. But Butt said sermon-listening can be an "escape." He said: "God wants transformation from listening into living."

In contrast to spiritual sloth, consider the example of one of the greatest missionaries of all time—the legendary David Livingstone, whose 200th birthday we celebrated this past year. He plodded along into the interior or unchartered territory in Africa for the gospel's sake.

Here's what he wrote in his diary: "I place no value on anything I have or may possess, except in relation to the kingdom of Christ. If anything will advance the interests of the kingdom, it shall be given away or kept, only as by giving or keeping it I shall promote the glory of Him to whom I owe all my hopes in time and eternity."

The good works I'm talking about are not sufficient to earn our way to heaven. Only Jesus could do that for us on the cross. Once we're redeemed, good works become our Thank You to Him.

To overcome sloth, here's a portion of the classic Serenity Prayer: "God, grant me...the courage to change the things I can..." That's not a bad petition at the outset of 2014.

Part 12.

Apologetics, the Defense of the Faith

Is Heaven Just a "False Hope"?

4/9/13

It's an incredible tragedy that mega-pastor Rick Warren's son committed suicide recently. Our prayers are with the family through this difficult time. His son was 27 and struggled for years with mental illness.

While many well-wishers have tried to give solace to the grieving family, others have heaped scorn---especially through the means of social media.

One person from Cincinnati posted this: "Either there is no God, or God doesn't listen to Rick Warren, despite all the money Rick has made off of selling false hope to desperate people." That same person told Warren he should "abandon primitive superstitions and accept the universe for what it is—a place that is utterly indifferent to us." Talk about kicking a man when he's down.

But is it true? Is Rick Warren and all the others who claim to speak for God just "selling false hope to desperate people"? Is the universe just "a place that is utterly indifferent to us"? Is death just the end? Is there any rational reason to believe that there is a life after this one?

As far as the notion of "selling false hope," I think the states that sell lottery tickets are selling false hope---consider the odds of winning.

But is heaven just a false hope? At the end of the day, all that counts is what is true.

The Bible is clear that there is life after this one. There are rewards and punishment---heaven and hell. There's a day of Judgment coming, and Jesus will be that judge.

Jesus said, "I am the way, the truth, and the life. No one comes to the Father, but through Me."

Salvation is by works---the finished work of Jesus on the cross on behalf of sinners. True faith in Jesus results in good works, but it's not our works that save our soul---His do. The urgency and importance of this message is what motivates Rick Warren and others to share it.

But who says the Bible is true?

Rick Warren et al., including me, believe that 2,000 years ago, ours became what theologian J. B. Phillips called "the visited planet." Jesus of Nazareth came into our world as a baby. His birth, life, death, and resurrection were foretold in hundreds of prophecies written down long before.

Because Jesus rose from the dead, because He actually walked out of that tomb days after the Romans killed Him, and there is ample evidence of His resurrection, we believe that everything else He taught is true.

I once interviewed Lee Strobel, who has worked with Rick Warren at Saddleback Community Church in southern California.

Strobel worked as the legal affairs editor of *The Chicago Tribune* earlier in his life. A graduate of Yale Law School, Strobel was an atheist for years.

He admits he had a mean streak, relishing the power he wielded in his position at the Tribune: "What I really savored was making big shots dance to the newspaper's tune." For example, he purposefully postponed calling a prominent businessman until Thanksgiving day, just before the family feast, to inform him that the paper was going to run a major story the next day on how the man was under investigation for fraud.

But when Lee Strobel's wife, Leslie, went to church one Sunday morning, he was taken aback. "You didn't give those guys any of our money, did you?" he asked. She soon had a come to Jesus moment, and this led him to do an historical search on Jesus. He wanted to debunk Christianity once and for all: "No resurrection, no Christianity," he reasoned---which is correct.

Lee Strobel meticulously engaged in the type of careful research that had made him a respected reporter. But the more he studied, the more convinced he became of the veracity of Jesus Christ.

He was amazed to learn that hundreds of years before Jesus was born, much of His story was foretold by the Hebrew prophets in the Old Testament. As Strobel studied the prophecies that Jesus fulfilled, he found that they weren't easily dismissed. He writes: "The more I studied them, the more difficulty I had in trying to explain them away."

Strobel says the Hebrew Bible (the Old Testament) gave humanity a thumbprint: "It says that when you find the person that fits this thumbprint, that's the Messiah. That's the Son of God, and throughout history, only Jesus Christ has had that thumbprint."

As he looked at the odds of any one person fulfilling these prophecies, he was stunned at the scientific evidence that Jesus was the Messiah. Strobel was shocked by the work of mathematician Peter Stoner, who proved that the chance of any one person fulfilling even eight of these Old Testament prophecies was one in 10^{17} —that is 10 with seventeen zeroes after it.

If that was not mind boggling enough, Stoner demonstrated that the chances of any one fulfilling 48 prophecies were 10^{157}. Strobel realized the incredible implications of that. He said it would be like finding "a single predetermined atom among all the atoms in a trillion, trillion, trillion, trillion, billion universes the size of our universe." Well, other than that…

Lee Strobel finally did the intellectually honest thing—he recognized Jesus as the Lord. He has now written such classics as *The Case for Christ and The Case for Faith.*

The truths that he has uncovered and now helps to promote are proof that the message of his friend, Rick Warren, are based on historical realities. Please keep the Warrens in your prayers.

Why Does God Allow Hurricanes?

8/28/12

The shortest sermon I ever heard was delivered whimsically.

On a Sunday night, many years ago, an associate pastor of a popular mega-church got up to preach. He said that the topic of his sermon was, "Why Do Bad Things Happen to Good People?" Then he said, "The answer to that question is very simple: There are no good people." Then he pivoted and began to walk away.

A half minute later, he returned to the pulpit and delivered his actual message. I don't remember a word of what followed, but I've never forgotten his humorous prelude.

With Hurricane Isaac causing some havoc and threatening a lot more (as of this writing, it seems to be following the path of Katrina), we remember again the problem of reconciling a good God with suffering.

Some politicians have weighed in on the hurricane, tying it into the Republican Convention in Tampa. On August 24, US Congressman Danny Davis (D-IL), told WLS radio in Chicago, "Well, it means that the gods are favoring Democrats. Not that we wish any kind of difficulty in terms of the weather." The next day, former Michigan Governor Jennifer Granholm tweeted, "R convention delay due to Isaac: I guess God has ways to shut the whole thing down."

When it looked like the GOP convention was going to be spared and New Orleans might be hit, actor Samuel L. Jackson tweeted in a profanity-laced message on Monday that it was "unfair." And an actress tweeted a message, also with swearing, regretting that Isaac wasn't going to wash away the pro-lifers, et al, into the ocean.

All politics aside, how could a good God allow hurricanes or other forms of natural disasters?

This is a core question that keeps resurfacing. Presumably, it is part of what keeps some from believing the Gospel of Jesus Christ.

There's only so much you can say in this type of forum. But here are a few observations I make, as a student of the Bible and as a student of history.

1) Ultimately, we don't know why God allows these things. His ways are not our ways.

The whole book of Job deals with the issue of Job's suffering—why did God allow it? Throughout the book, Job's "friends" or "comforters" insist he must be guilty of secret sin; otherwise he wouldn't be going through all this pain. Job maintains his integrity throughout the ordeal, but does question God's justice in all this.

At the end of the book, God rebukes Job's comforters. But He also asks Job many pointed questions, such as, "Where were you when I created the heavens and the earth?" Over and over, for four chapters, God puts Job in his place. He also says words to this effect: Will you condemn Me to justify yourself? That's precisely what many do today.

2) We live in a fallen world. Fallen because of humanity's sin. Bad stuff happens to everyone. So does good stuff. Someone once said, "The real question isn't, 'Why do bad things happen to good people? But, why do good things happen to bad people?'" In any event, hurricanes are a reminder that things are not right between us and the Creator. Jesus said the rain falls on the just and the unjust.

Despite the hurricane, or anything bad that may come our way, faith can provide comfort. Even in the midst of the storm, God can help. It's reported that minutes before Dr. Martin Luther King, Jr. was shot on that hotel balcony in Memphis in 1968, he was requesting the hymn, "Precious Lord, Take my Hand," to be sung at that night's meeting.

The words are instructive: "Precious Lord, take my hand. Lead me on; let me stand. I am tired; I am weak; I am worn. Through the storm, through the night, lead me on to the light. Take my hand, precious Lord, lead me home."

Come what may, even a hurricane, faith in the Lord produces endurance, even in very difficult circumstances. As is often said, "There are no atheists in foxholes."

3) Christ experienced suffering on the cross for the sake of our salvation. To paraphrase the late Dr. D. James Kennedy, Jesus experienced the hurricane of God's wrath when He died for sinners. So in Jesus, the God of the universe experienced things even worse than a hurricane, so that He might secure our salvation. We are blessed to know that Christ will never leave or forsake us during our time of suffering.

4) Believers can bring glory to God's Name through the storm. And when the storms are over, we can provide needed help. Frankly, millions of faithful Christians rise to the occasion, storm after storm. Even an atheist marveled at this. When Hurricane Katrina hit, skeptic Roy Hattersley wrote an editorial for the UK *Guardian* (9/11/05), in which he said of the groups providing post-hurricane relief: "Notable by their absence are teams from rationalist societies, free thinkers' clubs and atheists' associations—the sort of people who not only scoff at religion's intellectual absurdity but also regard it as a positive force for evil."

He added, "... faith comes with a packet of moral imperatives that, while they do not condition the attitude of all believers, influence enough of them to make them morally superior to atheists like me." I appreciate his honesty.

A hurricane might be a wake-up call from on high, and when (and if) it comes, I hope you'll join all those of good will who will do what they can to improve the circumstances for those hurt and needy.

God Is Not a "Psychotic Mass Murderer"

3/19/14

Comedian and leading skeptic Bill Maher called God a "psychotic mass murderer."

292

He said that in the upcoming *Noah* movie, God---not Russell Crowe (playing Noah)---had an anger problem.

On his HBO program on Friday (3/14/14), Maher said about the Noah story, "It's about a psychotic mass murderer who gets away with it, and his name is God."

He adds, "What kind of tyrant punishes everyone just to get back at the few he's mad at?"

The "few"? The few were those who He wasn't mad at---the ones He saved on the ark.

Maher also said, "Conservatives are always going on about how Americans are losing their values and their morality, well maybe it's because you worship a guy who drowns babies."

I was a guest four times on his show when it was on ABC. Bill Maher seems to hold to moral relativism. Therefore, he does not believe there is a real right and wrong. Then who is he to say that God was wrong to judge humankind in the flood?

Ironically, he uses a Judeo-Christian criterion of right and wrong to judge the God of the Judeo-Christian Scriptures. Yet that very God asks Job: Would you condemn me to justify yourself?

I'm glad Bill has discovered it's wrong to kill babies, so he's against abortion now. Oh wait. Implied in Bill's complaint is that God was being unfair in His judgment. When God judges all of us, He will be completely fair and totally just. And therein lay our problem.

We all know instinctively that there is right and wrong. Certainly, our forebears knew that.

Thomas Jefferson wrote in *Notes on the State of Virginia* in 1781: "God who gave us life gave us liberty. And can the liberties of a nation be thought secure when we have removed their only firm basis, a conviction in the minds of the people that these liberties are of the Gift of God? That they are not to be violated but with His wrath? Indeed, I tremble for my country when I reflect that God is just; that His justice cannot sleep forever." On this point, he was spot on.

As noted before, on September 7, 1864, President Lincoln received a copy of the Holy Bible and said: "In regard to this great book, I have but to say, it is the best gift God has given to men. All the good the Savior gave to the world was communicated through this book. But for it we could not know right from wrong."

Here's a newsflash to Bill Maher and any of his followers. The God of the Bible hates sin. While He is not accountable to us, we are accountable to Him. The Hebrew prophet Habakkuk said of God, "Your eyes are too pure to look on evil; you cannot tolerate wrong."

I have not seen the upcoming *Noah* movie, and I understand by their own admission the producers have taken many liberties with the text. (With virtually Bible movies, it's hard not to quip, "The book is better.")

But [SPOILER ALERT] one liberty the producers have apparently taken with the text is that a character sneaks on the ark. Noah finds out and kills him! (This is in early versions seen in pre-screenings. Hopefully, the producers will cut it out.) That implies that Noah and God were trying to keep people off the ark. But that's not at all in the spirit or text of the Noah story.

The Bible says it took Noah and his sons 120 years to build the ark. That was a long time for his neighbors to see the storm coming---and repent, if they wished. It also says (in St. Peter's second letter) that Noah was a "preacher of righteousness." To whom? The animals on the ark? No, presumably to those around who could see the coming judgment as Noah was preparing the ark.

So to imply that Noah and God were trying to keep people from being saved is a sad distortion.

This reminds me of something Jesus said, right after He made the famous statement of John 3:16. (For God so loved the world He gave His one and only Son that whoever believes in Him will not perish but have eternal life). He said: For God did not send His Son into the world to condemn the world, but to save it.

The world is already condemned. For there is no one good. No, not one. But Jesus (who is fully God and fully man) lived a perfect life and then voluntarily received the due penalty of our sins on Himself. He became sin for us---and for that horrible moment---God forsook Him.

But God raised Him from the dead on that first Easter Sunday. He will one day come back to judge the living and the dead.

Noah's ark is a symbol of the cross. You're in or you're out. Therefore, choose wisely.

It's like the Passover lamb. Jesus was killed on Passover, the ancient Hebrew celebration when they took the blood of an innocent lamb (without breaking its bones) and put the blood on the top and two sides of their doorway (indirectly forming the sign of the cross). They were either covered by that blood or they were not.

It was interesting to note in the recent *Son of God* movie that as Jesus was being crucified in the background, you could see a Passover lamb being slain in the foreground.

750 years before Jesus, Isaiah said it all, "All we like sheep have gone astray...But the Lord has laid on him the iniquity of us all." I pray for Bill Maher to see this one day.

Whatever Happened to Hell?

7/18/12

Many years ago, when cartoonist Johnny Hart was alive, he had a comic panel that was misunderstood. One of his caveman characters in *BC* was standing behind a rock (like a store counter) with the slogan saying in effect, "Gospel available here." The next panel showed another caveman asking, "What's the Gospel?" And the final frame showed the first caveman saying, "beats the Hell out of me."

Understandably, some conservative religious leaders thought Johnny was being sacrilegious and called for a protest against him and his newspaper syndicate. Thankfully, it never went anywhere because Johnny had been misunderstood.

I know for a fact Johnny was a man of faith, and his point was that the Gospel was the solution to the problem of Hell, which Johnny took very seriously.

Hell is not a popular doctrine for obvious reasons. Just this month, we saw the republishing (into paperback) of a major seller that for all practical purposes denies Hell (or the import of it). What makes this more difficult to stomach is that it was written by "an evangelical pastor."

Sixteen months ago, Rev. Rob Bell published the book, *Love Wins*, which denied a critical aspect of Hell. He didn't deny it exists; he denies essentially that any people will go there.

Its success was phenomenal in that the book spent twenty weeks on the *New York Times'* bestseller list.

Belief in Hell doesn't seem to be taken too seriously these days. Millions of high school students have been taught about Jonathan Edwards' famous sermon, "Sinners in the Hands of an Angry God," as a supposed example of Puritan excess. For instance, near the very end, he rebuked his own church (which later fired him): "Therefore, let everyone that is out of Christ, now awake and fly from the wrath to come. The wrath of Almighty God is now undoubtedly hanging over a great part of this congregation."

Difficult words. Yet this man's preaching in Northampton, Massachusetts helped spark the Great Awakening. George Whitefield helped spread this awakening up and down the Atlantic seacoast. John Adams said the push for American Independence was a political move that came a generation or so after the spiritual revolution that took place in the hearts of many of the colonists---which we now call the First Great Awakening.

In his 1974 book, *The God Bit*, the late comedian Joey Adams writes, "I love the attitude of my good friend Father Bob: 'Since I believe in the Bible, I'm sure there is a Hell. But I also believe in God's mercy---and therefore I'm sure it's empty."

Sounds nice. But is it true? That makes me think of the line from a Simon and Garfunkel song, "A man he hears what he wants to hear---and disregards the rest."

I keep reading these stories of some unhappy person blowing away a bunch of people---it even happened recently at a Christian college in California. Where's the fear of God in our society? I don't think people would do those sorts of things if they truly understood the reality of Hell.

In America's early years, a "future state of rewards and punishment" was an important concept. For example:

· In 1786, founding father Benjamin Rush wrote: "Such is my veneration for every religion that
reveals the attributes of the Deity, or a future state of rewards and punishments..."

· Noah Webster's first Dictionary (1828) had many Bible verses. He said one aspect of "Religion" includes "a belief in a state of rewards and punishment, and in man's accountableness to God..."

· The Constitution of the State of Maryland, adopted in 1864, required political officials to hold to a belief "in a future state of rewards and punishments." The same held for South Carolina's 1778 constitution, as did Tennessee's constitution of 1796.

· The Pennsylvania Supreme Court stated in 1817: "Laws cannot be administered in any civilized government unless the people are taught to revere the sanctity of an oath, and look to a future state of rewards and punishments for the deeds of this life."

In short, Hell is a part of divine accountability.

When Osama bin Laden was finally killed in May 2011, a CNN/Opinion Research Corporation poll released shortly after found that 61 percent of the public thought he went to Hell, thus showing that a lot of Americans still believe in Hell.

CNN's Polling Director Keating Holland said this: "Not all Americans believe in Hell---a point of view reflected in the relatively large number of 'don't know' responses---and many religions don't include punishment in an afterlife as part of their teachings. Nonetheless, the six in ten who say bin Laden is in Hell reflects how strongly many Americans feel that bin Laden was an evil figure." And, as I say, it also reflects how many Americans believe Hell exists.

In short, Hell is the ultimate accountability. By Jesus dying for sins, love wins---for those who repent and believe on Him. For those who don't, Hell awaits. Thus, divine justice wins too. No wonder He said, "What does it profit if you gain the whole world and lose your soul?"

The Apostles' Creed says about Jesus that He "suffered under Pontius Pilate; was crucified, dead and buried: He descended into Hell." In other words, Jesus went to Hell for us on the cross, so we don't have to. That's why the Johnny Hart caveman could so cheerfully say that the Gospel "beats the Hell out of me."

A Dark Night Indeed:
Trying to Make Sense Out of Another Senseless Act of Violence in Modern America

Another senseless act of random violence in America has made the headlines. This time there was a random shooting in a movie theatre, during the opening night of *The Dark Knight*. This was the midnight showing in Aurora, Colorado, just outside of Denver.

As of this writing, 14 people are reported to be dead, and 50 injured. The alleged shooter was a 24-year old white male, who was wearing a bulletproof vest and a gas mask. He reportedly acted alone, using tear gas, and firing three guns.

How do we make sense out of this kind of thing? Why do things like this happen?

I can't help but feel that to some extent, we're reaping what we've been sowing as a society. We said to God, "Get out of the public arena." Lawsuit after lawsuit, often by misguided "civil libertarians," have chased away any fear of God in the land---at least in the hearts of millions.

The shooting was like a scene out of a scary movie. One witness said, "It was very hard to breathe. I told my brother to take cover. It took a while. I started seeing flashes and screaming, I just saw blood and people yelling and a quick glimpse of the guy who had a gas mask on. I was pushed out. There was chaos, we started running." (*ABC News*, 7/20/12).

Recently, I wrote on the subject of Hell and how our society has generally lost its cognizance of it.

We've lost this cognizance to the point that a recent bestseller was a book by an "evangelical pastor," who for all practical purposes denied Hell (or the import of it). (It exists, but don't worry---supposedly nobody's going there.) When the book was first published sixteen months ago, it made the cover of *TIME* magazine. This month it was republished as a paperback.

This makes me think. "Wow, what the heck happened to Hell?" What---was there some new revelation that changed what the Lord warned about? To me, what He said 2000 years ago is still worth heeding: What does it profit you if you gain the whole world and lose your soul?

Tens of millions of young people in this culture seem to have no fear of God. It's becoming too commonplace that some frustrated person will go on a killing spree of random people. If they kill themselves, they think it's all over. But that's like going from the frying pan into the fire.

Where's the fear of God in our society? I don't think people would do those sorts of things if they truly understood the reality of Hell.

I'll never forget what an Alabama black pastor said to me one time when I interviewed him about Judge Roy Moore, the Ten Commandments judge. He said, "All across American people should stand with Judge Moore about the Ten Commandments. Why? Because when they took prayer out of school, you didn't hear about kids killing each other, about them bringing dope to school, shooting the teachers, you didn't hear about that. You see what I'm saying? That's what's wrong. We need more God-fearing."

Roy Moore (former Chief Justice of the Alabama Supreme Court) once told me, "In my tenure as a circuit judge, I've handled all kind of violent crimes. I had one case where a mother drowned her child face up in a bathtub of water between her legs, so that her father could not get custody. We've had terrible crimes and I seriously wonder why the ACLU is attacking me for, posting of Commandments which read, 'Thou shall not kill.'"

The founders gave us a system where voluntary God-fearing was the underpinning of civility in society. The more internal restraints people have, the less need they have for external restraints. (And the converse is true.) That's why I can't understand the ongoing crusade of those who want to remove any vestige of Judeo-Christian in the public arena. All they're doing is making everything worse for everyone else.

Religion and morality were key to the founders' vision for a civil society. In his Farewell Address, George Washington highlighted the source of morality: "Whatever may be conceded to the influence of refined education on minds of peculiar structure, reason and experience both forbid us to expect that national morality can prevail in exclusion of religious principle." Will somebody please tell that to these civil libertarian lawyers always suing against public displays or the Ten Commandments and the like?

I know in my natural state I am worthy of Hell before a holy God, who doesn't grade on the curve. I am eternally grateful that on the cross Jesus went to Hell for me, so I don't have to. The next time someone wants to take out their frustrations on others by killing innocent victims, they ought to consider the eternal consequences of their evil actions.

Does Believing in Hell Make One "Evil"?
4/2/13

Recently, it was brought to my attention that, supposedly, those who believe in a real Hell are evil. And so is our God.

Let me get this straight. The Son of God leaves the glories of Heaven and subjects Himself to life on planet earth---which includes (to paraphrase Shakespeare): "the heartache and the thousand natural shocks that flesh is heir to." To these and worse, Jesus voluntarily submits Himself.

Jesus lives a perfect life, and then offers Himself as a sacrifice for sins, so that those who trust in Him for eternal life will be able to go to Heaven to be with Him forever. This salvation from Hell (which is separation from the source of life, God) is by good works---His, not ours. (True belief in Him, of course, will always result in good works.)

In short, Jesus went to Hell for us on the cross, so we don't have to. But now some people want to reject His once-and-for-all sacrifice out-right and then turn around and blame Him, should they wind up there, where they will be punished for their own sins.

They also want to deny that Hell is real (or that anyone goes there) and marginalize anybody who dares say it is. Sometimes, they even make a caricature of those who dare mention that Hell is real, so they can then easily dismiss this nut-job or malicious malefactor. Church Lady might say, "How conveeeeenient!"

Through the centuries, down to our present day, many people who believe in historical Christianity have done (and continue to do) many positive things in our world. Of course, included in the historic Christian faith would be the belief in what Jesus Himself said about Hell.

Consider just a preliminary list of men and women who through the centuries---and even today---have embraced the historic Christian faith, which includes the now politically incorrect view of the afterlife.

That list would include Peter, Paul, and Mary (not the singing group, but the saints---the original ones). Now that we're at it, virtually all the apostles and believers dubbed as saints.

Included in that list are many great religious leaders through the centuries, including Polycarp, Ignatius, Justin Martyr, Augustine, Athanasius, Ambrose, John Chrysostom, Thomas Aquinas, Francis of Assisi, Thomas More, Martin Luther, John Calvin, Ignatius Loyola, Blaise Pascal, John Wesley, George Whitefield, D. James Kennedy, Francis Schaeffer, and Billy Graham.

Also included are many great writers, including Dante, Geoffrey Chaucer, John Milton, John Bunyan, Fyodor Dostoyevsky, Chuck Colson, Oswald Chambers, G. K. Chesterton, C.S. Lewis, Dorothy Sayers, Flannery O'Connor, and J.R.R. Tolkien.

You can add William Shakespeare. Note what he said in his Last Will and Testament: "I commend my soul into the hands of God my Creator, hoping and assuredly believing through the only merits of

Jesus Christ my Saviour, to be made partaker of life everlasting; and my body to the earth, whereof it is made."

Musicians would include Johann Sebastian Bach, Felix Mendelssohn, Franz Joseph Haydn, and George Friedrich Handel. Meanwhile, who can forget the classic scene (featured in Amadeus) from Mozart's *Don Giovanni*, where the unrepentant Don Juan gets cast into Hell?

The list would include many great scientists, including Johannes Kepler, Michael Faraday, Robert Boyle, Gregor Mendel, Lord Kelvin, Louis Pasteur, and Joseph Lister, along with many great political leaders and reformers, including Constantine, Justinian, Alfred the Great, Charlemagne, St. Louis (Louis IX), George Washington, Queen Victoria, and, of course, William Wilberforce.

Ten years ago I had the privilege of interviewing the international leader of the Salvation Army at the time, Gen. John Gowan. He said, "There wouldn't be a Salvation Army without a Savior!"

He also added, "Without any question, there are millions of people today, as we're sitting here, who are receiving something beautiful either of a physical or a spiritual kind from compassionate Christians. If there were no compassionate Christians, there would be many of those million who would not receive what they desperately need to face today."

Even an Orthodox Rabbi, Daniel Lapin of Toward Tradition, recognizes the many good things done by those who believe in historic Christianity. He cites one example, "Every time there is a natural disaster, who is on the spot? Numerous American religious Christian-driven charities bringing relief; that is where it is coming from."

If I needed to go the hospital, I could go to Holy Cross, Good Samaritan, St. Luke's, or Baptist Hospital. But I won't be going to the Madalyn Murray O'Hare Clinic any time soon, because it doesn't exist.

Have there been Christian believers (real or fake) who have done atrocious things---even sometimes in the name of the Savior? Of course, but that's not because of Him, but despite the One who taught us to love even our enemies.

On balance, historic Christianity has greatly benefitted humanity. About a hundred years ago, James Russell Lowell, who wrote the hymn "Once to every man and nation" (which Dr. Martin Luther

King, Jr. quoted when he made it to Selma) once said this: "I challenge any skeptic to find a ten square mile spot on this planet where they can live their lives in peace and safety and decency, where womanhood is honored, where infancy and old age are revered, where they can educate their children, where the Gospel of Jesus Christ has not gone first to prepare the way. If they find such a place, then I would encourage them to emigrate thither and there proclaim their unbelief."

Part 13.

Death

Entrepreneur Wants to Find "Cure" for Death
9/24/14

The man who co-created PayPal helped solve a big problem, how to make trustworthy payments on the Internet. This successful solution has enriched the lives of everyone---himself included.

Now, he wants to think outside the box to solve another problem: Death.

Writing for the *Telegraph* of the UK (9/19/14), Mick Brown penned, "Peter Thiel: the billionaire tech entrepreneur on a mission to cheat death; The co-founder of PayPal and likely the most successful venture capitalist in Silicon Valley is on a mission to change the world through technology – and to find a cure for death."

When Brown interviewed Thiel, the topic turned to "the question of death. 'Basically,' Thiel says earnestly, 'I'm against it.'" Thiel reportedly returns to this topic often.

Thiel adds, "I think there are probably three main modes of approaching it. You can accept it, you can deny it or you can fight it. I think our society is dominated by people who are into denial or acceptance, and I prefer to fight it."

I'm reminded of the old story about our 30th president, Calvin Coolidge, a man of few words, who attended church one Sunday morning. When he returned, he was asked what the sermon was about. "Sin," replied Coolidge. "What did the minister say?" Response: "He's against it."

And so Thiel is against death. Well, good luck with that. I am sure there are ways to increase the length and quality of the life that we have and to reduce some of the diseases that prematurely bring death. But ultimately all of these things will only prolong the inevitable.

Studies repeatedly show that getting more exercise within reason, that prayer and meditation, and having an optimistic outlook improve the quality of your life. Attending church on a regular basis tends to lengthens one's life and also improves the quality of life. This is a repeated finding. It is a God-given desire to want to live forever. But none of this spells the death of death.

Wisdom from the Bible sheds light on this. It is written, "...it is appointed for men to die once and after this comes judgment." Death is a fact, and it is universal. Yet death is the great enemy of humanity---certainly no friend. Proverbs says those who hate God's wisdom love death.

Death entered into the world because of sin. In that sense, it is profoundly unnatural. Death is indeed the final enemy to be defeated. However, in one sense, death has already been defeated. Jesus defeated death both on the cross and in His resurrection.

Christ rose from the dead bodily and changed all of history because of it---and the Bible tells us His resurrection is the "firstfruits" of the Christian's own bodily resurrection to come. How great to know that recently David Limbaugh's book, *Jesus on Trial: A Lawyer Affirms the Truth of the Gospel*, which includes historical evidence for the resurrection, shot up to #1 on Amazon.

C. S. Lewis once wrote: "...this universe is at war...it is a civil war, a rebellion [against God]...we are living in a part of the universe occupied by the rebel. Enemy occupied territory---that is what this world is. Christianity is the story of how the rightful king has landed, you might say landed in disguise, and is calling us all to take part in a great campaign of sabotage."

Man's works are like beautiful sand-castles, the elaborate kind, with all sorts of intricate details. But eventually they'll crumble. They're like beautiful sculptures of ice, destined to melt one day.

C. T. Studd once said, "Only one life, 'twill soon be passed. Only what's done for Christ will last." It isn't how long you live. It's what you do with the life you have.

Consider the great Christian hero, Jim Elliot. He and four other young men died as missionaries to Indians in the jungles of Ecuador in 1956.

His widow and female family members of some of the other dead missionaries returned to that place and lived among the tribes-people and brought the gospel to them. Some of the very men who had speared the missionaries to death found new life in Christ through these efforts.

These five missionaries who died so heroically helped spark a new interest in Christian missions at that time. I mention all this because Jim Elliot said famously, "He is no fool who gives what he cannot keep to gain that which he cannot lose."

Reinhold Niebuhr wrote the famous serenity prayer: "God grant me the serenity to accept the things I cannot change; courage to change the things I can; and wisdom to know the difference."

Despite the noble-sounding aspirations of those like Peter Theil, death--at least this side of Christ's return---is one of those things we "cannot change."

If you want to live forever, then believe in Jesus Christ who alone has conquered death and will raise to new life all who believe in Him when He returns.

Reflections on Death with the Passing of my Mother
9/6/11

In Ricky Gervais's 2007 movie, *The Invention of Lying*, an interesting thing happens as his mother faces death.

Here she is in the hospital about to die, and she's mortally afraid.

But he reassures her: "You're wrong about what happens when you die, Mum. It's not an eternity of nothingness."

She hangs on every word he says---so does the hospital staff.

He continues, "When you die you're going to go to your favorite place in the whole world. And you're going to be with all of the people you've ever loved and who have ever loved you....and there will be no sadness, no pain, just love and laughing and happiness."

She dies contentedly.

It turns out he was making it all up just to provide comfort to her.

The actor himself professes to be an atheist, so he himself doesn't believe the comforting words his character was saying in this moving scene.

But what if it is true? What if it's not? How can we know?

My own mother died last Friday, so death is definitely on my mind.

Death is a sword of Damocles that hangs over all of us. We're not getting out of this thing alive. The question is, Do we need to get ready somehow?

Woody Allen supposedly said, "I'm not afraid of dying. I just don't want to be there when it happens."

My mom was ready to die. It was a long time in coming---as she had been struggling with Alzheimer's for years.

In that sense, by the time the end came, it was a relief.

Ann Lombard Newcombe was born on December 7, 1922. She died September 2, 2011.

She was married to Leo R. Newcombe since May 1, 1948.

She was the mother of eight children---six boys and two girls. As Dad once jokingly said, he had married "Fertile Myrtle."

Her first cousin was William F. Buckley, Jr. Her husband was a newspaper executive for years---serving as Vice President, General Manager of *The Chicago Sun-Times* and *The Chicago Daily News* (defunct since 1978).

One of her sons (Richard) founded one of only two successful newspaper syndicates since the 1930s that is still in business today---Creators Syndicate (established in 1987). Today, Creators Syndicate is the third largest newspaper syndicate in the world.

In one of Buckley's books, he talks about the remarkable family of sisters that his mother came from. They all loved God. One of those sisters was my grandmother.

That love for Jesus was passed on from mother to daughter---that daughter being my mother.

Her enthusiasm and love for Jesus has rubbed off on me. Not that I'm as devout as she. But I wish I were.

She reminds me of the classic statement from the *Confessions of St. Augustine*: "You have made us for Yourself, O God, and our hearts are restless until they find their rest in You."

I have every hope, based on historical facts, that she is with Jesus.

Why? Because she trusted in Christ for her salvation.

When Jesus conquered the grave, He gave a reason for hope beyond the grave---based on historical facts.

To me, this isn't just pie in the sky, when you die, by and by.

This is hope based on facts of history. There would be no Christianity, in all its manifestations, had Jesus Christ not walked out of the tomb, bodily, 2,000 years ago. The first skeptics of the resurrection were the disciples themselves, including Doubting Thomas, but they came to believe when He appeared to them over and over.

So convinced did they become that they went out and told the world. Most of them were martyred for their efforts, but none of them recanted.

Mom believed deeply in Jesus Christ.

According to eyewitnesses, including my sister and brother-in-law, my mom---after about four or five days of having her eyes shut and being completely "out of it"---suddenly opened her eyes (with her pupils slightly dilated---"like when you see someone you really love," to quote my sister). She began to stare intently at something for about five minutes. She didn't blink. Was she looking at Jesus?

307

My wife says that when her father was little, in Norway, in the late 1940s, his 22 year old sister, Kirsten, was dying of heart failure. The whole family (all seven siblings and the parents) gathered around her bed. Although she had been in a coma for three days, just before she died, she sat up in bed and stared intently at something.

Then she raised her arms and with a big smile said, "Jesus, you're coming to get me!" Then she died. My wife can't tell this story without her eyes getting moist.

If ever someone was ready to die, I believe it was Ann Newcombe.

When I think of her death, I'm reminded of the beautiful poem by the 20th century African-American writer, James Weldon Johnson, called "Go Down, Death," which starts this way:

> Weep not, weep not,
> She is not dead;
> She's resting in the bosom of Jesus.
> Heart broken husband---weep no more;
> Grief stricken son---weep no more;
> Left lonesome daughter---weep no more;
> She's only just gone home.

Chuck Colson, Trophy of God's Grace

4/25/12

An outstanding man died on April 21, 2012. Chuck Colson (born in 1931) was a great author, speaker, and prison reformer.

He had gone from being a high-priced lawyer to senior counsel for President Nixon to an inmate in federal prison, sentenced for Watergate-related crimes.

Before he went to prison, he had a dramatic conversion after a friend gave him a copy of C. S. Lewis' classic book, *Mere Christianity*. He describes the transformation Christ made in his life in his book, *Born Again*, the first of about 30 titles he produced.

I have had the privilege of interviewing Chuck Colson about half a dozen times for Christian radio and television programs. He was always a great and insightful guest.

I remember one of those times in the mid-1990s. As I recall, it was a Saturday night, I got to interview him after he spoke at a conference at the Broward County Convention Center. His assistant told him that there was a crowd waiting for him outside the room where we were doing the interview. But he told Mr. Colson he knew a way the two of them could escape through a back exit.

It was late. Colson had just given a long public speech, then he had to endure a TV interview with me. One could easily see how he would have chosen to simply slip away with his aide.

But Colson preferred to go meet with the crowd to talk with them. He was a very nice man---the man I got to see on camera and off-camera.

Having served for seven months, after Chuck Colson got out of prison, he went on to found Prison Fellowship in 1976. This is a ministry that has had tremendous impact in touching the lives of hundreds of thousands of inmates around the world. The main goal has been to change convicted criminals into godly men and women through the power of the gospel of Jesus Christ.

Chuck told me in a 2009 interview that Prison Fellowship is established in 114 countries across the globe. Just in the U.S., it has a presence in more than 1300 prisons. Among many of their activities is providing Christmas gifts each year for the families of incarcerated men and women through the Angel Tree Project.

Chuck Colson did a daily three minute radio commentary on some 1,400 outlets across the country, reaching about eight million listeners a week.

And Colson was the driving force behind the Manhattan Declaration—a statement geared toward uniting Protestant, Catholic, and Orthodox Christians to take a stand for life, for marriage, and for religious liberty in a culture that is increasingly hostile to them.

In his book, *Loving God,* Colson reflected back on his life, "my mind began to drift back in time…to scholarships and honors earned, cases argued and won, great decisions make from lofty government offices. My life had been the perfect success story, the great American dream fulfilled. But all at once I realized that it was *not* my success God had used to enable me to help those in this prison, or in hundreds of others just like it. My life of success was not what made this morning so glorious---all of my achievements meant nothing in God's economy" [emphasis his, p. 24].

Colson had begun to learn that God could use his shortcomings more than his accomplishments. He continues, "No, the real legacy of my life was my biggest failure---that I was an ex-convict. My greatest humiliation---being sent to prison---was the beginning of

God's greatest use of my life. He chose the one experience in which I could not glory for His glory."

This is a great lesson for all of us. Even we mess things up, if we turn it all over to the Lord, He can use our lives for His glory and others' good. As has been said so often before, the ability God cares about the most is our *availability*.

Chuck Colson was a great trophy of the grace of God. He will be greatly missed.

Shakespeare and "Death with Dignity"

10/15/14

Recent events have brought the debate on so-called "death with dignity" and assisted suicide into the spotlight again. And yet, the argument is not really a new one. No less a light than William Shakespeare extensively dealt with the subject in his writing.

"Death with dignity" is essentially a code word for suicide, sometimes in the face of a terminal illness. As one humanist put it, he wants to kill himself on his own terms rather than die from some disease. He said it would be like telling God, "You can't fire me---I quit."

In the Netherlands, they accepted the basic concept of doctor-assisted suicide ("death with dignity") many years ago. But they have now reached the point where the level of involuntary deaths has exceeded the number of voluntary deaths.

Breitbart.com (10/3/14) notes, "Dr. Peter Saunders of the Christian Medical Fellowship told the *Daily Mail* that euthanasia in the Netherlands is 'way out of control,' saying that it proves that assisted dying is impossible to regulate."

The Breitbart article adds that earlier this year a Dutch official told the British Parliament, "Don't go there," when he was asked about England's consideration to legalize assisted dying.

"Death with Dignity" is gaining greater traction in Western society---especially as we move away from God and Judeo-Christian morality, which states in the Ten Commandments: Thou shalt do no murder. That includes murder of self. It is God's prerogative to give and to take life.

This may seem harsh to our culture, but what in God's revelation has changed? There's no divine sanction for suicide. I remember when a distraught believer once asked me if he would still go to heaven if he killed himself. I told him one sure wouldn't want to find out the hard way that he would not. Thankfully, he chose to live. (Later, his problem resolved itself very well.)

Suicide is one of the themes of one of the greatest plays in the history of the world, Shakespeare's *Hamlet*.

There was a lot of biblical influence on William Shakespeare. Even the leading atheist of our time (Richard Dawkins, former Oxford professor) notes that there are some 1300 biblical quotes and references in the writings of the bard from Statford-upon-Avon. Dr. George Morrison wrote *Christ in Shakespeare*, noting the Bible's impact on numerous passages where we can "trace its phraseology, and beyond its phraseology we can detect its thought."

So what does Shakespeare, particularly in *Hamlet*, have to say about "death with dignity"? He obviously doesn't use the phrase. What he does talk about is "self-slaughter." The famous soliloquy of Hamlet (Act III, Scene I): "To be or not to be" can be paraphrased as: "Should I or should I not commit suicide?" Of course, the original sounds better.

This life, contends Hamlet, is filled with all sorts of problem that he catalogues: "The slings and arrows of outrageous fortune;" "a sea of troubles;" "The heartache, and the thousand natural shocks That flesh is heir to;" "the whips and scorns of time, The oppressor's wrong, the proud man's contumely [i.e., contempt], The pangs of despis'd love, the law's delay, The insolence of office, and the spurns That patient merit of the unworthy takes."

Life stinks, says Hamlet. To paraphrase the references above: There's bad luck; there are the bad things that naturally happen to us; we grow old; we deal with oppression and contempt; there are those we love who hate us; justice is denied because it is delayed; those in charge do what they want; and there are "the insults which the hard-working, patient person receives from the one who does not deserve credit" (Source for this last phrase: forum.wordreference.com).

In short, Hamlet asks, should I or should I not "shuffle off this mortal coil"? With a "bare bodkin" (an unsheathed knife), I could end it all, says Hamlet, and find "quietus" (release from life). So why not end it all and thus lose all these "fardels" (burdens), rather than "grunt and sweat under a weary life"? This would be "Devoutly to be wish'd."

But what happens after death? "To die,—to sleep;—To sleep: perchance to dream:—ay, there's the rub; For in that sleep of death what dreams may come, When we have shuffled off this mortal coil, Must give us pause."

He adds, "But that the dread of something after death,—The undiscover'd country, from whose bourn No traveler returns,— puzzles the will, And makes us rather bear those ills we have

Than fly to others that we know not of?" What if I kill myself, and God turns out to true after all?

He concludes this passage, "Thus conscience does make cowards of us all..." Better to not kill yourself than to find out the hard way that it was wrong---with tragic consequences---concludes Shakespeare's Hamlet, thus ruling out "death with dignity," in the way the phrase is used today, i.e., suicide.

Earlier, in his first soliloquy in the play, Hamlet laments: "O that this too too solid flesh would melt, Thaw, and resolve itself into a dew!" I wish I were dead, he cries. And then comes the rebuttal: "Or that the Everlasting had not fix'd His canon [i.e., His law] 'gainst self-slaughter!" Translation: Oh that God had not decreed His law against suicide! But He has indeed done that.

In his last will and testament, Shakespeare himself wrote: "I commend my soul into the hands of God my Creator, hoping and assuredly believing through the only merits of Jesus Christ my Saviour, to be made partaker of life everlasting; and my body to the earth, whereof it is made."

While our debate on "death with dignity" may seem new, it's as old as God's law on Mt. Sinai and as old as Shakespeare's 17th century dramas. Our lives are not ours to take with impunity.

Omnipresent: Video Cameras---And the Lord
3/15/15

If it weren't for a short video-clip captured on a cell phone, the recent shooting of an unarmed, fleeing black man by a white police officer in South Carolina might not have been reported and acted upon. The man who videotaped the incident even considered deleting it.

Providentially, this alleged criminal act can be evaluated based on that tape. I say alleged because as of this writing the cop has not had his day in court. But that video is key.

Apart from all privacy concerns (of which there are many), this gets me to thinking about daily living in light of omnipresent video cameras. I can't drive by an intersection where I live without seeing those ubiquitous cameras.

- Suppose you knew that everything you did and said was captured on videotape, would you live any differently?
- Suppose everything you said, including gossip behind someone's back, were to be broadcast, would you say anything different?
- Suppose every word you wrote, even in private emails, were to end up being blasted throughout the media, would you reword anything?

Of course we would. I must confess that I drive more carefully when I'm followed by a police car. With that last question, the recent Sony hacking scandal comes to mind.

Tom Johnson, former head of CNN, once gave this great piece of advice: "Do what is right. If you aren't sure, ask yourself this question: 'How will my actions, taken in private, look if published on the front page of the newspaper my mother and father read?' You never need to lie or cheat to succeed in life." As has been said, character is what you are when no is watching.

I just heard a 30-year old story about a young man who passed his first driver's test with flying colors. After the driving instructor who tested him left, he was relieved that he didn't have to drive so perfectly now that the instructor was gone.

We're all like that. It's easy to get back to normal, as if no one is watching us. But Someone is.

In some ways the ethic of our age is do what you will, even if it's wrong---only don't get caught. The unspoken assumption of all this is that we will not one day give an account for our lives.

But that's not true. Jesus said what we whisper in secret will one day be shouted from the housetops. He also spoke of the day of reckoning we will all face one day---standing before Him. On that day, the books will be open, and no fancy lawyering can change the outcome. We're all sinners; but only the blood of Jesus will save any of us, and it is available to all who call on Him.

What we do in secret is seen by God. Thus, we should strive to be the same in private as we are in public.

Previous generations understood all this better than ours does. In my wife's hometown of Kristiansand, Norway is a thousand-year old church. I've attended services there. On the ceiling is an old painting of a human eye---representing the eye of God. It has reminded people for centuries that God sees all.

Generally, our nation's founders believed in divine accountability. They believed that the people needed to be good of their own accord---knowing full well that we will all stand before God one day.

Bill Federer, historian, author, and speaker, has compiled great information in his book, *The Original 13: A Documentary History of Religion in America's First Thirteen States.*

Federer told me: "It's interesting to see how so many of the constitutions of the original thirteen states of our country mentioned the importance of belief in God, because it was viewed as a requirement for moral behavior. Because to God, we will one day give an account. As the constitutions changed over time, becoming less religious and more secular, there was still this angle of divine accountability."

For instance, he cites the Pennsylvania Constitution of 1776, which required officeholders to acknowledge "one God, the Creator and Governor of the Universe, the Rewarder of the good and the Punisher of the wicked. And I do acknowledge the Scriptures of the Old and New Testament to be given by Divine Inspiration." Even Ben Franklin signed this.

Federer adds, "Later, Pennsylvania's 1790, 1838, 1874 and 1968 Constitutions contained the wording: 'That no person, who acknowledges the being of a God and a future state of rewards and punishments, shall, on account of his religious sentiments, be disqualified to hold any office or place of trust or profit under this commonwealth.'"

Knowledge of our accountability to God should change how we act.

Smile. You might be on candid camera.

Breaking News From AD 33

7/8/14

In a sense, we're all on death row. Death is on my mind because of the recent death of my much-missed older brother, Doug. I am so grateful he died as a Christian. To die in Christ is gain.

In our culture, we do just about everything we can to push death away from our thoughts. Often we don't even use the words. We'll

314

say things like, "He passed away" or just "he passed." But these are just euphemisms for "he died."

There is an interesting contrast between the Puritans and us, when it comes to sex and death. Sex was all hush-hush, while death was front and center.

When the Puritans learned their ABCs through *The New England Primer*, how did they learn the letter X? "Xerxes did die, and so must I," in reference to an ancient King of Persia written up in the Bible. Death was not hidden from the Puritans, not even their children.

Sex was reserved for marriage and was not to be displayed out in the open. (I'm sure that on average they enjoyed intimate relations significantly better than do modern Americans.)

Today, death is hushed up, euphemized, put away from our cognizance as much as possible. Often old people are warehoused in nursing home situations. Out of sight, out of mind. (That's obviously not true in all situations, thankfully. But it does happen all too often.)

And sex today is front and center. You can't even drive down the highway without some reminder about it. Even ads for burger joints say things like, "Get some in the sack."

The Puritans chose better in this matter. They chose to be reminded that in this life, all the clichés are true---we're only just passing through.

You can't cheat death by one minute. If you had all the wealth in the world, you couldn't buy one more minute of life if you wished.

"A horse, a horse," cries Shakespeare's Richard III who wants to escape sure death as his enemies close in on him, "my kingdom for a horse." Really, what he's pleading for is his life. But not one minute more is granted him.

Think of some incredibly wealthy people. They can't take a penny with them. Jesus said it all, "What does it profit a man if he gains the whole world but loses his soul?" It was noted that when John D. Rockefeller died, some businessmen were arguing amongst themselves as to how much he left behind. But the real answer was he left it all.

I read recently about a woman who hoarded stuff, a lifetime of stuff---whatever she could store in her house. Eventually, her stuff caused the floor of her house to cave in (with her on that floor). As I recall the news, she was found dead in the basement, surrounded by all her stuff.

You can't take it with you. The best you can do is to send it on ahead.

In Christ is a philosophy to live by and a philosophy to die by. As painful as death is, the real sting of that sorrow is removed by Christ, who conquered the grave. That is the "Breaking News from AD 33," as James Taranto might put it. When Jesus walked out of the tomb, He ultimately created the timeline (Anno Domini, in the year of our Lord).

The difference between being ready to die and not ready is huge. Behind George Washington and Martha's sarcophagi in Mt. Vernon, chiseled in stone, are these words from Jesus in John 11 (the raising of Lazarus chapter): "I am the resurrection, and the life: he that believeth in me, though he were dead, yet shall he live." His last words were, "'Tis well."

But contrast that with a decidedly anti-Christian perspective, that of British atheist Bertrand Russell (1872-1970), who said, "That man is the product of causes which had no prevision of the end they were achieving..." Evolution says we're here by accident.

Continues Russell: "...that his origin, his growth, his hopes and fears, his loves and his beliefs, are but the outcome of accidental collocations of atoms; that no fire, no heroism, no intensity of thought and feeling, can preserve an individual life beyond the grave..." The grave stops it all.

Death not only overtakes us all, but everything else too, says Russell: "...that all of the labour of the ages, all of the devotion, all of the inspiration, all the noonday brightness of human genius, are destined to extinction in the vast death of the solar system, and that whole temple of Man's achievement must inevitably be buried beneath the debris of a universe in ruins..."

He concludes, "Only within the scaffolding of these truths, and on the firm foundation of unyielding despair, can the soul's habitation henceforth be safely built." Begin with the premise that life is meaningless and then you can build meaning into it. In one sense, you could say Russell is right...if Jesus didn't rise from the dead. But He changed all history when He did.

There is no way we would even have heard of Jesus of Nazareth if He hadn't convinced His disciples of His resurrection. Even

Doubting Thomas was so convinced he made up for lost time, by preaching the gospel all the way to southern India, until he was put to death as a martyr.

I once saw a grave from the 1860s in New Jersey. It said this, "This world is vain and full of pain, with care and trouble sore. But they are blessed, which are at rest with Christ forevermore." My brother Doug himself wrote two months before his death, "Please don't be sad over this. I know my Redeemer and am confident where I will be going soon. It's actually kind of exciting."

Are You Ready for the Test?

7/29/15

As I read the news, I am dismayed to see how few people seem to be preparing for the only day in their lives that matters more than any other---the day they give an account to God.

I live in Ft. Lauderdale and about 20 years ago there was a series of billboard ads on behalf of God. Someone anonymously donated money to have these ads created.

The billboard and inside-bus ads included such messages as:
* "What Part of 'Thou Shalt Not...' Didn't You Understand?"- God
* "Keep Using My Name in Vain And I'll Make Rush Hour Longer" - God
* "That 'Love Thy Neighbor' Thing, I Meant It." - God
* "You Think It's Hot Here?" - God

But the one I found most memorable in that whole series of ads was this one: "Have You Read My #1 Best Seller? There Will Be A Test." – God. Indeed, there will be a test.

The only important day in your life---the day by which every day should be measured---is the day of accountability when you stand before Jesus Christ, who is God. He has been entrusted as judge of the whole world. It is to Him we shall all give an account, regardless of our beliefs or denomination or religion or country of origin or anything else.

Jesus is the inescapable imperative. If you think I'm wrong, then you are staking your whole eternal future on the prospect that Jesus Christ did not rise from the dead. As the saying goes, "Good luck with that!"

A couple of years ago Ron Reagan, Jr., the rebellious son of one of America's greatest presidents (my favorite since Lincoln), cut an on-camera ad on behalf of an atheist organization.

His tag line at the end said he's not afraid to burn in hell. He could only say that because he doesn't believe it's real. At this point in his life (and he still has the chance to repent), he is staking his eternal well-being on the idea that Jesus didn't walk out of His tomb 2,000 years ago.

Some of the most hope-filled words ever spoken are when Jesus told the thief on the cross who repented of his sins and believed in Him, "I tell you the truth, today you will be with Me in paradise." Last minute sincere repenters are welcome in. Wow.

None of us on our own merits are able to stand before a holy God. This is why Jesus died for sinners. Those who knowingly reject His offer of forgiveness will be cast from His presence, where there is no light, no laughter, no joy, no quenching of thirst, no reprieve...nothing good. Jesus is the source of all good. Remove His presence, and it all is bad.

Thus, Dante could write in his classic *Inferno*, "Abandon all hope, ye who enter here."

I just finished listening to a wonderful series of lectures on CD, "Jesus: Legend or Lord?" by D. Paul L. Maier, professor of ancient history at Western Michigan University. I have interviewed him many times. He points out that historians can't prove miracles, like Christ's resurrection, but they can prove that the tomb of Jesus was empty on that first Easter Sunday.

They can't prove that Jesus did miracles, but they can prove that even hostile sources acknowledge that Jesus did such extraordinary things---things that were beyond natural.

For example, as noted before, Dr. Maier mentions the arrest warrant for Jesus of Nazareth (listed here as Yeshu Hannozri) while He was on earth:

Wanted: Yeshu Hannozri

He shall be stoned because he has practiced sorcery and enticed Israel to apostasy...Anyone who knows where he is, let him declare it to the Great Sanhedrin in Jerusalem. (*Sanhedrin* 43a, Babylonian Talmud)

So here we have a hostile source traced back to the first century providing attestation that Jesus did supernatural works---which they wrongly attributed to demonic, not divine, power. Clearly, what Jesus did went beyond natural events.

Historians can't prove that Jesus rose from the dead *per se*, but they can prove that the disciples changed dramatically based on their claimed experience of having seen Him after He rose. Those previously cowering disciples went and boldly laid the foundation of much of Western civilization.

The founders of America believed that we would all give an account for our lives one day, and they gave us limited government based on the notion that we would govern ourselves. The system doesn't work without that notion of divine accountability.

That's why John Adams could say, "Our Constitution was made only for a moral and religious people. It is wholly inadequate to the government of any other."

Scan the headlines and see for yourself how few seem to be ready for the test. I hope you'll be an exception.

Epilogue:

"The Stone That Became a Mountain"

About 500 years before Jesus was born, Daniel, the Hebrew prophet, foretold the coming kingdom of Jesus Christ.

In the 6th century B.C., many Jews were living in exile in Babylon. The Jews back home were under a puppet king, who had been appointed by the king of Babylon, Nebuchadnezzar. Daniel was an exceptional young man among those living in exile.

One night, King Nebuchadnezzar was troubled by a dream. When he awoke, he wanted to learn the meaning of it. There was only one problem. He couldn't even remember what the dream was.

Nonetheless, he demanded of his wise-men, magicians, and sorcerers that they not only interpret his dream, but that they tell him what it had been in the first place. He demanded they tell him this or he would execute them.

Somebody remembered Daniel, one of the Hebrew exiles who had a reputation for having a unique relationship with God. They "volunteered" him to help solve the problem. The king summoned Daniel and made the same demand of him.

Daniel asked for an opportunity to pray that night for God to show him the answer, and indeed God revealed to Daniel what Nebuchadnezzar had dreamt. The Hebrew prophet told the Babylonian ruler:

> As you were lying there, O king, your mind turned to things o come, and the revealer of mysteries showed you what is going to happen....You looked, O king, and there before you stood a large statue—an enormous, dazzling statue, awesome in appearance. The head of the statue was made of pure gold, its chest and arms of silver, its belly and thighs of bronze, its legs of iron, its feet partly of iron and partly of baked clay. While you were watching a rock was cut out, but not by human hands. It struck the statue on its feet of iron and clay and smashed them. Then the iron, the clay, the bronze, the silver and the gold were broken to pieces at the same time and became like chaff on a threshing floor in the summer. The wind swept them away without leaving a trace. But the rock that struck the statue became a huge mountain and filled the whole earth (Daniel 2:29-35).

Daniel told Nebuchadnezzar about four kingdoms to come. While there are different interpretations of this passage, many scholars and commentators have tied those parts of the statue to different earthly kingdoms. To wit:

* The head of gold. This was Nebuchadnezzar and his kingdom. Interpreters believe this to be the contemporary rule of the Babylonians (612-539 B.C.).

* The midsection of silver. This is interpreted to be the reign of the Medes and Persians (539-331 BC).

* The legs of bronze. This is held to be the rule of the Greeks (331-63 B.C.). In a later chapter, Daniel spoke quite vividly about the rise of Alexander the Great about two hundred years later, who he likened to a rushing ram with a strong horn in front of him. The ram crushed everyone and everything in its way, just as Alexander the Great did in his far-reaching conquest. Then, says Daniel, the ram will suddenly die, and his power will be divided and shared by four military leaders. This is precisely what happened. No wonder liberal scholars believe Daniel was written so late, but again, that is only speculation on their part; there is no archaeological, textual, literary, or historical evidence that it was. It simply reflects their anti-supernatural presuppositions (and that's not evidence).

* The feet made of iron mixed with clay. This is believed to be the Roman Empire (63 B.C.-A.D. 476). Rome ruled with an iron fist. Yet half the Roman Empire, historian Will Durant tells us, were slaves.

Daniel says of the Roman kings, "in the days of those kings," the God of heaven will establish a kingdom which will begin small (like a stone), but eventually it will become big (like a mountain filling the whole earth).

This is the kingdom of Jesus Christ, which began in an inauspicious way during the days of the Roman "kings."
Daniel says:

"In the time of those kings, the God of heaven will set up a kingdom that will never be destroyed, nor will it be left to another people. It will crush all those kingdoms and bring them to an end, but it will itself endure forever. This is the meaning of the vision of the rock cut out of a mountain, but not by human hands—a rock that broke the iron, the clay, the bronze, the silver, and the gold to pieces."

Daniel tells us that this stone was essentially a kingdom. A kingdom not of this earth—this stone was not made by human hands. Its roots were small, but of divine origin.

The stone not made by human hands hit the statue, and ancient Rome in all its power and glory eventually subsided into the ash-heap of history. It did not happen overnight, but it did happen eventually.

It's interesting to note that the secular historian Edward Gibbon once sneered that it was the Christian religion that ultimately caused the downfall of ancient Rome—mainly because its widespread acceptance weakened the Roman army and its conquering cruelties. I remember a very anti-Christian professor, Nels M. Bailkey, when I went to Tulane University gleefully reporting this point to our class on ancient history. Little did he or Gibbon (or I at the time) consider the possibility that these secular historians might well have been confirming biblical truths.

Gibbon said: "As the happiness of a future life is the great object of religion, we may hear without surprise or scandal, that the introduction, or at least the abuse of Christianity, had some influence on the decline and fall of the Roman Empire." He added, "...the last remains of the military spirit [of Rome] were buried in a cloister..." So instead of joining the army, young men were joining the monastery.

H. G. Wells said, "So far as it challenged the divinity of Caesar and the characteristic institutions of the empire, Christianity is to be regarded as a rebellious and disintegrating movement, and so it was regarded by most of the emperors before Constantine..." Wells continued, "...Christianity was a rebellious and destructive force towards a pagan Rome."

Like my undergrad history professor, there's a smug jab at the Christian faith on the part of both Gibbon and Wells, both of whom were skeptics. Little did they realize that the notion of Christianity destroying ancient Rome was the fulfillment of ancient Bible prophecy.

The Caesars are long gone. Their remains disintegrated centuries ago. No one worships them now. No one vows to live for them. No one serves them. Meanwhile, there are hundreds of millions of human beings all around the world, from every nation and virtually every culture, who commit themselves to serve Jesus of Nazareth.

The carpenter's son who was born in a humble cave and placed in a filthy feeding trough for animals has won out, while even the statues of the emperors of ancient Rome lay in disrepair.

Despite setbacks here and there, even seemingly significant ones, Jesus and His kingdom are indeed unstoppable. You're encouraged to join the winning team if you have not already.

~ ~ ~

Acknowledgments

I am most grateful to my employer, D. James Kennedy Ministries, based in Ft. Lauderdale for the opportunity to publically express my opinion in these columns. As one friend of mine puts it, writing like this can be a form of therapy---especially in these trying times. I am grateful to two employees at the ministry in particular who have taken the time to go through many of these columns and edit them, John Rabe and Susie Dzuro. On occasion, Dr. Karen Gushta has edited some of them. I am also grateful to my older brother Rick, founder of Creators Syndicate. He is the one who initially suggested I write a weekly column. I am also grateful to worldnetdaily.com, townhall.com, christianpost.com, newsmax.com, and the many other outlets that run these articles. I am also grateful to my wife, Kirsti, who is a great sounding board for all my creative work. Above all, I am grateful to my Lord and Savior Jesus Christ, by whose grace I enjoy the gift of life---all this and heaven too.

About the Author

Dr. Jerry Newcombe serves as the senior producer and as an on-air host and a columnist for D. James Kennedy Ministries. Jerry has produced or co-produced more than 60 one hour television specials that have aired nationwide. Jerry is the author or co-author of twenty-six books, at least two of which have been bestsellers, *George Washington's Sacred Fire* (with Dr. Peter Lillback) and *What If Jesus Had Never Been Born?* (with Dr. Kennedy). Jerry has also written *Doubting Thomas? The Life and Legacy of Thomas Jefferson* (with Mark Beliles). Jerry has appeared on numerous talk shows as a guest, including *Politically Incorrect with Bill Maher* (4x), the Janet Parshall radio program, Point of View, the Moody radio network, TBN, the Fox News Channel, the Fox Business Channel, C-Span2's "Book Notes," etc. Jerry hosts a weekly radio program, Vocal Point, with archival audio available at jerrynewcombe.com. Jerry is happily married with two children and two grandchildren. The Newcombes reside in South Florida. For more information, see www.jerrynewcombe.com

Index

A

Abdulazeez, Mohammod Youssef, 213
ACLU, 33-34, 129, 245, 299
Adams, Samuel, 34, 63
Adam of Baghdad, 206-208
Adams, John, 40, 71, 117, 243, 319
Adams, Joey, 296
Agassiz, Louis, 186
al-Assad, Bashar, 234
Alexander the Great, 165, 322
Alfred the Great, 89, 301
Ali, Muhammad, 226, 262
Allen, John, 275
Allen, Woody, 45, 306
Ambrose, St., 98, 237, 300
Amish Grace, 125-126
Andreeva, Nellie, 39-40
Andrewes, Lancelot, 89
Andrews, Julie, 181
Anis, Mouneer Hanna, 230
Aquinas, St. Thomas, 155
Archer, Gleason, 80
Aristedes, 12
Aristotle, 53, 132
Armenian massacre, 210-212
Athanasius, 175,300
Atta, Mohammed, 226
Augustine, St., 98, 300, 307
Avila, Ross, 241-242

B

Babbage, Charles, 186
Bach, Johann Sebastian, 187, 301
Bacon, Francis, 190
Baehr, Ted, 5-6, 41-43, 45, 46, 47, 52, 65
Bailkey, Nels M., 323
Barber, Matt, 5, 262
Barr, Roseanne, 54-57
Barrett, David, 211-212
Baylor, Greg, 116-117
Beamer, Todd, 230
Beck, Glenn, 40
Beethoven, Ludwig von, 187
Behe, Michael, 197
Beisner, Cal, 195
Bell, Rob, 295
Berle, Milton, 198
Bernardone, Francis (See Francis of Assisi, St.,)
Bhutto, Benazir, 223
bin Laden, Osama, 223-225, 297
Bloomberg, Michael, 116-117
Bock, Darrell L., 20-21, 46
Boice, James Montgomery, 46
Bonhoeffer, Dietrich, 210
Born Again, 308
Boyle, Robert, 186, 300
Bozell, Brent, 62-63
Brewster, David, 187
British Museum , 188
Broadwell, Paula, 275
Brown, Dan, 130
Brown, Michael, 123
Brown, Mick, 304

Brown, Tim, 120
Buckley, Reid, 174
Buckley, William F., Jr., 11, 62, 174, 307
Bunyan, John, 300
Burkett, Larry, 285
Bush, George W., 120, 152, 225
Butler, Daniel Allen, 177
Butt, Howard E., Jr., 286

C
Cacioppo, John, 105
Cahill, Thomas, 169-170
Calvin, John, 300
Cambrian Explosion, 192
Cameron, David, 213
Cameron, Kirk, 259-260
Camping, Harold, 26-28
Canby, William, 34
Carney, Art, 279
Carney, Jay, 232
Carter, Jimmy, 276
Casablanca, 257
Case for Christ, The, 30, 290
Cass, Gary, 104, 129
Cassels, Louis, 83
Cassidy, Jennifer Kennedy, 6
Castro, Fidel, 55, 153
Catt, Michael, 65
Cecil the lion, 61-62
Centers for Disease Control and Prevention, 282
Chafets, Zev, 122
Chamberlain, Neville, 201
Chambers, Oswald, 300
Chang, Jack, 257
Charlemagne, 165, 224, 301
Charles, Prince, 237

Chaucer, Geoffrey, 300
Chernow, Ron, 39
Chesterton, G. K., 97, 123, 185-186, 220, 256-257, 300
Chinese Cultural Revolution, 55
Christ in Shakespeare, 311
Chrysostom, John, 300
Churchill, Winston, 89, 174, 176-177, 201
Clement of Rome, 12
Climate Research Unit at the University of East Anglia (U.K.), 22-23
Climategate, 22
Clinton, Hillary, 48, 68, 231, 232
Cohen, Betsy, 272
Collins, Francis, 197
Colson, Chuck, 29, 263-264, 300, 308-310
Columbus, Christopher, 28
Comfort, Ray, 64, 269
Connor, Steve, 105
Constantine, 130, 301
Coolidge, Calvin, 304
Cook, Alan, 191
Creators Syndicate, 307
Crouch, Andre, 361
Crouse, Janice, 129
Crowe, Russell, 293
Crusades, 213-214
Cuvier, Georges, 86

D
Dante, 300, 318
Dark Knight, The, 297-298
Darwin, Charles, 71-72, 190, 191-193
Darwin's Doubt, 191-193

DaVinci Code, The, 84, 97, 130
DaVinci, Leonardo, 284
Darwish, Nonie, 221, 223
Daughters of the American Revolution, 56
Daunt, Tina, 48
Davis, Danny, 290
Dawkins, Richard, 11, 51, 88, 121, 173, 185, 186, 227, 260, 311
Day America Told the Truth, The, 269
de Leon, Ponce, 100-101, 103
de Wesselow, Thomas, 30, 32, 33
Dean, Howard, 217
Depp, Johnny, 41-42
DiMucci, Dion, 160
Diognetus, 12
Dickens, Geoffrey, 231
Dobbs, Julian, 207, 229
Dobson, James, 60
Doherty, Glen, 231, 232
Dostoyevsky, Fyodor, 300
Dreisbach, Daniel, 88
Duche, Jacob, 34
Dugard, Martin, 278
Durant, Will, 10, 11, 322
Dys, Jeremy, 136-137

E
Edison, Thomas, 55
Edvardsen, Aril, 33-35
Edwards, Jonathan, 295-296
Egues, Jorge, 152-153
Ehrman, Bart, 76-77, 79-83, 85
Eiesentein, Paul A., 278
Eldredge, Niles, 188

Elliot, Jim, 305
Erdoes, Richard, 258-259
Escobar, Samuel, 256
Esquivel, Jose Manrique, 257
Evans, Pippa, 96
Everett, Carol, 121-122
Exodus: God and Kings, 64

F
Faber, Frederick William, 254
Fabre, Henri, 186
Facing the Giants, 64
Fairfax, Sally, 40
Falwell, Jerry, 46, 47
Faraday, Michael, 186, 301
Farah, Joseph, 68
FAU, Florida Atlantic University, 9
FCC, 57
Federer, Bill, 1-3, 162, 167, 234, 240-241, 314
Ferguson, Niall, 261
Fields, W. C., 44
Fireproof, 64, 65
First Amendment, 34, 68, 219
Fitna, 200
Fjeldstad, Arne, 236
Flaccus, Gillian, 96
Fleming, John Ambrose, 186
Foley, James, 213
Fort Hood, 215, 216
Fountain of Youth, 101
Fox-Genovese, Eugene, 49
Fox-Genovese, Elizabeth, 49
Foxx, Jamie, 9
Francis of Assisi, St., 255-257, 300
Francis, Pope, 237, 255-257

Franklin, Ben, 71, 95, 253, 256, 277, 314
Free speech, 120, 243-245
Freedom From Religion Foundation, 129
Freeman, Richard, 102
French Revolution, 54-57, 271

G
Gaddafi, Muammar, 201, 240
Galli, Marc, 255, 257
Gallienus, 167
Galloway v. Greece, 33
Gates, Bill, 270
Geller, Pamela, 244-245
George, Francis, 126
Gervais, Ricky, 306
Getty, Keith, 128
Gibbon, Edward, 323
Gibbs III, David, 6, 34-35
Gibson, Mel, 47, 58, 64
Gleason, Jackie, 279
Global Warming ("Climate change"), 21-23, 48, 135, 193-195
Gnosticism, 83-86
Gore, Al, 152, 194
Gould, Stephen Jay, 188
Gowan, John, 301
God's Not Dead, 52-54
God's Not Dead 2, 17
Goodwin, Doris Kearns, 57
Gospel of Thomas, 85
Gods of Egypt, The, 72-74
Goebbels, Joseph, 66
Graham, Billy, 270, 300
Graham, Franklin, 128, 244
Graham, Mrs. Billy, 168

Granholm, Jennifer, 290
Greenleaf, Simon, 147-149
Greenstreet, Sidney, 58
Grey, Tom, 181

H
Habermas, Gary, 11-12, 17, 18, 20, 30, 46, 97
Hadrian, Emperor, 12
Hague, Canon Dyson, 144
Hainline, Charlie, 90-92
Hamilton, Alexander, 40
Hamlet, 311-312
Hammond, Peter, 233
Hancock, John, 71
Handel, George Friederich, 156-158, 164, 301
Handel's *Messiah*, 156-158
Harris, Sam, 280
Hart, Johnny, 295, 296
Harvard, John, 53, 54
Harvard Law School, 148
Harvard University, 45, 54, 102, 132, 253
Hasan, Nidal, 216
Hattersley, Roy, 292
Haydn, Franz Joseph, 301
Haykin, Michael, 127
Henry VIII, 89-90, 98
Herschel, William, 186
HHS-mandate, 35
Himmler, Heinrich, 183
Hitchens, Christopher, 260
Hitler, Adolf, 28, 66, 123-124
Holland, Keating, 297
Holocaust, 3, 204, 245
Holt, Andrew, 242
Hughes, R. Kent, 250, 269

Hume, David, 15
Hussein, Saddam, 235

I
Ignatius, 300
Inhofe, James, 154-156

J
Jackson, Samuel L., 291
Jasser, Zhudi, 216-217, 228
Jay, John, 98
Jefferson, Thomas, 34, 35, 117, 218, 284, 293
Jeffress, Robert, 98
Jennens, Charles, 158
Jennings, Peter, 15
Jesus Seminar, 46
Johnson, Byron, 102, 104-105, 114-116
Johnson, James Weldon, 308
Johnson, Leo, 125
Johnson, Tom, 313
Jones, Hillary, 107-109
Jones, Sanderson, 96
Jones, Terry, 202-204
Josephus, 12, 75, 76, 149
Judas of Galilee, 28
Justin Martyr, 12, 300
Justinian, 301

K
Kaufmann, Eric, 111
Kavanaugh, Patrick, 157-159
Kelvin, Lord, 186, 301
Kendrick, Alex, 63-66
Kendrick, Stephen, 63-66
Kennedy, D. James, 53, 58, 60, 62, 73-74, 90, 100, 113, 127, 129, 132, 142, 163, 170, 172, 185, 191, 210, 213, 238, 252, 285, 292, 300
Kennedy, John F., 1
Kepler, Johannes, 132, 186, 190, 301
Kerry, John, 204
Khomeini, Ayatollah, 205
Killing Jesus, 278
Kibbutzim, 49
King, Martin Luther, Jr., 7, 99, 125, 132, 251, 266, 291, 301-302
Kinneer, Jack, 171-172
Kivel, Paul, 131-135
Kluth, Brian, 151
Knight, Robert, 44, 220
Koba, Mark, 268
Koenig, Harold G., 101-102
Koppel, Ted, 90
Koran (see Qur'an)
Koyaanisqatsi, 276
Kulze, Elizabeth, 60

L
Laaser, Mark, 273-275
Lamerson, Sam, 78, 81
Lapin, Daniel, 124, 187, 238, 301
Last Temptation of Christ, The, 46, 47, 202
LeFan, Michael, 252-255
Lehman, David, 250
Lehrer, Tom, 206
Lenin, Vladimir, 49
Lerner, Harriet Goldhor, 278
Levin, Mark, 63
Lewis, C. S., 29, 131, 133, 161, 163, 203, 266, 268, 305, 308

Lewis, John, 95
Lewis, Tanya, 189
Liberty University, 11, 30, 46
Licona, Mike, 12, 19, 20, 30, 80-82
Liddington, David, 227
Lillback, Peter, 40-41
Limbaugh, David, 4, 305
Limbaugh, Rush, 63
Lincoln, Abraham 57-58, 59, 61, 88, 266, 293
Lincoln's Second Inaugural Address, 88, 90
Lister, Joseph, 186, 301
Livingstone, David, 286
Lorre, Peter, 58
Louis (Louis IX), St., 301
Lowell, James Russell, 7, 301-302
Lowry, Rich, 229
Loyola, Ignatius, 300
Lucian, 12
Luther, Martin, 41, 125, 300
Lutz, Donald, 99-100

M
Maclaren, Ian, 255
Madison, James, 34, 256
Maher, Bill, 185, 213-214, 292-295
Mahoney, Pat, 1-4
Maier, Paul L., 15, 16, 19, 45-46, 54, 76, 77, 80, 83, 160, 318
Malik, Faisal, 241
Mao, Chairman, 50
Mara Bar-Serapion, 12
Marcus Aurelius, 75
Marsh v. Chambers, 33

Martel, Charles, 224
Marx, Groucho, 44, 83
Marx, Karl, 2
Massood, Stephen, 226
Mather, Cotton, 28
Maury, Matthew Fontaine, 187
Maxwell, James Clerk, 186
Mayo Clinic, 86-88, 196-197
Maya, 257-259
McCain, John, 237
McClintock and Strong, 50
McCorvey, Norma, 125
McDowell, Josh, 29
McGrath, Alister E., 158
McKay, Hollie, 57
McPherson, James, 58
Mead, Walter Russell, 238
Media Research Center, 61-63, 231
Medved, Michael, 123
Meese, Ed, 63
Melito of Sardis, 12
Mendel, Gregor, 186, 301
Mendelssohn, Felix, 301
Menninger Clinic, 13
Menninger, Karl, 13
Meyer, Steven, 191-193
Milton, John, 300
Milton, Michael, 4-5
Moore, James, 191
Moore, Roy, 298, 299
More, Thomas, 98, 300
Morgenthau, Henry, 211
Morrison, George, 311
Morsi, Mohammad, 229-230, 235-236
Movieguide, 6, 42-43, 45, 46, 47, 52, 65

Mozart, Wolfgang Amadeus, 301
Muravchik, Joshua, 48-49
Murray, Alexander, 53-54
Muslim Brotherhood, 229-230

N
Nag Hammadi, 84-86
Napoleon, 7, 164
Napolitano, Janet, 121
NASA, 257
Nassif, Elizabeth, 196
Nathanson, Bernard, 12
National Cathedral, 89-90, 219-221
Nazi-Ali, Michael, 241
Nazis, 76-79, 134, 179-181, 183, 210
Nelson, Robert, 195
Netanyahu, Benjamin, 205
New England Primer, 81
New Harmony, 49
Newcombe, Ann, 306-308
Newcombe, Doug, 314-317
Newcombe, Kirsti, 105, 167-168, 173, 308, 313-314
Newcombe, Leo, 306-307
Newcombe, Richard, 307
Newton, Isaac, 28, 190
Nicene Creed, 43, 129-131, 175, 252
Nicholas, St., 151
Niebuhr, Reinhold, 305
Niemoller, Martin, 124
Nietzsche, Friedrich, 52
1984, 2
Nixon, Richard, 29
Noah, 64, 292-295

None Dare Call It Islam, 213
Norges Hjemmefront Museum (Norwegian Resistance Museum), 180
Northwest Ordinance, 154

O
Obama, Barack, 48, 176, 225
Objective Hope, 102
Ocean, Stephen, 103-104
Occupy Wall Street, 94-96
O'Connor, Flannery, 247, 300
O'Gorman, Tom, 260-261
O'Hare, Madalyn Murray, 301
Old Deluder Satan Act, 154
"Once to Every Man and Nation," 250-252, 301
O'Reilly, Bill, 278
Orwell, George, 2, 247
Oxford University, 51, 54, 131, 132, 203, 260
Owen, Robert, 49
Owens, Jimmy and Carol, 205-206

P
Pacquiao, Manny, 261
Pagels, Elaine, 85
Papias, 12, 77
Parks, Rosa, 99
Pascal, Blaise, 97, 187
Passion of the Christ, The, 47, 58, 64
Passover Plot, The, 16, 140
Pasteur, Louis, 186, 301
Patrick, St., 169-171
Patterson, Colin, 188-189
Perkins, Tony, 62, 125

Peterson, J. Allan, 275-276
Petraeus, David, 275
Pew Research, 114-115, 185
Phares, Walid, 207-208
Phillips, J. B., 129, 288
Phlegon, 12
Piltdown man, 72
Planned Parenthood, 61-62, 107
Pliny the Younger, 12, 97, 130-131
Polycarp, 12, 77, 210, 212, 300
Pompeii, 60-61
Pope, Alexander, 60
Pot, Pol, 133
Powers, Kirsten, 235
Prayer of Saint Francis, The, 255
Prison Fellowship, 309
Punctuated Equilibrium, 188

Q
Quisling, Vidkun, 179
Quadratus, 12
Qur'an (Koran), 35-37, 200, 202-203, 244-245

R
Rabbae, Mohammed, 200
Rabe, John, 213
Ramsey, William, 197
Rawlings, Harold, 90
Ray, John, 187
Rayleigh, Lord, 186
Reagan, Ronald, 1, 63
Reagan, Jr., Ron, 318
Rhodehamel, John, 34
Riemann, Bernard, 187
Robinson, James M., 85
Rocheleau, Matt, 247

Rockefeller, John D., 315
Roe v. Wade, 12
Rose, Charlie, 214
Royal Society of London for Improving Natural Knowledge, 191
Rush, Benjamin, 296
Russell, Bertrand, 316
Russia Today, 54

S
Saebo, Kirsten, 308
Saebo, Leif, 67
Safe Haven, 50
Sandburg, Carl, 2
Sanders, Bernie, 48-49
Sanford and Sons, 50
Saturday Night Live, 10, 23-24, 232
Saunders, Peter, 310
Saved, 47
Savit, Adam, 228
Sayers, Dorothy, 300
Schaeffer, Francis, 300
Schenck, Rob, 126
Schlesinger, Arthur, 1
Schut, Mike, 21
Scorsese, Martin, 47, 202
Seidler, David, 39-40
Selma, 251
Sero, Junipero, 132
Shackelford, Kelly, 136
Shakespeare, William, 299, 300-301, 310-312, 315
Sherman, Allan, 283
Shimron, Aryeh, 19, 20
Shroud of Turin, 31-33
Siegel, Mark Alan, 122-124

Siller, Stephen, 230
Simon and Garfunkel, 296
Simpson, James, 186
Smith, E. J., 178
Smith, Rod, 122
Smith, Sean, 231
Smith-Crowe, Kristin, 268
Smothers Brothers, 272
Snyder, Tom, 42-43
Socialism: A Clear and Present Danger, 49
Sorbo, Kevin, 52, 54
Soviet Union (see USSR)
Sparks, Nicholas, 50
Spencer, Michael, 113
Spencer, Robert, 204, 226, 242-243, 245
Spielberg, Steven, 57
Spurgeon, Charles Haddon, 266
Stalin, Josef, 49, 271-272
Stanford, Peter, 31
Stark, Rodney, 108-111, 135
Staver, Mat, 4
Steen, Sverre, 172
Stetzer, Ed, 111-114
Stevens, Chris, 231
Stokes, George, 186
Stoner, Peter, 143-144, 290
Strickland, Scott, 231, 232
Strobel, Lee, 17, 29-30, 289-290
Studd, C. T., 305
Suetonius, 12
Sufra, Tite, 103-104
Summa Theologica, 155
Sunderland, Luther, 188-189
Sun-Tzu, 218
Sussman, Brian, 22-23
Swindoll, Chuck, 281, 282

T
Tacitus, 12, 149
Tadros, Samuel, 229
Talmud, 12
Talpiot Tomb, 19, 20
Tamerin, John, 86
Tarantino, Quentin, 23
Taranto, James, 316
Telemachus, 263
Ten Commandments, 24-25, 48, 57, 270, 272, 276, 285, 298-299, 310
Teresa, Mother, 150, 176
Thallus, 12
Theodosius, Emperor, 98, 131
Theudas, 12
Thiel, Peter, 304-306
Tillis, Murray, 13-14
Titanic, 177-179
Tiberius, Emperor, 12
Toastmasters, 43
Tobin, Gary A., 243
Tolkien, J.R.R., 300
Townend, Stuart, 128
Trajan, Emperor, 12, 130
Trotsky, Leon, 271-272
Trump, Donald, 62, 86
Turner, Steve, 28
Twain, Mark, 116, 253
Tyndale, William, 89-90, 228

U
USSR (Soviet Union), 49, 133, 256, 271-272

V
Valentine, St., 167, 169, 209
Van Biema, David, 52

Verhoeven, Paul, 45-47
Victoria, Queen, 159, 301
Vikings, 171-173
Virginia Statute for Religious
Freedom, 35, 218
Von Trapp, Georg, 182-183
Von Trapp, Maria, 181-183

W
Wall Street, 94-96
Wallace, Lew, 39
Wallis, Jim, 94-96
Walton, Bill, 63
War Room, 63-66
Warren, Rick, 256, 288-290
Washington, George, 33, 34, 39-41, 58-59, 90, 137, 154, 164, 219, 221, 248, 299, 301
Wasner, Father, 182
Webster, Noah, 296
Weigel, George, 248
Welch, Derek, 131
Wells, H.G., 323
Wells, Jonathan, 71-72
Wesley, John, 175-176, 252, 300
Westcott, Brooke, 89
Whitefield, George, 296, 300
Whitehead, Alfred North, 186
Whanger, Alan, 31-32
What If Jesus Had Never Been Born?, 53, 129, 132, 172, 185, 191, 238
Wilberforce, William, 175-176, 252, 301
Wilders, Geert, 200-202, 240, 244-245
Will, George F., 68
Wilson, Woodrow, 219-221

Winthrop, Robert, 278
Witherspoon, John, 256
Wohlstetter, John, 205, 217-218
Wolf, Frank, 231
Won By Love, 125
Woods, Ty, 231, 232
Woody, Jeriah, 103-104
Wright, N. T., 10
Wycliffe, John, 89, 228

Y
Yamauchi, Edwin, 127-128
Yeats, W.B., 250

Z
Ziglar, Zig, 249, 276

~ ~ ~

"THE UNSTOPPABLE JESUS CHRIST" IS ALSO AVAILABLE AS AN E-BOOK FOR KINDLE, AMAZON FIRE, IPAD, NOOK AND ANDROID E-READERS. GO TO WWW.CREATORS.COM/BOOKS.

~ ~ ~

66652034R00191

Made in the USA
Charleston, SC
26 January 2017